GUIDE TO BUSINESS MODELLING

OTHER TITLES FROM
THE ECONOMIST BOOKS

The Economist Desk Companion
The Economist Economics
The Economist Guide to Economic Indicators
The Economist Guide to the European Union
The Economist Numbers Guide
The Economist Style Guide
The Guide to Analysing Companies
The Guide to Financial Markets
The Guide to Management Ideas
The Dictionary of Economics
The International Dictionary of Finance
Going Digital
Improving Marketing Effectiveness
Management Development
Managing Complexity
Measuring Business Performance

Pocket Accounting
Pocket Advertising
Pocket Director
Pocket Economist
Pocket Finance
Pocket International Business Terms
Pocket Internet
Pocket Investor
Pocket Law
Pocket Manager
Pocket Marketing
Pocket MBA
Pocket Money
Pocket Negotiator
Pocket Strategy

The Economist Pocket Asia
The Economist Pocket Europe in Figures
The Economist Pocket World in Figures

GUIDE TO
BUSINESS MODELLING

John Tennent
and
Graham Friend

THE ECONOMIST IN ASSOCIATION WITH
PROFILE BOOKS LTD

Published in 2001 by Profile Books Ltd
58A Hatton Garden, London EC1N 8LX

Reprinted 2002

Typeset in EcoType by MacGuru
info@macguru.org.uk

Printed in Great Britain by
St Edmundsbury Press, Bury St Edmunds

A CIP catalogue record for this book is available
from the British Library

ISBN 1 86197 126 5

For information on other Economist Books, visit
www.profilebooks.co.uk
www.economist.com

Contents

Preface

Business models have become the primary tools for the financial analysis of nearly all major business decisions. Unfortunately, the structure and design of most models have evolved without reference to an effective business-modelling methodology. In writing this book we hope to provide the first terms of reference for best-practice business modelling.

The structure and content of the book have been derived from our years of experience of working with business models and training others in the arts of business modelling. We set out to describe the essential principles that underpin the building of any business model, the things you may want a model to do and the elements that may need to be included in it, the most useful spreadsheet functions to incorporate, and how you go about testing a model to ensure that it works, is reliable and is easy to use. In short, we have tried to produce a concise, accessible and relevant guide that touches on every aspect of business modelling. We also hope that we have succeeded in conveying our passion for building effective decision support tools and that this guide will help others to enjoy creating a "virtual world" where they can explore and evaluate their business ideas.

A book with so many formulae, like a business model, must be accurate if it is to be useful. This book has been through several detailed checking stages, so we hope that it is both accurate and useful. If you spot any errors that have slipped through the net please inform us, or the publisher, so that we can correct them in the next edition. Furthermore, in such a fast-developing field, we would welcome feedback from readers of any kind that will help us improve the book and make it even more useful in future. You can contact us at the e-mail addresses below.

john-tennent@corporateedge.co.uk
graham.friend@coleago.com

All books, but perhaps this more than most, are not just the work of the authors but the result also of the contributions of many others. We would like to thank our publishers for the support they have given us, particularly Penny Williams, for her role in editing the book, and Jonathan Harley, who did the page make-up. Special thanks are due to Derek and Jennifer Friend for their invaluable contributions in reading, checking and commenting on the various drafts the book went through. Lastly, we are grateful to all of our colleagues and clients who gave us the opportunity to develop our thinking and our own business modelling skills.

John Tennent and Graham Friend, June 2001

1 Introduction

In all organisations, from self-employed sole traders through to major multinational companies, nearly all new ideas or initiatives require some form of financial or commercial analysis, possibly as part of a business plan. The analysis is often performed through the creation of a business model in a spreadsheet package. Unfortunately, great business ideas do not always receive the support they deserve. The business models that provide the commercial justification for the idea are often poorly structured and, in some cases, simply inaccurate. The result is a misleading view of the financial strength of the idea. This book provides a guide to the development of business models that is relevant to all sizes of organisation and business modelling problems. It examines all the common aspects of a business model, such as forecasting the size of a market and managing stock and working capital through to developing a profit and loss account and a balance sheet and even valuing the company. The last chapters of the book show how a few basic macros (simple computer programmes) can turn a simple spreadsheet into an impressive business application.

HOW MODELS SUPPORT DECISION-MAKING

Models can be used to help with all kinds of business decisions. In today's complex and fast-moving business environment, firms may have a wide variety of strategic and operational choices. A business model helps managers to explore complex choices, using different assumptions to represent different future operating environments. It also helps to develop a clearer understanding of the inherent pattern of relationships between the variables and the likely outcomes. In the end, it is the judgment of the decision-makers that is crucial, but a well-designed model can make the exercise of that judgment easier. A model can help with all three stages of decision-making: analysis, choice and implementation.

Analysis

A business model must be flexible enough to enable those working with it to explore a range of alternatives. The breadth of options must cater for flexing internal and external factors, such as changes in the business environment (for example, inflation, customer demand and taxes), the organisation (for example, automation and synergies) and resources (for example, labour and costs of materials).

Often it is only during the process of building the model that it becomes possible to understand some of the complexities of the project and how different attributes and external factors relate to each other. The success of any business modelling project depends on getting the various assumptions and relationships (or at least the important ones) as accurate as possible. Careful and critical analysis of which attributes and factors require modelling and how they link or may link to each other is fundamental. It may be establishing the relationship between price and sales, or it may involve facts that are harder to pin down, such as the effect of weather patterns or changes in fashion.

Choice

A business model must be constructed in a way that allows alternative sets of data to be input, so as to, for example, include or exclude particular options or grow the business at different rates. This gives a good idea of the risks and rewards attached to different courses of action. It should also ensure that when the decision is made everyone is as comfortable as possible with it because the alternatives have been thoroughly examined.

Implementation

If the model has been built with sufficient detail, such that it shows each of the revenues and costs over the life of the project, it can become the template for the project's budget. Variances in the actual results achieved against the ones predicted by the model will help measure the project's success or will provide early warnings of unforeseen problems. The lessons learnt from such monitoring should also help to improve the decision-making process in the future.

SPREADSHEETS

This book focuses on building business models using spreadsheets because of the widespread access to and familiarity with spreadsheet software among business people throughout the world. It bases its examples and illustrations on Microsoft Excel, although users of other spreadsheet products will be able to achieve much of the same functionality.

The development of the spreadsheet over the last 20 years has made the feasibility of modelling complex projects open to all managers, but in practice there is wide variation in the ability of managers to build robust models. Growing evidence suggests that large numbers of spreadsheet models contain serious errors in their construction. John Sterman, a professor of management at the Massachusetts Institute of Technology (MIT), has commented that "as a result of the introduction of the spreadsheet the average quality of financial models has plummeted and many models are not only useless but downright harmful to decision-makers". Few spreadsheet builders and users are aware of this comment, and fewer still are aware of the simple but powerful techniques covered in this book that can be used to reduce the sources of error.

Anyone involved in business modelling should have firmly in mind the principal advantages and disadvantages of using spreadsheets to construct business models as detailed in Chart 1.1.

Chart 1.1 **Advantages and disadvantages of using spreadsheets**

Advantages	*Disadvantages*
Widely accessible and installed on computers as a standard package in most companies	Wide range of abilities among users; some novices operate in an unstructured and detrimental manner
There are many operators in an organisation thus reducing the need for new product training	The majority of the package's power and functionality is not known about or used by operators
Easily changed to meet the evolution of situations	A lack of standard structure in construction leads to amateurish evolution
Has become a standard format for downloading the output from other packages including most accounting packages	Weak annotation by developers makes it difficult for new users to understand the structure of the spreadsheet
Incorporates a wide variety of mathematical and statistical functions for analysing and evaluating data	Errors can easily be made and lie undetected in cell co-ordinates that are difficult to verify
Passwords can be used to protect user access and preserve the logic. This helps ensure robustness of use	Considerable duplication of effort as so many spreadsheets are started from a blank sheet
Considerable formatting and graphical functionality for impressive presentation	Pride in detail that adds aesthetics rather than enhanced decision support
	Spreadsheets do not easily handle text if more than a few sentences are required

Other platforms can be used for building models. These are examined in Appendix 2.

THIS BOOK

This book is intended principally as a practical guide aimed at those with little experience of business modelling as well as experienced practitioners seeking to hone their skills and add clarity of structure. It combines financial and business analysis with software techniques and an awareness of corporate politics. Its principles apply equally to straightforward business projects as they do to mergers and acquisitions. Although each sector has its own characteristics and set of relationships between assumptions, the process for understanding risk, sensitivity and key determinants of success are identical.

Chapter 2 provides an overview of the steps involved in planning, building, testing, using and presenting a business model. These steps are then explored in more detail throughout the rest of the book. Chapters 3–5 explain how scenario planning can be used to identify the outputs from the model, the required inputs and the economic and logical relationships that link the two in an uncertain business environment. Scenario planning is a powerful technique for developing "the story" that supports and explains the results of the business model.

If readers have already developed a good understanding of the business environment to be modelled, they may prefer to begin with Chapter 6. Chapters 6–8 examine the process for constructing the model and the fundamental principles of good spreadsheet design, as well as providing a review of some useful spreadsheet functions that are used throughout the remainder of the book.

Chapters 9–15 provide detailed examples of spreadsheet solutions that address the elements common to nearly all business models. The remaining chapters help readers to use the model as part of their decision-making process and show them how to add the finishing touches that turn a basic spreadsheet into an impressive business application.

Conventions

In this book, several conventions are used to display data.

- Range names (see Chapter 7) are shown in italics, though in Excel they will appear as normal text.
- Functions, such as CONCATENATE, are in capital letters to distinguish them from other text. (Note that when entering data in formulae there should be no spaces in the entry.)
- Within functions, commas are used to separate attributes. In some countries these can be ; (semicolon) or . (full stop). Please check by clicking on the Paste Function button *fx* on the toolbar. In the "Paste Function" box select Function category: "All" and Function name: "SUM". Below the Function category list it will show SUM(number1,number2...) with the appropriate punctuation symbol as the separator.
- Numbers within a formula are shown without commas as thousand separators and no superfluous decimal places. Negative numbers have a preceding – (minus) sign.
- Numbers for an output or for printing are shown with commas as thousand separators and a fixed number of decimal places. Negative numbers are in brackets.

Chart 1.2 shows a recommended set-up for your PC for business modelling purposes. If you follow this set-up, with its toolbars, formulae bars, status bar, and so on, you should easily be able to replicate all the examples and illustrations given in this book.

Chart 1.2 **Business modelling set-up**

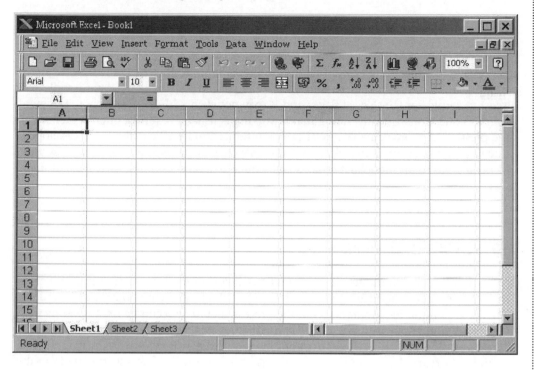

2 The business modelling process

Many managers, when faced with assessing a business opportunity or risk, will begin to develop a spreadsheet model with little or no preparation. A poorly planned model may contain a number of weaknesses: it may be incompatible with available data; it will almost certainly contain logical flaws; and it may not even address effectively the original business issue. Consequently, substantial reworking is usually required, often under severe time pressure. A more valuable model can be produced more efficiently if it is developed through a robust business modelling process. This chapter presents a general process that can be applied to all modelling projects. Subsequent chapters examine each stage of the process in detail.

THE STAGES OF THE PROCESS

The stages of the business modelling process are shown in the process map in Chart 2.1. The first stage in any modelling process is to define the fundamental business question being asked; all the remaining stages of the process should concentrate on answering this question. A simple question might be: Should the business launch a new product? The next step is to identify all the outputs from the model that are required to answer the question. For example, the decision-maker might wish to see the forecast revenue from the new product launch. The outputs themselves are determined through a combination of input variables, such as the selling price of the product, and spreadsheet formulae. Once the outputs have been determined, all the input variables should be identified. Before proceeding to the next stage it is important to establish whether the input data can actually be collected. Data collection can be one of the most challenging stages of the process and is discussed in the next section.

Once a list of input variables has been established the possible future behaviour patterns for each variable should be described. For example, severe competition in the market may imply that prices will fall in the future. Before starting the construction of the model, the economic and financial relationships and logical flows between the inputs and outputs should be determined. For example, the number of customers multiplied by sales revenue per customer would give total revenue for the new product. These relationships provide the logic behind the formulae that ultimately determine the outputs. The process of constructing the model is the subject of Chapter 6.

The final stages of the process involve entering, or populating, the model with the collected data. The model can then be used to help answer the original question by testing the sensitivity of the outputs to different input assumptions. The final results, and also the model itself, should be documented. If the project is subsequently approved, it then moves into the implementation phase. Lastly, a post project review is often valuable to capture any insights that will be of benefit to future business modelling projects.

Chart 2.1 **The business modelling process**

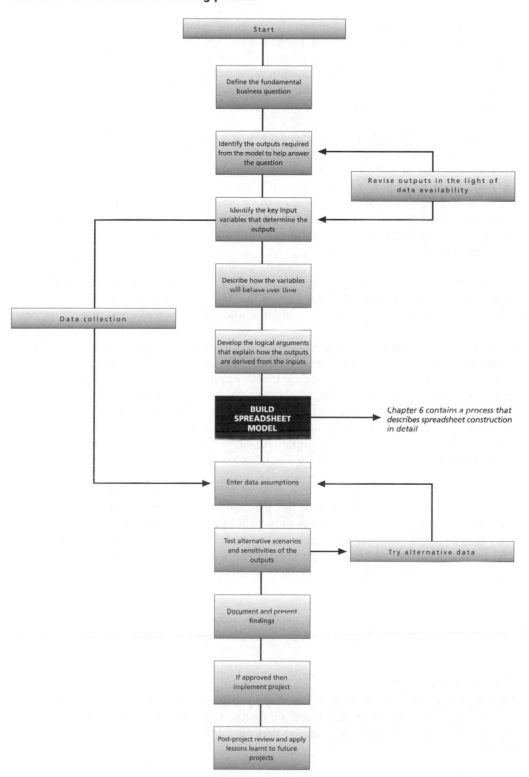

DATA COLLECTION

The value of a well-designed and accurately developed business model will be considerably lower if the data used to derive the outputs are of poor quality. The data needs of the model must be clearly specified, and it is vital to check whether the required data is available and can be collected within the time scale of the project. Although data collection can prove to be time consuming, the activity can often be performed in parallel to the construction of the model.

The sources of available data will be specific to each project. Some data will be drawn from internally held sources, such as data warehouses or financial database systems. External data may be gathered from industry bodies or research agencies. A considerable amount of external data can be located on the Internet. Macroeconomic forecasts for inflation, exchange rates and interest rates can be obtained from governmental departments and also from stockbrokers. Stockbrokers' research notes can also be a useful source of industry information. Increasingly, stockbroking firms are making their research available, free of charge, on the Internet.

In some cases, no suitable existing data will be available and primary research may be required to generate the relevant information. The brief to the research agency should specify the format of the final results in order to allow for easy data entry into the model.

Initial results from the data collection exercise should be reviewed as early as possible to ensure that they meet the original specifications; that they are in the correct currency and units; and that they cover the appropriate time horizon and do so for the correct time period. They should be reviewed for reasonableness and accuracy. They should also be compared with expectations, and if there are significant differences, explanations should be obtained to validate the quality of the information. Ideally, from the outset existing data should be used to populate the input templates and any completed workings can then be reviewed to examine whether the anticipated results are being achieved.

In some cases it will not be possible to collect all the desired information. The data may simply not be available or it may not cover the required time horizon, products, customer segments or geographical regions, for example. Under these circumstances the modeller must reconsider the design and structure of the model to allow for the limitations in the dataset. The potential need to redesign the model highlights the importance of an early review of the outcomes from the data collection process.

CREATING THE RIGHT BUSINESS MODELLING TEAM

The project manager

The person with the responsibility for managing the business modelling process and co-ordinating the business modelling team is the project manager. In many small organisations one individual may have to perform all the stages of developing a business model.

The business modelling team

In larger organisations the size and members of the team will depend on the complexity and perceived importance of the project. In selecting the team, the project manager should consider three key milestones:

- The development of the business model.
- Approval of the plan.
- Implementation of the plan.

The team should include experienced representatives from all of the major disciplines likely to be involved were the project to be implemented. In the case of a telecommunications company, for example, the team is likely to include members from marketing, sales and customer relationship management, strategy, finance, human resources, information technology and engineering. It is also helpful to appoint one member of the team as the data collection manager. This person will have overall responsibility for specifying the data requirements, sourcing the data and potentially liaising with outside agencies if primary market research is being conducted. Finally, the involvement of those who will have a say in the final decision – at least in the early stages of the project – should help ensure a smooth passage through the approvals process.

The model developer

The developer is the individual who will actually create the model. The level of skill required by the developer depends on the proposed complexity of the model and who will actually be using it. Where the expected users have little experience of manipulating spreadsheets the developer may decide to make use of menus and buttons to make the model easier to use. In this case the developer will require knowledge of more advanced spreadsheet features and techniques and perhaps some knowledge of a programming language such as Visual Basic.

DEVELOPING A BUSINESS MODELLING PROJECT PLAN

In the case of large and complex business modelling assignments, the creation of a Project Plan will help ensure the most effective use of resources and the timely co-ordination of the different activities involved in producing the completed business model.

Define the scope and goals of the project

A successful project requires a clearly defined goal from the outset. In large organisations, it is particularly important that goals are clearly stated and effectively communicated. When defining your goals, make them SMART:

- Specific
- Measurable
- Achievable
- Relevant
- Time-bound

Defining the scope of the project is also essential. For example, when reviewing the profitability of a new product launch, should the analysis be conducted at a national, regional or global level?

Plan the work

The project manager, having described the goal and scope of the project, should ask the team to list (perhaps through brainstorming) all the potential risks (such as delays in data collection) and constraints (such as lack of resources) that may affect the successful completion of the project. In the light of the identified risks and constraints, the project's goals and scope may need to be altered to balance the end results against the time and resources available.

Next the team should list all the tasks and activities that need to be done to achieve the goal. Tasks are pieces of work carried out by one person. Activities are defined as a package of work comprising several tasks, carried out by one or more persons. Activities may include data collection, model building, meetings with suppliers, product testing and the various stages of the corporate approvals process.

A useful technique is to write each task or activity on a note and stick it on a flip chart on the wall. The team should then be asked to cluster groups of related tasks and activities to define the stages of the project. These stages should then be put in sequence, with the stage that must be completed first placed on the left-hand side of the flip chart. Working from left to right, the remaining stages should be placed on the chart depending on what must or can be done next. Once this has been completed for the stages of the project, the process is repeated, first for the activities and then for the individual tasks.

The project manager can then link all the tasks in a logical sequence, each having an input and an output. Once this has been completed and the flow of activities reviewed and tested the project logic will be agreed.

Milestones (points in the plan that indicate when a group of related tasks have been completed) should then be identified and the responsibility for their completion, or their ownership, allocated to individual team members. There should only ever be one owner of a milestone.

The owners can then look at the tasks and activities required to reach their milestones and estimate how long each task will take. Team resources can then be allocated to the delivery of each task or activity.

Produce the plan

A project plan should be produced showing the path of the project, start and completion dates, milestones and their owners, and the allocation of resources to tasks and activities. The clearest way to present this information is in a Gantt chart, which is a horizontal bar chart representing the time relationship of the tasks in a project. It allows people to study quickly the people, resources, dates, overlaps and key elements of the project. An example of a Gantt chart for a high-level third-generation licence bid model is shown in Chart 2.2. (Other techniques can be used to show the dependencies between tasks, such as PERT

(Performance Evaluation and Review Technique), developed by the US navy, and CPM (Critical Path Method), developed by Du Pont. These techniques have not been included in this book.)

Chart 2.2 **Gantt chart for a high-level third-generation licence bid model**

Project name	Third-generation licence bid model
Project sponsor	A N Author
Version number	3
Date	08/05/2000

Task	Owner	Time	Week 1	Week 2	Week 3	Week 4	Week 5	Week 6
			M T W T F	M T W T F	M T W T F	M T W T F	M T W T F	M T W T F
Define problem	GH	1.0						
Identify outputs	GH	0.5						
Identify inputs	AS	0.5						
Check data availability	NH	1.0						
Review outputs and inputs	AS	1.0						
Describe input behaviours	GH	1.0						
Identify economic logic	GH	2.0						
Business model specified		**7.0**						
Data collection	NH	16.0						
Data collected		**16.0**						
Model construction	AS	14.0						
Model built		-						
Data entry	AS	1.0						
Scenario testing	AS	2.0						
Report writing	GH	2.0						
Report presented		**5.0**						
Review project	GH	1.0						
Project reviewed		**1.0**						
Total project time		**29.0**						

Key

Task/activity

Milestone

The project plan in Chart 2.2 was produced using a spreadsheet package. Although using a spreadsheet to produce a project plan is quick and easy and does not require the purchase of new software, it will not update timings automatically, unlike dedicated project planning tools. A spreadsheet is usually adequate for most modelling exercises; however, for large, complex projects or for those responsible for a lot of project management, a dedicated package may be a useful investment.

The project manager should also develop contingency plans for the risks that have been identified, and then review the plan in the light of the resource constraints identified earlier.

Managing the project

The project plan should be used to monitor progress and it should be adapted to take into account unforeseen events. Everyone with a stake in the project should be regularly informed of progress and any changes to the plan.

Sharing the lessons learnt and the knowledge acquired

When the project has been completed a debriefing session should be held with the team to identify what went well and what could – or should – have gone better. The debriefing report together with items such as the project plan, templates, market research briefs and models should be filed and made available to the rest of the organisation, perhaps by placing them on the company Intranet.

3 Defining the ouputs

A clear understanding of the fundamental question being asked or the decision to be made must be established from the outset. The question or decision should be written down precisely and agreed on by all the team members, including those who will ultimately make the decision. Some examples of fundamental questions are as follows:

- What maximum price should a business be prepared to pay to acquire a competitor?
- Which is the most financially efficient method of purchasing a new fleet of vehicles?
- Should the US market be targeted?
- Should a new product be launched?

The question used to illustrate the techniques presented in this and the following two chapters is: Should an existing mobile telecommunications operator launch a third-generation mobile telecommunications video telephony service?

ALIGNMENT WITH THE BUSINESS'S OVERALL OBJECTIVES

In small businesses, there is usually little risk of the modelling objectives being misaligned with those of the business as a whole. In larger organisations, however, it is important to ensure that the strategic objectives implied by the business modelling exercise are aligned with the overall strategic plan for the business. Business modelling can take place anywhere within the pyramid of corporate planning activity depicted in Chart 3.1.

Chart 3.1 **The corporate planning pyramid**

The nearer the apex of the pyramid, the more business modelling is related to determining the strategic direction itself. Towards the base of the pyramid, models become more reporting oriented and may be used to perform variance analyses, identifying how far actual performance diverges from the forecast contained in the budget.

DEFINING THE OUTPUTS REQUIRED TO ANSWER THE QUESTION

The modeller must define the outputs from the model that will be used to answer the question. If the question concerns the valuation of a competitor, for example, the output required may be the net present value (NPV) of the future cashflow or the internal rate of return (IRR) of the project. Alternative valuation approaches are discussed in Chapter 15.

The modeller should also identify the additional information the ultimate decision-makers will require in order to make their decision. A small business may be examining the cheapest route to acquiring a new fleet of company vehicles. It may wish to examine whether it is cheaper to buy, rent or lease the new vehicles. The model may use a NPV calculation to compare the options. The NPV may indicate that the lease option is the cheapest over the lifetime of the vehicles. However, the business may also be concerned with its cashflow. The decision-makers may also wish to ask what will be the level of monthly payments under each option. At the outset, therefore, the modeller should define not only the outputs required to help answer the fundamental business question, but also the additional information the decision-makers are likely to require in coming to their final decision.

In some cases, the modelling exercise may not produce an answer to a specific business question. The model may be constructed simply to enhance the business's understanding of its operating environment.

Model outputs and corporate decision-making

Large organisations often have to make important decisions swiftly. Considerable effort will have gone into streamlining the decision-making process to allow organisations to react rapidly to their fast-changing environment. The pressures on the decision-makers are such that the reports on which they rely must often be no longer than a few pages. The structure and content of these reports will have been determined in advance. Furthermore, before a report is presented, it must usually be approved by a number of departments which all have different evaluation criteria. Organisations often develop a set of templates with specific financial input requirements to speed up the approvals and decision-making process. The business model must produce all the outputs required by the corporate decision-making process.

Specify the time frame and period length

Business models are often used to forecast the future. The modeller needs to know how far into the future the forecast should extend. In the case of a business examining whether to bid for a licence to operate a train network, the model may be based on the period specified by the licence, which could be 10, 15 or even 20 years. In the case of company valuations there is no finite life for the business. The model will typically produce detailed forecasts for around ten years with further assumptions made about the value of the business after that period – the terminal value. (The calculation of the terminal value is discussed in detail in Chapter 15. The calculation makes a number of simplifying assumptions including the assumption that the business has reached maturity and continues to grow at a steady rate of growth.) The number of years of detailed forecasts required must therefore be sufficient to ensure that the business has reached maturity or a "steady-state".

Strategic business questions, such as whether to acquire a company, will typically involve more years of detailed forecasts than more tactical questions, such as whether to reduce the selling price of a product, for which the time frame may be only one year or even less.

A further time-related issue is the length of each period that is represented by one column in the spreadsheet. Short-term, tactical modelling problems may have a two-year time frame, but the forecast might have to be made on a monthly basis, that is, 24 columns with each column representing one month. In the case of valuation problems, periods of 12 months are usually sufficient.

Establish the basics

The modeller should also check some basic output considerations. These include:

- period ends – calendar or fiscal;
- the currency in which to produce the outputs;
- the units – millions or thousands;
- whether the forecast should take account of inflation (a nominal forecast) or be presented entirely in today's, or constant prices (a real forecast).

Real versus nominal forecasts

Forecasts can be produced in either real or nominal terms. In most modern economies with low levels of inflation, there are a number of reasons why it is usually preferable to forecast in nominal terms. First, most managers, when they form their expectations about revenues and profits for the coming years, do so in nominal terms. Second, historic revenues, costs and profits are often used as a basis for projecting trends into the future. These historic results are recorded in nominal terms and so forecasting on the same basis is usually easier. Third, interest rates are normally quoted in nominal terms and so forecasting on the same basis can make interest calculations more straightforward.

In countries suffering from high levels of inflation, however, it is usually preferable to forecast in real terms, as the nominal forecast soon becomes meaningless. Furthermore, when forecasting revenues it is often easier to think about customers' expenditure levels, or the price of goods, at constant prices. The task of predicting consumer expenditure on your product, ten years from now, after taking into account the effects of annual inflation, is considerably harder than thinking about it in constant prices, or in real terms.

IDENTIFYING THE CRITICAL FACTORS THAT DETERMINE THE OUTPUTS

This involves asking the question: What do we need to know about the future in order to answer the fundamental business question? The modeller must identify all the critical factors that must be forecast before the outputs can be produced and the question answered. At this stage the term forecast is used quite loosely. Some of the critical factors will be related to regulatory, political or legal concerns and may not be directly associated with a particular element within the model. These factors, however, will be crucial in describing fully the context for the answer and will influence how variables within the model are forecast.

The focus should be on external factors. Macroeconomic variables such as gross domestic product (GDP), interest rates, inflation, exchange rates, income levels and income distribution are likely to be important factors. Population growth, urbanisation and trends in transport may also be relevant. At a microeconomic level, customer needs, market size and market growth will be essential. Current and future competitors, the nature of their product offerings and their positioning in the market place should be identified.

Once all the critical factors have been identified they should be divided into those that will be explicitly modelled and those that simply provide the context for the forecast and are likely to be described in a business planning document.

Critical factors in the mobile telecommunications industry

Chart 3.2 shows some of the critical factors for a company examining the launch of a mobile telecommunications third-generation video telephony service. The telecommunications industry is usually carefully scrutinised by governments and so the regulatory regime is always a crucial factor. Furthermore, governments have been anxious to foster competition in the sector and so most markets feature a number of competing players. The number of players in a market and their respective market shares are important considerations. So too are the ownership, or penetration, of mobile devices capable of delivering video telephony among the population and the average revenue generated per user or customer per month (ARPU). Crucially, the company must predict how much demand there will there be for video telephony and how much cash will be required to create the required network infrastructure. There are many factors that will determine the success of such a product launch, but these are some of the most critical.

Chart 3.2 **Third-generation mobile video telephony service critical factors**

Business model	Context
Population size and growth	Regulatory environment
Mobile penetration of the population	Health issues
Number of competitors	Consumer lifestyle trends
Market share	Mobility among workers
Average revenue per user (ARPU)	Availability of content
Demand for video telephony services	
Average spend per customer	
Speed of network roll-out	
Network creation capital expenditure	
Device or mobile handset availability	
The difference between the selling price of a device and the purchase cost to the business, known to the business as a subsidy	
Size of the operating cost base	

CREATING AN OUTPUT TEMPLATE

To ensure that all the required outputs have been identified, a template reflecting the design and content of the final output sheet should be produced. No figures are required at this stage, simply the row descriptions and the column headings. This template should include the main outputs, the evaluation criteria and any information that helps answer the decision-makers' likely additional questions. The template should also incorporate the critical factors that were used to derive the outputs.

The output template can then be presented to the ultimate decision-makers to ensure that the outputs from the model will be sufficient to allow them to make their decision. Revealing early what form the output from the model is going to take is an effective method of managing people's expectations of the modelling process. An example of an output template is presented in Chart 3.3.

RUNNING A WORKSHOP

When a modelling project involves a number of people it can be useful to run a workshop to define the fundamental business question, the model outputs and the critical factors. The decision-makers should also be present to ensure that their expectations of the outputs from the model are appropriately managed.

Before the start of the workshop the team should be provided with some or all of the following:

- The business's vision, mission and goal statements.
- An overview of any current strategic and tactical plans.
- A summary of recent financial performance and any corporate statements.
- Market forecasts, assessments or results of recent market research projects.

Newspaper articles could be useful and may provide context and expert opinion on any important trends, such as market liberalisation or socio-economic and demographic shifts.

The team should then work together to produce the final output template. During the workshop, the team should discuss (perhaps brainstorm) all the critical factors and their trends that will affect the business in the future. Team members should remember that these factors may not be present in the current market and they should be challenged to think widely and laterally around the business problem.

Chart 3.3 **Third-generation mobile telecommunication video telephony output template**

	A	B	C	D	E	F	G	H	I	J
1	**Third-generation mobile video telephony**									
2	(All figures in millions of local currency unless otherwise stated)									
3										
4										
5	**Valuation**									
6							Discount rate			
7	Net present value					7%	8%	9%		
8										
9	Internal rate of return (%)									
10	Peak funding requirement									
11	Payback period (years)									
12										
13										
14	**Summary financial results**									
15							Year ended March 31st			
16					2000	2001	2002	2003	2004	2005
17										
18	Revenue									
19										
20	Operating costs									
21										
22	EBITDA (1)									
23	EBITDA margin (%)									
24										
25	PBT (2)									
26										
27	Capital expenditure									
28										
29	Free cash flow (3)									
30										
31										
32	**Critical factors**									
33										
34	Population (000)									
35	Penetration (%)									
36	Market size (000)									
37	Market share (%)									
38	Customer base (000)									
39	ARPU (local currency)									
40	Video telephony expenditure (local currency)									
41										
42										
43	**Definitions**									
44	1) Earnings before interest, tax, depreciation and amortisation									
45	2) Profit before tax									
46	3) Operating profit plus changes in working capital less capital expenditure									

BUSINESS MODELLING OUTPUT CHECKLIST

Before proceeding to the next stage of model development, the modeller should ensure that all the items in Chart 3.4 on the next page have been prepared, reviewed and approved.

Chart 3.4 **Business model output checklist**

	Prepared/documented	*Reviewed/approved*
Fundamental business question		
Model outputs and additional information needs		
Time frame		
Time periods		
Period end – calendar or fiscal		
Currency		
Units		
Real or nominal		
Critical factors		
Output template		

4 Uncertainty, scenario planning and model inputs

DEFINING THE INPUTS

The final outputs of the business model and many of the critical factors are derived from a combination of model inputs and formulae, although in some cases it may not be possible to derive a critical factor in this manner. In these instances, the critical factor will also be a direct input into the model. Inputs can be viewed in two parts:

- The seed, which is the initial starting point for a particular input.
- The behaviour, which describes how the input develops over time.

Although the initial starting point for most inputs can be observed directly from the real world, the future behaviour of the input may be subject to considerable uncertainty.

UNDERSTANDING THE NATURE OF UNCERTAINTY

Uncertainty is a lack of understanding of which markets, competitors, customers and products, for example, will constitute the future. For stable, mature industries, such as steel production, levels of uncertainty are low, which makes the task of forecasting fairly straightforward. In other industries, however, especially those close to the information technology, media and telecommunications sectors, the business landscape has been changing dramatically. These industries do not experience slow, steady, incremental changes in their day-to-day operations, but major discontinuities. The creation of Amazon.com introduced an entirely new form of bookselling. A brief glance at the statistics presented in Chart 4.1 reveals how dramatically the book retailing landscape has shifted. For many firms, tomorrow may be unrecognisable from today, and a forecast based on past experience may be a poor basis for decision-making.

Chart 4.1 **The changing structure of the US book retailing industry**

	Amazon.com	Barnes & Noble
Number of stores	1 website	1,011
Titles per superstore	3.1m	175,000
Book returns	2%	30%
Sales growth	306%	10%
Sales per employee (annual)	$375,000	$100,000
Inventory turns per year	24	3
Long-term capital requirements	Low	High
Cashflow	High	Low

EXAMINING DIFFERENT APPROACHES TO UNCERTAINTY

A number of approaches to forecasting uncertain events have been developed over the years. Many approaches are based on probability models. Probability-based models quantify the likelihood of future events based on the statistical occurrence of past, similar events. These models are valuable when the past provides a good predictor of the future, and extrapolative approaches to forecasting are explored in Chapter 10. However, in industries faced with dramatic and discontinuous change, the future will be determined by a set of circumstances that currently do not exist and, therefore, cannot be quantified, measured or predicted. In these cases, it is not possible to assign a probability based on an observation of the past. So an alternative approach to forecasting is required, which must be flexible and able to accommodate drastically different operating environments.

A SCENARIO-BASED FORECASTING APPROACH

Scenario-based forecasting provides a structured approach for thinking about uncertainty. The development of scenario planning can be attributed to Herman Kahn, who worked for the RAND Corporation in the 1950s. The approach was formalised by Shell during the 1970s, and its use has become increasingly pervasive in recent years in response to the dramatic changes that many industries and business must now contend with. For a more detailed understanding of scenario-based forecasting techniques, *Learning from the future: Competitive Foresight Scenarios* is an excellent reference.[1]

Scenarios are pictures, painted in words, of vividly different, contrasting and relevant environments in which the business may have to operate. They describe the key trends and interactions that may characterise the development of a particular future environment. Usually, no more than three or four alternative scenarios will be developed.

There are a number of benefits of using scenario planning to support the modelling process:

- Scenario planning ensures that a detailed, consistent list of model inputs is produced.
- Scenario descriptions provide context for the forecasts and make them easier to understand and explain to the various audiences.
- The decision-maker is presented with more choice through the creation of alternative scenarios.
- The economic understanding contained within the scenarios provides the foundations for the formulae within the model as well as a check on the logic and consistency of the model's outputs.

The process of developing each of the scenarios can be valuable as it increases the understanding of the forces shaping the industry, how the industry might evolve and what the future business environment may look like.

---

1   Liam Fahey and Robert M. Randall (eds), *Learning from the future: Competitive Foresight Scenarios*, John Wiley & Sons, 1997.

The stages of a scenario-based forecasting approach

Chart 4.2 presents the five stages of a scenario-based forecasting approach. This chapter focuses on stage 1, identifying the key inputs. The remaining stages are presented in Chapter 5.

Chart 4.2 **Stages of scenario planning**

Stage	Description
1	Identify key inputs with a high degree of uncertainty that have a high impact on the business
2	Describe alternative behaviour patterns for the key inputs
3	Select the three or four most informative scenarios
4	Develop the scenario story including the relationships between the key inputs, the critical factors and the model's outputs
5	Develop appropriate business strategies

STAGE 1: IDENTIFYING HIGH IMPACT, HIGHLY UNCERTAIN INPUTS

Identify all the variables that influence the business

The first stage in identifying the model inputs is to identify all the variables that could have an impact on the business now or in the future. It is important to think laterally at this stage as some future influences on the business may appear obscure and even ridiculous from today's perspective.

Not all variables will be associated with an observable and measurable model input. The cost of raw materials to the business is an observable, measurable and quantifiable variable that will feature in the business model. In the case of some lifestyle trends, there are no obvious, quantifiable variables that could easily be incorporated into the model. It is equally important, however, to identify both types of variable during this stage of the process. Although not all variables may be entered directly into the business model, they will provide a useful context for the results of the model.

The acronym PEST may prove a useful starting point for this exercise. PEST analysis relates to factors classed under the following headings:

- Political
- Economic
- Social
- Technological

The variables that are likely to affect the current and future performance of a mobile telecommunications business are listed in Chart 4.3 on the next page.

Chart 4.3 **Variables influencing the mobile telecommunications industry**[a]

Population growth	M-commerce expenditure	Number of competitors
Demographic trends	E-commerce expenditure	Regulatory environment
Gross domestic product	Leisure time	Health issues
Income distribution	Worker mobility	Device availability
Mobile enabled machines	Fixed/mobile substitution	Network infrastructure costs
Internet penetration	Spectrum allocation	Infrastructure availability
Fixed line prices	Churn	Advertising trends
Mobile penetration	Data application availability	Transaction commissions
Interconnect costs	Call centre costs	Supplier contract terms
Interconnect income	Licence fees	Distribution channels
Staff availability	Accounting policies	Dealer commissions
Web-based servicing	Tax rates	Billing costs
Customer service staff	Import duties	Billing system capabilities
Land area	Population density	Capacity
Content prices	Roaming agreements	Billing system costs
Coverage of population	Geographic coverage	Demand for voice services
Demand for data services	Mobile wallet	Partnerships & joint ventures
Mobile video tariffs	Availability of content	Calling patterns
Fixed-line penetration	Mobile browser technology	Speed of roll-out
Number of transactions	Data tariffs	Average transaction value
Type of competitors	Device subsidies	Market share
Site availability	Mobile encryption	Voice minutes of use
Broadband penetration	Currency movements	Advertising revenues
Voice revenue per customer	Customer numbers	Topography

a This list is certainly not exhaustive and readers are not expected to understand the exact meaning of every term.

The list will inevitably include variables, the level of which can be set directly by management – these are called strategic variables. At this stage these variables are uncertain because it is not known at which level management and the competitors will set them.

Identifying the relationships between variables

Within the list of variables, there will be a number that are closely related to others listed. It is important to identify these relationships for two reasons. First, it may help reduce the amount of data that needs collecting. Second, it allows the model to capture these relationships so that as many important variables as possible can be derived within the model.

The variables whose behaviour is derived within the model are called endogenous. The variables that are direct inputs into the model, and that cannot be determined through the use of formulae and other inputs, are called exogenous. For example, in many businesses the number of customer services staff can represent a significant cost, but it is related to the number of customers that they have to service. Therefore, by using a ratio of customers to customer services staff, the number of customer services staff can be derived from the number of customers. In this case, the ratio of customers to customer services staff is the exogenous variable, because it is input directly into the model, and the number of customer services staff is the endogenous variable, because it can be determined within the model by combining customer numbers with the ratio of customers to customer services staff.

The benefit of a model with a large number of endogenously determined variables is that the outputs from the model will remain valid over a wider range of inputs. This makes the model much more useful for modelling alternative scenarios, as key inputs can be changed and the resulting, final outputs will remain coherent and logically consistent. In the customer services example above, the ratio of customers to customer services staff may remain relatively constant over time. However, by using a ratio in the model, rather than directly entering the number of customer services staff, the number of staff will change depending on the total number of customers. Customer numbers, in turn, will partly be based on the level of market share. The modeller can now use the model to run sensitivities on the level of market share and the model will automatically calculate the number of customer services staff. If customer services staff had been a direct input into the model, the number of staff would not have altered with a change in the market share assumption.

The modeller should review all the variables in the original list (Chart 4.3) and identify whether a relationship can be established between groups of closely related variables. Those variables that can be derived from others should be removed from the list and the approach to deriving them recorded. It may be necessary to add additional variables to the list if they are required to derive the variable that has just been removed. For example, the number of customer services staff would be removed from the list but the ratio of customers to customer services staff would be added as an input into the model. Chart 4.4 provides three examples of how variables and their relationships may be recorded.

Chart 4.4 **Variables and relationships**

Derived variable	Related variables and inputs	Additional input requirements
Number of customer services staff	Customer numbers	Ratio of customers to customer services staff
Voice revenue per customer	Minutes of use, customer numbers, calling patterns	Mobile call tariffs
Customer numbers	Population and penetration	None

Review the data collection requirements

The list in Chart 4.3 should now contain only direct inputs into the model. Of these inputs, some will be directly observable and measurable and will explicitly feature in the business model. The remainder will provide the context for the forecast but will not form part of the data collection exercise.

The list of inputs should be reviewed and potential sources of data for each input should be identified. Where no source can be located, the modeller should attempt to identify an alternative input that can be collected and that could act as a proxy for the original input. For example, in developing economies it can be difficult to obtain accurate income data; information on education attainment is usually more readily available. Education levels and income are often closely related, so education can be used as a proxy for income. If no obvious proxy is available, the modeller will have to consider deriving the input as a discrete modelling exercise in itself. The modeller should examine how best to forecast this variable based on data that are available, and this process may identify additional data requirements that should be incorporated into the table.

When finalising the data input requirements for the model, two well used but highly pertinent adages should be borne in mind. First, that "rubbish in results in rubbish out", and second, that "it is better to be roughly right than precisely wrong".

Analyse variables according to uncertainty and impact

In developing scenarios the modeller will focus on the variables that have the highest degree of future uncertainty and also the greatest impact on the business. This ensures that the range of scenarios will reflect the most diverse possible future environments in which the business may have to operate, as well as those that have the greatest potential impact on the performance of the business.

The list of inputs should now be analysed between the four quadrants of the impact/uncertainty matrix shown in Chart 4.5. Uncertainty relates to how easy it is to predict the future behaviour of a variable. Impact relates to how significantly a variable influences business performance. In the model, business performance is represented by the critical factors and the model's outputs.

Chart 4.5 **The impact/uncertainty matrix for a mobile business**

		BUSINESS IMPACT			
		Low		**High**	
UNCERTAINTY	**High**	Mobile browser technology Mobile encryption technology Billing costs E-commerce expenditure Speed of roll-out Billing system capabilities	Web-based servicing Fixed/mobile substitution Device availability Infrastructure availability Billing system costs Partnerships and joint ventures	Mobile-enabled machines Demand for video services Mobile video tariffs Number of competitors Type of competitors Advertising revenues	M-commerce expenditure Churn Licence fees Health issues Market share Mobile wallet Device subsidies Mobile data tariffs
	Low	Population growth Demographic trends Gross domestic product Income distribution Fixed-line penetration Leisure time Supplier contract terms	Content prices Internet penetration Customers to customer services agent ratio Cable penetration Broadband penetration Calling patterns	Mobile penetration Interconnect rates Interconnect income rates Fixed-line prices Staff availability Land area Worker mobility Accounting policies Tax rates Import duties Currency movements Data application availability	Regulatory environment Infrastructure costs Distribution channels Dealer commissions Capacity Roaming agreements Population density Price elasticity of demand Transaction commissions

When performing this task the modeller must look to the future, because those variables that today are certain and benign may be highly volatile and influential by the end of the forecast period. Some inputs may be uncertain and pervasive in the short term, but in the long term they are unlikely to have a major impact on the long-term performance of the business. For example, the lack of availability of personal devices with video telephony capabilities may have an impact on the business in the next few months. In the long term, however, device availability will improve significantly and the overall impact on the business will not be dramatic. Those variables that are placed in the upper-right quadrant are those that could have a long-term, fundamental impact on the performance of the business.

BUSINESS MODELLING INPUT CHECKLIST

Before proceeding to the next stage of model development, the modeller should ensure that all the tasks in Chart 4.6 have been performed.

Chart 4.6 **Business model input checklist**

	Completed
Identify all the variables that influence the performance of the business	
Identify and record relationships between variables	
Remove derived variables from the list	
Add additional input requirements to the list	
Review the data collection requirements	
Analyse inputs using the impact/uncertainty matrix	

5 Developing the scenarios

STAGE 2: IDENTIFY ALTERNATIVE DEVELOPMENT PATHS FOR KEY INPUTS

The upper-right quadrant of the uncertainty/impact matrix (see Chart 4.5 on page 25) contains a list of all the inputs that have, not only the greatest potential impact on the business, but also the highest level of uncertainty about their future behaviour or development path. The business modeller must now describe a number of alternative paths for each of the inputs in that quadrant. For each input the paths should be as contrasting as possible while remaining realistic. Two, often diametrically opposed, paths are usually sufficient to generate interesting scenarios; ideally, there should be no more than three. It is best to avoid a description that reflects the middle ground as this will result in uninteresting scenarios and allow little scope for creative or innovative strategic thinking in the later stages of the process. Chart 5.1 shows the development descriptions for the mobile video telephony example developed in Chapters 3 and 4.

Chart 5.1 **Potential input development paths**

Input variable	Path 1	Path 2	Path 3
Demand for video telephony services	Demand is from only corporate users.	Corporate and small and medium enterprise users demand a range of video services, and high-end consumers demand limited video telephony services.	Business customers demand full video conferencing facilities. The majority of mobile consumer users demand a range of video services.
Mobile video tariffs	Tariffs fall slowly as video telephony remains a premium service.	Tariffs fall rapidly as video telephony becomes a mass-market product.	
Mobile enabled machines	A small proportion of luxury cars and some commercial vehicles and a low number of specialist applications demand mobile enablement.	All new cars, motorcycles, commercial vehicles, vending/ticket machines, security cameras, parking meters, etc, become mobile enabled.	

Input variable	Path 1	Path 2	Path 3
Number of competitors	Competition is restricted to the 3–4 existing mobile network operators and one new entrant.	The number of network operators increases to 5–6. Service providers also compete in the market, and alternative wireless technologies compete in local, corporate markets.	
Type of competitor	Traditional mobile operators.	Competitors enter from the media, IT and banking sectors with high levels of potential mobile content.	
M-commerce expenditure	Mobile users remain wary of transacting over a mobile phone, and only a low number of low-value transactions are conducted via the mobile.	The mobile becomes the electronic wallet, replacing debit and credit cards as the preferred payment device for most users.	
Churn (the rate at which customers leave a network)	Churn increases with the award of licences but settles to the pre-licence award average.	The creation of mobile portals and the development of highly tailored applications result in closer relationships with the customer and virtually no churn.	
Licence fees	A beauty contest is used to allocate the spectrum and no licence fees are payable.	An auction is used to allocate spectrum and licence fees are bid up to very high levels.	An entry fee is charged and a revenue-sharing agreement with the government signed.
Health issues	Mobiles are shown to be harmless.	Mobiles are shown to cause mild short-term effects if used over an extended period of time.	Mobiles are deemed to have moderate long-term effects on memory.

Input variable Market share	Path 1 The business continues to maintain the same level of market share.	Path 2 The business suffers a considerable fall in market share.	Path 3 The business grows market share.
Device subsidies	The industry continues to subsidise the price of new devices to the customer.	The industry does not subsidise new devices.	

During the process of developing alternative development paths, the modeller may well revisit the original classification of variables. Attempts to identify alternative paths for a particular variable often result in the conclusion that there is only one path. These variables should be moved into the bottom-right quadrant.

STAGE 3: SELECT THE THREE OR FOUR MOST INFORMATIVE SCENARIOS

Managing the potential number of scenarios

Many scenarios could be developed from Chart 5.1. The objective is to identify, from the multitude of potential scenarios, no more than three or four of the most interesting, thought-provoking, contrasting and relevant scenarios that will help to answer the fundamental business question.

The modeller can generate scenarios by selecting two key inputs from Chart 5.1 and creating a matrix representing all the possible combinations of development paths for each input. If there are two alternative development paths for each of the two inputs, the result will be a two-by-two matrix. If there are three alternative development paths for each of the inputs, the result will be a three-by-two matrix. If more than two inputs are used, the scenario matrix rapidly becomes unwieldy, and it becomes difficult to examine the multitude of scenarios effectively. An example of a two-by-two matrix is presented in Chart 5.2.

During the initial scenario development phase, the scenarios are derived from combinations of just two inputs. Once the most informative scenarios have been identified, the remaining inputs will be incorporated into the full scenario descriptions so none of the key inputs will be excluded from the modelling process.

Chart 5.2 **Initial scenario matrix**

		MOBILE VIDEO TARIFFS	
		Path 1	**Path 2**
DEMAND FOR VIDEO TELEPHONY SERVICES	**Path 1**	▱ Tariffs fall slowly as video telephony remains a premium service. ▱ Demand is only from corporate users.	▱ Tariffs fall rapidly as video telephony becomes a mass-market product. ▱ Demand is only from corporate users.
	Path 2	▱ Tariffs fall slowly as video telephony remains a premium service. ▱ The majority of mobile customers demand a range of video services.	▱ Tariffs fall rapidly as video telephony becomes a mass-market product. ▱ The majority of mobile customers demand a range of video services.

Generating the most informative scenarios

Generating the most informative scenarios can be made easier by ranking all the inputs in the upper-right quadrant of the matrix in descending order of influence on the business before starting to generate scenarios. This can be a valuable exercise in itself, often promoting considerable debate. Once ranked, pairs of variables from the table can be selected systematically, starting with the highest-ranked inputs. Scenarios should be developed quickly and those that offer little insight should be dismissed. The modeller should aim to create quickly some 10–12 potentially useful scenarios.

Scenario selection criteria

Only three or four scenarios should be taken forward to the business modelling stage. To identify these scenarios the following selection criteria should be used:

- ▱ The scenarios should be realistic. Scenarios that are extremely unlikely to unfold are of little value to the modelling exercise.
- ▱ Each scenario should be dramatically different from the others to provide the business manager with both insights from looking at the business from a number of different perspectives and a wider range of options.
- ▱ The scenarios must be relevant to the fundamental business problem or question that the scenario planning and modelling exercise is attempting to resolve or answer.

The scenario from the bottom-right quadrant of the two-by-two matrix in Chart 5.2 is used as the example for the remainder of this chapter. This scenario envisages video calls falling rapidly in price as video telephony becomes a mass-market service.

STAGE 4: DEVELOP THE SCENARIO STORIES

Use evocative names for the scenarios

Each of the selected scenarios should be given an evocative name. The name should be a vivid description that captures the essence of the scenario. Descriptions that say something about the assumptions and the business context are much more valuable as a communications tool than the traditional base case and the inevitable low and high case variations. For this reason the example scenario has been given the name "Consumers go face-to-face".

Describe the essence of the scenario

The modeller should narrate, at a high level, the essence of how the scenarios will evolve over time and provide a description of the changing business landscape. In each scenario description the modeller should describe the behaviour patterns of the key inputs. Chart 5.3 provides the initial description for the "Consumers go face-to-face" scenario.

Chart 5.3 **Consumers go face-to-face**

Having invested heavily in their new telecommunications networks, which are capable of supporting video telephony, the operators are anxious to promote the use of the service by as many customers as possible. To encourage the adoption of video telephony, the service is provided at affordable tariffs from launch to generate appeal in the mass market. Customers enjoy the opportunity to go face-to-face with their friends and are attracted by the new, stylish video phones. Fierce price competition among a widening range of wireless communcation providers, desperate to retain and grow their customer bases, drives the cost of video telephony rapidly downwards.

When writing the scenarios do not use bullet points but maintain the discipline of writing complete prose. The use of bullet points often results in less coherent and logical scenario descriptions.

Introducing additional inputs

Once the development paths of the inputs that provided the original inspiration for the scenarios have been described, the scenarios can be developed further by including additional inputs from the impact/uncertainty matrix. Additional inputs from the upper-right quadrant should be included first, before moving on to the bottom-right quadrant, then the top-left and lastly the bottom-left. As the impact and uncertainty of the inputs diminishes less detailed descriptions are required for the development of the inputs. The behaviour of the additional inputs should be consistent and supportive of the original scenario. Chart 5.4 describes how device subsidies evolve in the example scenario.

Chart 5.4 **Device subsidies and consumers going face-to-face**

The current mobile operator's strategy of reducing the cost of mobile handsets to the customer through subsidies remains. The importance of mobile devices as a fashion item grows and the levels of subsidy and the rate at which handsets are changed for the newer model increase. To meet the rising costs of subsidising handsets, mobile operators increasingly form joint branding agreements with the TV and media companies that supply video images for phones. The mass production of handsets leads to economies of scale, which eventually reduce the cost of subsidies.

Input timelines

To simplify the modelling process, for those variables that are to be modelled explicitly, the scenario narratives should be translated into numerical inputs for the business model. The numerical values should be consistent with the scenario. The level of the inputs is required for the entire forecasting period. Chart 5.5 gives the input levels for video tariffs and handset subsidies that are consistent with the consumers go face-to-face scenario.

Chart 5.5 **Input timelines**

	2000	2001	2002	2003	2004	2005	2006	2007	2008	2009
Industry video tariff	1.50	1.25	1.00	0.80	0.60	0.50	0.45	0.40	0.40	0.40
Industry handset subsidies	125.0	135.0	150.0	200.0	220.0	250.0	250.0	230.0	210.0	190.0

Identifying the workings of the model

The modeller should now begin to explore in detail the rationale and logic that lie behind the scenarios. The resulting understanding will provide the basis of the formulae that link the inputs to the critical factors and the final outputs of the model. This step ensures that the model's outputs have an internally consistent and logically sound basis. Many of the formulae will already have been identified during stage 1 of the process when the relationships between the identified variables were examined.

During this stage the modeller should concentrate on the derivation of revenue, operating costs and capital expenditure, as these will inevitably form part of the critical factors if not the final outputs of the model. In the case of mobile video telephony revenue the economic model is fairly simple.

1. The number of customers who could potentially generate mobile video telephony revenues must be established. The number of customers at the end of any period is derived from the number of customers at the start of the period minus the number of customers who leave (these customers are called "churners") plus the number of customers who join the network (these customers are called "gross additions").
2. Inputs will be required for the proportion of the customers who use their mobile phone to make video calls.
3. Inputs will be required for the number of calls per customer per month and the average spend per call. The multiplication of the customer base, the number of calls and the average spend per call will give the total value of video telephony per month.
4. An annual figure can be obtained by multiplying the total monthly revenue by 12.

STAGE 5: DEVELOP THE BUSINESS STRATEGY

Inputs under management control

The modeller can now use the detailed scenario descriptions to develop a strategic plan.
The modeller can review a potential strategy with the help of the detailed economic
understanding provided by each scenario description. The modeller should be able to
anticipate the likely competitor, supplier, customer and governmental reactions to the
strategic action plan in the context of the scenario. Once the business model has been
created the strategic choices can be reviewed and refined, as the model provides an
enhanced understanding of the economic implications of the different strategic
alternatives. For each strategic alternative there will be a set of specific strategic inputs that
can be controlled by the business. Some of the strategic inputs in a mobile
communications model are listed below:

- Voice tariffs
- Data tariffs
- Dealer commissions
- Transaction commissions
- Handset selling prices (handset subsidies)
- Network roll-out, coverage and capacity
- Marketing spend

The modeller should produce a timeline for each strategic input. The format of the
strategic input template is identical to the timeline in Chart 5.5.

BUSINESS MODELLING WORKINGS CHECKLIST

Before starting to construct the model, the modeller should ensure that all the tasks in
Chart 5.6 have been performed.

Chart 5.6 **Business model workings checklist**

	Completed
Three or four evocatively named scenarios	
Detailed descriptions of each scenario	
Input timelines	
Economic understanding of the drivers of revenue, operating costs and capital expenditure	
Strategic plans	
Strategic input timelines	

6 Managing the model development process

STYLES OF DEVELOPMENT

The prospect of building a model can appear quite daunting at first. To make construction more manageable and efficient it makes sense to follow a development process that breaks the task down into simple, structured stages. Chart 6.1 shows a typical business modelling process map.

Chart 6.1 **Business modelling process**

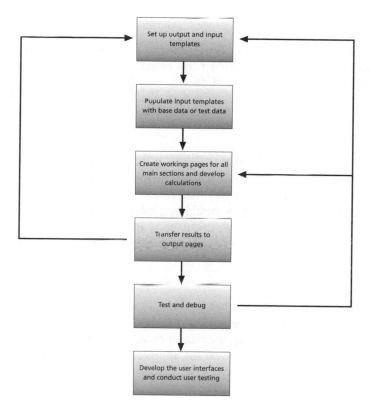

Free-form development

There are some instances where a structured approach to model development may not be appropriate. When relationships between variables are not immediately apparent, or there is uncertainty as to how to generate a specific piece of code, the modeller may choose to develop simple, unstructured models to help explore and identify the possible linkages or formulae. A free-form approach, in a separate workbook, allows the modeller to develop and test a spreadsheet solution that can subsequently be copied into the main model. Doing this "test" modelling in a separate workbook avoids the risk of corrupting existing, established code.

THE MODEL DEVELOPMENT PROCESS

Set up output and input templates

The first stage of the model development process is to set up sheets containing templates for all the outputs. The content of the output sheets was the subject of Chapter 3. Templates for the profit and loss, balance sheet and cashflow can also be created if these form part of the solution. During the model-building process the financial statement templates can be completed continuously, as if performing double-entry book-keeping. The modeller can ensure the accuracy of the work by checking that the balance sheet continues to balance throughout the development of the model. Sheets containing the input templates should also be created at the start of the process.

Populate input templates with base or test data

The input templates must be populated with data to allow model development to continue. Without input data the modeller will be unable to gauge the effectiveness and accuracy of the work done on the model. Ideally, real data should be used, but in the absence of such data, a test dataset, which reflects the likely trends of the actual data, can be used.

Create workings pages for all main sections and develop calculations

This stage of the development process contains the majority of the modelling work. First, separate sheets should be created for the main categories of calculations that will be required. For example, separate sheets should be established for employment cost workings, taxation and working capital calculations and depreciation computations. Once the sheets and their outline structure have been established the formulae and code can be developed.

Transfer results to output pages

In practice, it is better to transfer the results to the output pages as soon as the supporting workings are completed. Building up the output sheets as the model develops allows the modeller to identify early any issues with the approach to the modelling problem that were not foreseen during the planning phase. The sooner any problems are identified the quicker remedial action can be taken.

Test and debug

Once all the calculations have been performed and all the results transferred to the output templates, the modeller should test and debug the model. The testing and debugging stage is designed to ensure that the model is technically accurate and logically sound.

Develop the user interfaces and conduct user testing

The importance of this stage of the process will depend on who the ultimate user of the model will be. When the model is designed for inexperienced users, this stage of the process can be quite demanding. The user interfaces may include navigation and printing tools, online help and user input error-reporting messages. The modeller should identify the required user interfaces and develop the appropriate code. Once complete, a group of users should be invited to test the model to obtain their feedback, and the model amended accordingly.

A MODEL DEVELOPMENT PROJECT PLAN

The development of a business model in a small firm will not require a high level of co-ordination and a sophisticated model development project plan will be unnecessary. In large organisations with complex business modelling problems, however, a detailed model development project plan may prove invaluable. Complex modelling exercises may involve the simultaneous development of a number of models that must ultimately interface with each other. Several groups may provide input into the initial design of each model and then also form part of the user groups who test the various models. As well as the development work, the data collection exercise must be co-ordinated and controlled. If a model development project plan is deemed appropriate, then the project planning process described in Chapter 2 can be employed. The two areas where the modeller should ensure that sufficient time has been allocated are testing and debugging the model and data collection.

Using material from the modeller's library

Over time the modeller will develop a library of models. If the models have been created with a similar style and structure, it is often possible to save considerable time and effort by incorporating existing pieces of code into the current model. Generic code for areas such as discounted cashflow, taxation, working capital, depreciation, amortisation and finance calculations can often be reused with little additional development work. The modeller may also be able to incorporate existing financial statement formats and calculations directly into the current model with only cosmetic changes to the descriptions of items that make up the statements. Clearly, during the development of any new model the modeller should bear in mind the possibility of reusing the code later in other models and should structure and style the development accordingly.

BEST PRACTICE IN MODEL DEVELOPMENT

The basics of quality control

Model ownership

There should be just one person with overall responsibility for a model. The nature of spreadsheets is such that only one individual can work on a model at any one time. The openness of the spreadsheet format, however, can present problems if a number of individuals take it in turns to work on the model. It can become difficult for each developer to identify where changes have been made and co-ordinate their efforts accordingly. The simplest solution is to allocate specific components of the model to individual developers if the complexity of the model permits this. The model owner then simply combines their work into a master copy. Alternatively, they can be allocated specific sheets within the master copy if the modelling work must be performed sequentially. (See also Development log below.)

Version control

Version control is concerned with keeping track of the development process and ensuring that the appropriate version of the model is used for subsequent development work, user testing and finally generating the outputs. The first step in ensuring good version control is to use a file-naming convention. The file name should contain at least the following pieces of information:

- ☑ Title of the model
- ☑ Version number
- ☑ Date
- ☑ Last active developer

A typical example of a file-naming convention might be:

Mobile Telco V2.2 19_04_2000 AN Author.xls

Development log

During the initial stages of development the model will progress quickly and maintaining a record of the changes to each version would be onerous. Once the model has attained a reasonable degree of stability, however, a development log should be maintained. This development log can simply be a separate sheet in the model where the changes made to each new version are described and the date the changes were made and the modeller that made them are recorded.

Retaining old versions of the model

Once the structure of the model is nearly fully established, each old version of the model should be retained in case the modeller decides that the most recent development was unnecessary or created errors that could not be easily rectified. If the previous version has been retained, the current version can be abandoned and the modeller can revert to that previous version. During the final stages of development new versions can be created at the start of each day or even twice a day.

Retaining old versions of the model will quickly generate a large number of files that will need to be systematically stored. Chart 6.2 shows a typical file folder structure for a model development project.

Chart 6.2 **A file folder structure**

The current version of the model being developed is saved to the "Current development version" folder. This folder should only ever contain one file. Older versions of the model should be saved to the "History" folder. The "Releases" folder is useful for keeping track of the models issued for testing and providing an audit trail when the outputs of the model have been incorporated into presentations and board papers. The "Other" folder can contain test pieces of code, model documentation and any other relevant material. The "Master Copy" folder will eventually contain the finished model.

Regularly saving the model

During the development process the model should be saved regularly to reduce the amount of rework that will be required should the computer crash. Before making any significant changes to the model the modeller should save the current version. If the change severely damages the integrity of the model, the file can be closed without saving and the recently saved version reinstated. In the case of major changes to the structure of the model, a new copy should be created before undertaking this work.

Multiple models and dynamic links

Ideally, an entire spreadsheet solution should reside in one model, as the co-ordination of the development work and version control is considerably easier with just one model. Inevitably, complex modelling problems require a number of models that must pass information back and forth. To maintain the quality of the overall business model solution, the developers should agree, at the outset of the development process, the structure and content of the interface sheets that will be used to pass information. The model that generates the information and the model that receives the information should both contain identical interface sheets. Any changes to the interface sheets should be communicated immediately.

Once the interface sheets have been agreed, the modeller responsible for the model that receives the information must decide whether to link the interface sheet to that of the other model or simply copy the values. To create a link the modeller should select COPY→EDIT→PASTE from the toolbar. To copy only the values the modeller should use COPY→EDIT→PASTE SPECIAL→VALUES. The first approach creates a link that will allow the contents of the interface sheet to be updated by using the EDIT→LINKS command. Version control can be maintained reasonably effectively when the developer must specifically update the links to refresh the information in his model. A potential problem can arise when links have been used and both the receiving model and the source model are opened simultaneously in the same session. The links will automatically be updated and no warning will be given. The developer can easily forget that the model being worked on has been linked to another open model and may be unaware that the links have updated, potentially changing some of the information in the model. To minimise the risks associated with links during the development phase, the modeller should use the paste values option (highlight the material to be copied, right click, and then COPY→EDIT→PASTE SPECIAL→VALUES) to ensure more robust version control. The links (COPY→EDIT→PASTE SPECIAL→ALL) can be used when the model is nearer completion and the modeller wants to explore how changes in one model flow through to the other model.

Maintaining quality when under pressure

In an ideal world where the model development process has been planned and managed effectively, the development of the model should take place in an environment free from pressure and stress. In the world the modeller often has to operate in, this is unlikely to be the case, especially at certain times. For example, during negotiations that are supported by the analysis performed by a business model, sudden changes in the negotiating stance of one of the parties can create the need for major modelling work to be done to a tight deadline. When such changes are required the modeller should create a new version of the model and should attempt to plan the changes carefully and document the work done. The modeller should resist the temptation to overwrite formulae or "hard code" any results. However, if time pressures are such that hard coding results is the only solution, then the modeller should highlight the areas where hard coding has been used and document the areas in the development log. Once the time pressures have lifted the modeller should reproduce the hard coded results using the appropriate changes to the model and its calculations. The modeller should eliminate all hard coded entries before doing any further development work.

Avoiding some common pitfalls

Backing up the model

Modellers working in large organisations should ensure that they not only save their models on to their hard drive but also save the files to a network drive which will be backed up regularly. They are then protected if their hard drive crashes. Modellers in smaller organisations should use an alternative back-up medium such as a zip drive.

Group sheet function

Many spreadsheet packages have a group sheet function that allows changes to be made to a number of sheets simultaneously. This is a useful function, but it can be devastating if the modeller forgets to turn off the group function before continuing with normal development work. If possible, avoid using the group function, but if it is the most efficient option then save a new version of the model before using it.

Hiding rows and columns

During the development phase do not hide rows or columns within any sheet, as it is easy to forget this has been done. Once rows or columns have been hidden, formulae can be copied into them erroneously or they can unintentionally become part of a sum or similar function despite being hidden. To avoid these risks ensure that all development work is conducted with all rows and columns visible.

7 Useful items to include in the modeller's toolbox

Before starting to build a model it is useful to be aware of a range of functions and features that are available in Excel to help the model development process. They are described here with examples of where they could be applied.

NAMING SHEETS

Some of the conventions used in this book are to set up separate sheets for:

- Inputs – numerical data
- Workings – calculations
- Outputs – results for printing

These are explained in detail in Chapter 8, but references to these sheets will be made in this chapter.

To name a sheet

Double click on the sheet name "Sheet 1" and it will appear reversed out. Type in a new name, such as "Inputs". (An alternative method is to right click on the sheet name and select "Rename" from the pop-up menu.)

RANGE NAMES

The most frustrating part of picking up a model developed by someone else or returning to model that has not been accessed for some time is trying to understand what has been developed and how it operates. This is often complicated by long, unintelligible formulae consisting only of cell references, surrounded by arithmetic signs and functions.

Instead of using co-ordinates to refer to cells in formulae, name cells with clear words or phrases by using the RANGE NAME function. For example, a value for revenue could be calculated by the formula:

=Revenue_per_customer*Number_of_customers (rather than, say, D23*D24)

The benefit of this approach is the speed with which it can be interpreted and understood. It eliminates the need to track back and see what the reference cells (D23 and D24) contain.

The naming of cells can be done in several ways as explained below. This convention will be used throughout the rest of this book. For clarity, all range names will be shown in italics, although they will appear in normal type in Excel.

Naming one cell

Click on any cell and in the "Name box" it will show the cell co-ordinates (the "Name box" is shown on the left side of the formula bar – if the formula bar is not visible go to the menu option VIEW and tick FORMULA BAR). Click in the "Name box" and the cell co-ordinate will appear reversed out. Now type in a name for the cell and press RETURN at the end. (Note that range names cannot use punctuation and spaces. These are traditionally replaced with an underscore _ character.)

Chart 7.1 **Formula bar**

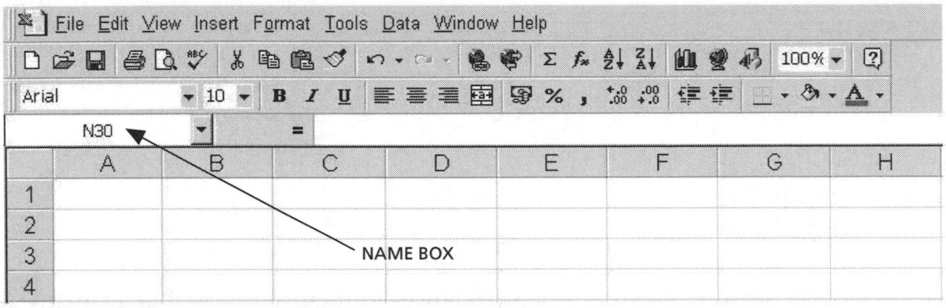

To see the names that have been created click on the list arrow at the right of the "Name box" and all defined range names will appear. Selecting a name from the list will move the cursor to highlight the cells to which the name refers.

The defined names can now be used in formulae to calculate results.

Naming one cell where the cell name is displayed to the left of reference value

If A25 contains the word "*Inflation*" and B25 contains 5%, the range name *Inflation* should refer to the number. Thus wherever *Inflation* is used in a formula it will mean 5% (or any other value subsequently put in cell B25).

Chart 7.2 **Naming one cell where the name is to the left of the value**

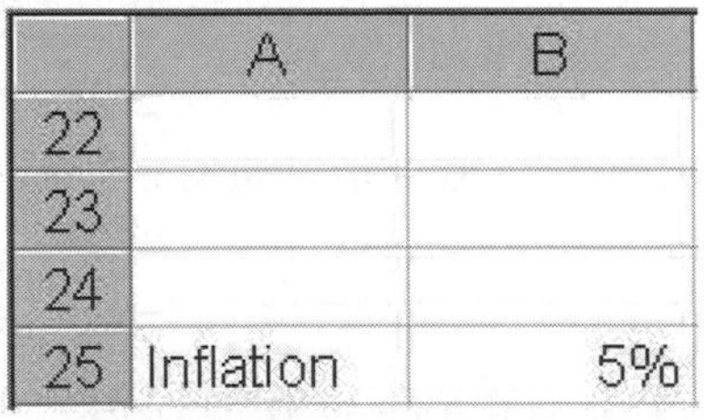

Highlight the cell B25 only and from the INSERT menu select NAME→DEFINE (or press CTRL F3). In the "Names in workbook" box at the top will be the name *Inflation*. In the "Refers to" box at the bottom will be the cell reference $B$25. Press "OK" to include it in the list of defined names.

Chart 7.3 **The Define Name box**

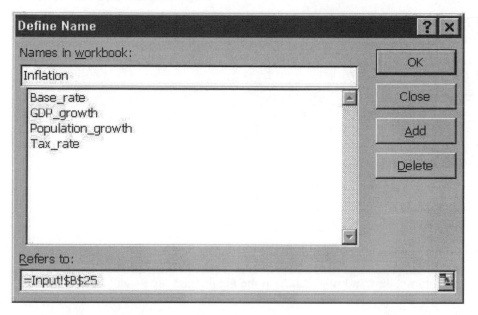

Defining several individual names

Once the "Define Name" box is visible it is possible to use it to define several names. Each range name will have to be manually keyed in the "Names in workbook:" box at the top and the cell reference entered in the "Refers to:" box at the bottom. Between each entry press "Add" to include it in the list. When the names have been entered press "OK".

For this type of naming the cell reference has to be entered in the absolute format of:

$$='sheet name'!\$'column'\$'row'$$

For example:

$$=sheet1!\$B\$25$$

The "Define Name" box can also be used to delete names that have been incorrectly entered. Highlight the entry on the list and press the "Delete" button. Press "OK" when complete.

Naming several values at once

The values should be set up in a group together with all entries below each other (blank lines can be left). As noted above, it is preferable to have the cell name on the left and the value in the adjacent cell to its right.

Chart 7.4 **Naming several values at once**

	A	B	C
24			
25	Inflation	5%	
26	Base rate	6%	
27			
28	Population growth	2%	
29	GDP growth	3%	
30			
31	Tax rate	30%	

To name all these values at once, highlight the whole block of both names and their numbers (A25:B31). From the INSERT menu select NAME→CREATE (or press CTRL SHIFT F3), tick the "Left column" box and press "OK". All the highlighted inputs will have been named.

Chart 7.5 **The tick box**

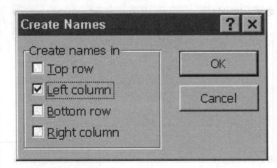

Naming whole rows

Select the row to be named, either by clicking on the row number at the left or by pressing SHIFT and SPACEBAR if the cursor is already in the row to be named.

From the INSERT menu select NAME→DEFINE (or press CTRL F3). In the "Names in workbook:" box at the top will be the text from the cell in column A (typically the row title). Whether the row is named or not, you can type in or edit the "Names in workbook:" box as required. In the "Refers to:" box at the bottom the row name will be entered. Press ADD to include it in the list.

To name part of a row the same procedure can be used, but before selecting the menu item or pressing CTRL F3, highlight the part of row and its name.

The benefit of naming whole rows is explained in Chapter 8 (see page 57).

Common range names

In many rows of the model it would be common for formulae to refer to the previous year and advance it in some way. To make the spreadsheet more intelligible, it is helpful if all the formulae say *Last_year* or *Previous_year* instead of the cell co-ordinate for the cell to its left. To achieve this effect it needs to be set up separately on each page of the workbook.

Take the following steps:

- ◪ Click the cursor anywhere on the spreadsheet except in column A.
- ◪ From the INSERT menu select NAME→DEFINE (or press CTRL F3).
- ◪ In the "Names in workbook:" field enter *Last_year*.
- ◪ In the "Refers to:" box remove the two $ signs (locating them with the mouse rather than the arrow keys) and change the column part of the cell reference to the previous character (for example, F would now be E).
- ◪ Click on the "Add" box.

Now whenever you refer to the cell *Last_year* it will always pick up the contents of the cell one to its left. So if you have a cost in the first year that you want to increase by inflation (already named *Inflation* above), in each subsequent year the following intelligible formula can be used:

$$=Last\_year*(1+Inflation)$$

Accessing the named inputs and rows

Whenever you need to refer to a pre-named cell while writing a formula just press F3 to access a drop down list of all the named ranges available. Click on the one required and it will be inserted into the formula. To speed up finding the right item when the list becomes long, press the first character of the name and it will automatically jump to that part of the list.

Sometimes modellers complain that setting up these range names is time consuming, which it is. But it has three advantages:

- ◪ Once set up it is quicker to model (time up-front pays dividends later).
- ◪ It provides wonderful clarity for users to explore and understand how the model works.
- ◪ It helps the modeller returning to enhance a model that has been untouched for several months to get back into its methodology.

When naming ranges it is important to use as much detail as possible to ensure that when the name is used in formulae it can be easily interpreted. For more complex models spanning several worksheets it can be helpful to precede each name with the sheet name, to aid traceability (and avoid duplication of common names).

USEFUL FUNCTIONS

CONCATENATE

This function allows text, numbers and formulae to be mixed in a cell (this can be achieved with the "&" symbol but CONCATENATE always appears much more tidy).

The benefit of this function is to have dynamic links between sheets. For example, if the assumption for the inflation rate on an input page were 5%, then it would be helpful if the heading on an output page stated this. Thus as the input assumption is changed so is the heading on the output.

Example

On the input page an assumption for inflation has been entered and using range names the cell has been named *Inflation.*

On the output page the dynamic link would be set up as:

=CONCATENATE("Cost inflation at ",*Inflation**100,"%")

If inflation were 5% this would read: Cost inflation at 5%

This can also be applied to range of variable expressions such as discount rates, growth rates, and so on.

MIN, MAX or IF statements

The IF statement provides an effective way to test and respond to attributes in a model. The syntax is:

=IF(Test,True,False)

The test is whether one attribute is equal to (=), greater than (>), greater than or equal (>=), less than (<), less than or equal (<=) or not equal (<>) to another attribute. The true/false parts are the separate results that will be put in the cell depending on the answer to the test.

A test can create repetition when a formula or function is used as part of the test as well as in the answer.

Example

=IF(complex formula>0,complex formula,0)

A more effective way to model this code is by using the MAX or MIN function:

MAX – which takes the highest value in a series separated by commas

MIN – which takes a lowest value in a series separated by commas

The IF statement could be replaced with:

$$=MAX(complex\ formula, 0)$$

Nested IF statements

For some types of inputs or situations there may be several choices for an entry, such as the currency to display outputs. This can give rise to a large nested series of IF statements. If a cell named ccy holds a three-letter currency type, the formula to identify an exchange rate could be:

$$=IF(ccy="USD", 1, IF(ccy="JPY", 100, IF(ccy="GBP", 1.6, \ldots\ldots$$

These are difficult to create and more difficult to review for error. An easier way is to set up a table and then refer to the preferred choice with an index number.

For example, the data in Chart 7.6 could be set up on the input page.

Chart 7.6 **A currency selection table**

	A	B	C	D	E	F	G
32	Report currency 4		Report_currency		Choice	Currency	Rate
33					1	USD	1
34					2	JPY	100
35					3	GBP	1.6
36					4	FFR	6

In cell B32 the user enters the preferred currency choice (1–4). This cell is named *Report_currency*. On the output sheet, set up a cell titled "Reporting currency". Next to this use the following code to identify the exchange rate.

To find out the exchange rate to apply to all outputs the INDEX function can be used. The syntax is:

$$=INDEX(range, row\ number, column\ number)$$

In this example it could be applied as:

$$=INDEX\ (Input!G33:G36, Report\_currency, 1)$$

It is also helpful to have some validation of the entry made to ensure it is in the range 1–4. This can be achieved by using the ISERROR function, which tests for a range of errors:

$$=IF(ISERROR(INDEX(Input!G33:G36, Report\_currency, 1)), "Warning\ message",$$
$$INDEX(Input!G33:G36, Report\_currency, 1))$$

The INDEX function will not allow a selection to be made outside of the defined range (in this case G33:G36) without showing #REF!, and therefore the ISERROR function detects the error and will handle it in a user-friendly manner.

OFFSET

For a model to have maximum impact it needs to be a highly flexible engine through which input data of scenarios or even fine tunings of scenarios can be passed. It would take a long time to record all the inputs for each scenario and enter them individually for each use of the model. Hence it can be useful to park all the scenarios in separate columns of the model and use a switch to select between them.

Chart 7.7 shows an example input sheet for a model where the working sheet is calculated from the inputs in column B (that are all individually range named by the words in column C). Alternative scenarios are set up in columns E to H..

Chart 7.7 **Setting up an OFFSET function to run scenarios through the model**

	A	B	C	D	E	F	G	H
1	Model title							
2						Scenarios		
3	Dataset	1	*Dataset*		1	2	3	4
4								
5	Price	5.0	*Input_price*		5.0	5.5	5.0	7.0
6	Price growth	3%	*Input_price_growth*		3%	3%	5%	5%

To drive the model from a variety of scenarios the values in columns E to H need to be able to be transferred into column B. The OFFSET function will enable this to be achieved. Its syntax is as follows:

=OFFSET(Reference cell,Rows away from reference,Columns away from reference)

The cell B3 is used to define which scenario will be used to drive the model. Assuming the content of cell B3 is range named *Dataset*, the formula in B5 would read:

=OFFSET(D5,0,*Dataset*)

The contents of cell B5 will therefore be filled by the contents of the cell defined by:

column: D + *Dataset*
row: 5 + 0

With *Dataset* set as 1 the content for cell B5 will be drawn from E5 (that is, the number 5.0), with *Dataset* set as 2 the content for cell B5 will be drawn from F5 (that is, the number 5.5), and so on.

This formula can be copied all the way down the input column. As the dataset number in B3 is changed so are all the inputs in column B that are used to drive the model.

This can be further enhanced and combined with the CONCATENATE function. Each of the datasets can be given a name entered in row 4 (such as "Best case" in E4 or "With Partnership option" in F4, and so on). On the output page the CONCATENATE function can be used to display which scenario is being used.

For example:

$$=CONCATENATE(\text{"These results have been created using Dataset: "},OFFSET(Input!D4,0,Dataset))$$

AVERAGE

Taking an average of two or more numbers is a common occurrence in many models. Often the AVERAGE function in Excel is forgotten and the mathematics is done manually with a division. The benefit of this function is that it adds and counts the number of items included and therefore is flexible to a range of data. The syntax is:

$$=AVERAGE(number,number,number...) \text{ for up to 30 numbers}$$
Though the number can be a range:Average(H61:H66) or a range
name:Average(*Prices*)

MOD

MOD is a useful function that provides the remainder of one number divided by another. For example, 7 MOD 3 is 1. The syntax is:

$$=MOD(number,divisor)$$

This can be used in modelling to trigger events at set intervals. For example, if a computer was replaced every three years MOD could be used to trigger the purchase by being applied to the year number.

Based on model years of 0,1,2,3... (rather than actual years) the formula would be:

$$=IF(MOD(Year\_number,Input\_life\_of\_computer)=0,Input\_new\_computer\_cost,0)$$

An asset would be bought in years 0,3,6... for an amount defined in the cell *Input_new_computer_cost*.

USEFUL FEATURES

Shortcut keys

In developing a model a lot of time can be spent moving between keyboard and mouse and back. A much more effective way of operating is to use the keyboard throughout. This can be achieved by using keyboard shortcuts that replicate mouse functions. It would take ten pages to list all the available options in Excel, whereas a simple use of the HELP function will reveal all of them. On the HELP index, select SHORTCUTS, KEYS and work through the available items.

Some of the most useful options are as follows.

F2	Edit cell contents
CTRL + C	Copy
CTRL + V	Paste
CTRL + PRINT	Print
CTRL + SPACEBAR	Select column
SHIFT + SPACEBAR	Select row
CTRL + SPACEBAR followed by SHIFT + SPACEBAR (or vice versa)	Select whole sheet
F10 followed by arrow keys	Select item on the menu toolbar

Divide by zero

In any division calculation there is a risk that the denominator is zero and this will cause the answer to result in a division by zero error. The ripple effect will cause all dependent cells to show similar division by zero errors, making it difficult to find the source of the problem. The TRACE ERROR button on the auditing toolbar will identify each incidence of the error.

To activate the auditing toolbar select menu option VIEW→TOOLBARS→CUSTOMIZE... and then check the tick box by "Auditing". To use the function, place the cursor in an error cell and press the TRACE ERROR button, which is a yellow diamond with an exclamation mark. The cursor will move to the cell creating the problem and highlight all connections from the errant cell over to the cell from where the function was called. The alternative is to set all division calculations within an IF statement:

=IF(cell reference for denominator=0,"warning message",division calculation)

Some modellers will use a more complicated solution that brings in the error test function 'ISERROR', which gives a true/false result for the outcome of a range of potential errors, including division by zero.

=IF(ISERROR(division calculation),"warning message",division calculation)

Format painter

On the toolbar is an icon of a wide paintbrush. It can be used to pick up and apply formats from one cell to another. This is particularly useful for number formats that have been created for certain styles and number of decimal places. It is much quicker than using the FORMAT→CELLS menu options.

To use the function follow these steps:

- ◪ Click on a cell that has the format you want to copy.
- ◪ Click on the paintbrush.
- ◪ Click on the destination cell where you want to replicate the format.
- ◪ To apply the format repeatedly, double click on the paintbrush and then everywhere you click thereafter the format will be applied.
- ◪ To stop repeated application click back on the paintbrush or press the ESC key.

Be sure that format painter picks up every attribute of format – colour, style, font, size, and so on.

Macros for repeated tasks

During detailed development work on a model the modeller will often need to perform a number of tasks repeatedly. An example in the early stages is the creation of an input cell that has a different font, background colour and border and is unprotected, compared with ordinary cells. Each time an input cell is required the modeller must go through the laborious task of formatting the cell accordingly. Fortunately, it is possible to record macros for this and similar tasks and assign them to a shortcut key so that the task can be performed with one or two keystrokes. The following steps explain how to record a macro to perform a sequence of formatting commands and to assign them to a shortcut key:

- ◪ TOOLS→MACRO→RECORD NEW MACRO.
- ◪ Enter a name for the macro in the dialog box.
- ◪ Enter the keystroke to which the macro will be assigned, CTRL + character. (It is often helpful to have it on the left side of the keyboard to enable the macro key combination to be actioned with the left hand.)
- ◪ Press OK.
- ◪ Perform carefully all the formatting or regularly repeated tasks that you want to be able repeat.
- ◪ Press stop.

The macro has now been recorded. To use the macro code simply select the cell that you wish to format and press the shortcut key combination. The macro will run automatically, performing the task for you. This technique can be applied to other tasks, such as formatting, printing or copying and pasting a formula cell in one year across all the remaining model years.

Using graphs

Often the most user-friendly way to display numerical information is graphically. Graphs make trends in the data easy to discern. They also make it easier to examine relationships and to spot potentially erroneous data inputs. Most spreadsheet packages have graphing tools. In Excel the creation of a graph involves the following steps.

1. From the INSERT menu select CHART (or press the CHART WIZARD button).
2. Select the appropriate chart type (column, bar, line or a host of others) by clicking on one of the options. The type of chart to use will depend on the data being displayed. Revenue and cost information on an annual basis is often best displayed in column or bar charts. Macroeconomic variables such as interest and exchange rates and inflation and microeconomic variables such as product prices are often best represented in a line graph. When the information focuses on a particular year, such as a summary of expenditure types, a pie chart can often be the most effective.
3. Select the sub-type of the preferred type of graph – vertical, horizontal, with or without markers, and so on. The choice is often a case of personal preference. Press NEXT.
4. Identify the information to be presented in the graph. Having pressed NEXT in the

previous step the user is automatically presented with the choice of entering a data range (or block of data) or series (several separate blocks of data). Select SERIES to allow more control over the information that is presented.

5. To add a data series click ADD.

6. Select the values required either directly from the spreadsheet by highlighting them or by typing in the data range.

7. Select a name for the series by either manually entering a name or linking to a name on the spreadsheet.

8. Steps 5–7 can be repeated until all the data has been identified.

9. The same section also allows you to select a series for the x or horizontal axis (usually years for most models).

10. The next step takes you into the options for the graph which appear on a number of tabs:

   ▪ Titles are always valuable, certainly a main title and usually a vertical axis title. The horizontal title may not be required especially if the values are years or dates.

   ▪ On the AXES tab it is usually preferable to check both x and y boxes and to select automatic

   ▪ The use of gridlines is a matter of personal preference. If a data table is provided to support the graph, then the gridlines could be excluded. Usually, graphs look better without gridlines.

   ▪ The legend (or key) is important if a number of different data series are presented on the same graph. It is usually better to position the graph at the base as this allows the maximum width for the graph itself.

   ▪ Data labels can make a graph look messy and are best avoided, especially if the data are also presented in a table.

   ▪ The presentation of a data table can be useful as it allows a much cleaner graph to be presented.

11. Once the options have been selected and OK has been clicked the package asks where you would like the graph to appear. Once the selection has been made the graph will appear in the appropriate sheet of the model.

Improving the appearance of the graph

By right clicking at any point on the graph you can gain access to location-sensitive menus. Depending on whether you have clicked on a data line, background, gridline, axis or labels the following option(s) will appear:

   ▪ CHART OPTIONS – changes can be made to legends (keys) and axes.

   ▪ FORMAT DATA SERIES – the presentation of the graph is usually improved if bright primary colours are used rather than the defaults. It can also be helpful in presentation to increase the weight of the line to make it stand out more significantly. Select this option when the cursor is over a data line.

   ▪ FORMAT PLOT AREA – the graphs stand out more if they are presented against a pale background rather than the default grey.

   ▪ SOURCE DATA – this can be used to add or delete displayed data series.

   ▪ FORMAT AXIS – as time is usually on the x-axis it can look better if the year-end numbers are on rather than between the markers. To achieve this select the FORMAT AXIS menu and the SCALE tab and deselect the check box with the heading "Value (Y) axis crosses between categories".

Chart 7.8 **Sales forecast**

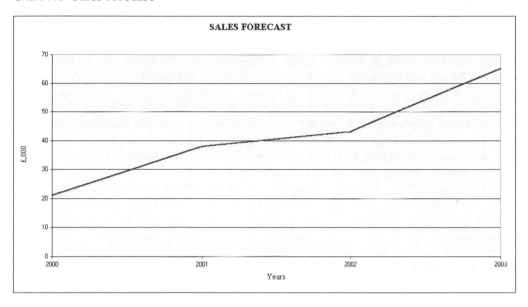

Eyeball lines

Excel may not always be the best judge of a line's fit to data or of the extrapolation of data. A helpful feature is Excel's ability to work backwards from a graph to generate data.

To create eyeball lines follow these steps:

- ▱ Beside the actual data for a line, manually enter a series of numbers that are approximately the same. Show this on the graph by adding it as a series and plot it as a trendline.
- ▱ On the graph line of this new series left click the mouse to highlight the individual data points.
- ▱ At a data point left click the mouse again to convert the cursor into an up-down arrow (↕).
- ▱ Keeping the left mouse button depressed move the data point up and down. The graph will change, the trendline will change and the trendline formulae will change. Back in the spreadsheet the data source will also change.

Eyeball lines can be used to support the generation of assumptions.

8 Style and outline

Having explored the background to model development and the process for its evolution, this chapter focuses on building the core structure of the spreadsheet. The overall aim is to:

- create a dynamic environment in which to test out scenarios and sensitivities;
- be able to change any one assumption and still have a valid answer;
- create a clear and logical structure that will enable easy adaptation and development;
- create legibility that will allow users to read the cells as well as the answers offered.

MODEL LAYOUT

The first stage is to set up a minimum of three sheets to separate out numerical inputs, workings and outputs for printing. The features of these are shown in Chart 8.1:

Chart 8.1 **Model layout**

INPUTS	WORKINGS	OUTPUTS
Numbers only **No** calculation formulae (all calculations to be done on workings sheet)	**Formulae only** **Never** any numbers (all numbers to be entered on input sheet)	Extracts from the workings sheet for printing

The benefit of the layout is to create a highly flexible "engine" through which sets of data can be passed. The logic may seem simple, but it requires discipline to apply.

Take, for example, an inflation rate that could be applied to all costs as they are projected forward. If the inflation rate were coded as a number in each of the cost cells, a change in rate would take considerable re-coding and potentially one or more uses of the percentage would be forgotten. However, if an inflation percentage is entered once as an input, applied to costs with formulae, it can be easily changed. This will enable the projections for all costs to be changed simultaneously, resulting in "a dynamic effect".

This layout should be applied without exception, even to the extent that the start year number or the number of days in the year should be placed on the input sheet. For inputs, all numbers means all numbers!

The discipline often breaks down in the heat of decision-making when an urgent response to a scenario is needed. The modeller may try to put in a "quick fix" by entering a hard coded number somewhere on the workings sheet. This is a fatal error that may go undetected for many a subsequent scenario, thus invalidating the use of the model.

The structure can be developed to match the scale of the model. For large models it may be helpful to create separate input and working sheets for types of assumptions such as revenue, capital costs and operating costs. Output sheets can be set up for profit and loss, balance sheet, cashflow, valuations, ratios and key graphs. Hence the number of sheets can easily rise. However, the most important points are to remember the status of each sheet (whether input, working or output) and to stick rigidly to the principles of that style of sheet.

In setting the design the golden rule is to develop a model that is fit for the purpose – the model should not be over-engineered. The point of the model should be kept clearly in mind and thus the component elements should only be those that are needed to achieve the objective. Other elements that are often "fun" to create, or "clever algorithms" developed to solve irrelevant details, should be avoided.

SHEET LAYOUT: INPUTS

The input sheet should consist of the base data to drive the model. All data should be entered into one column with each variable typically consisting of seed and behaviour attributes. In Chart 8.2 the seed is a price of 5 and the behaviour over time is a growth of 3% per annum.

Chart 8.2 **Input sheet layout**

	A	B	C	D	E	F	G	H
1	**Model title**							
2						Scenarios		
3	Dataset	1	Dataset		1	2	3	4
4								
5	Revenue							
6	Price	5.0	Input_price		5.0	5.5	5.0	7.0
7	Price growth	3%	Input_price_growth		3%	3%	5%	5%

Detailed attributes of the sheet

Row 1: The title of the model. Where possible enter this once on the input sheet and refer back to it for all other uses. Should the title change, one amendment will update the whole model.

Columns A and B: The names and values of the inputs that will be used to drive the model.

Row 5: Subheading to group inputs together by type.

Column C: The range names (see Chapter 7) given to the inputs for when they are used in formulae throughout the model.

Columns E to H: Data scenarios that can be pulled into column B to drive the model with alternative assumptions. This is done by using the OFFSET function (see Chapter 7) in column B that is referenced to the Dataset selection in B3.

An alternative style of input is to have error validation as part of the input with the scenario datasets starting in column I, as shown in Chart 8.3. Rows 9 to 35 are omitted as they contain other input assumptions.

Chart 8.3 **Input sheet layout with error validation**

	A	B	C	D	E	F	G	H	I
1	Model title								
2									Scenarios
3	Dataset	1	Dataset						1
4					Valid	Min	Max		
5	REVENUE								
6	Price	5.0	Input_price		Valid	3.0	8.0		5.0
7	Price growth	3%	Input_price_growth		Valid	0%	10%		3%
8									
39									
40	Data validity:	Valid input data							

Columns F and G: These are the minimum and maximum acceptable values that can be entered to run the model.

Column E: This tests the validity of the data driving the model in Column B. To do this Column B has a range name of *Model_data*, Column F has a range name of *Min_input* and Column G has a range name of *Max_input*. The formula for cell E6 (and subsequent rows) is:

=IF(AND(*Model_data*>=*Min_input*,*Model_data*<=*Max_input*),"Valid","Error")

Row 40: At the end of the input sheet a test can be done to check the validity of all data. Column E has a range name of *Input_validity*. The formula in cell B40 is:

=IF(COUNTIF(*Input_validity*,"Error")>0,"Invalid input data","Valid input data")

On the output sheet a link can be made to the text of cell B40 to alert users when the answers they are reviewing are built from erroneous input data.

SHEET LAYOUT: WORKING

The working sheet should consist of the calculations to create the lines for the output from the model, as shown in Chart 8.4. All cells (other than headings) should be formulae built up from numbers entered on the input sheet.

Chart 8.4 **Working sheet layout**

	A	B	C	D	E	F	G	H	I
1	**Model title**								
2									
3	Year number	*Year_number*			0	1	2	3	4
4	Years	*Actual_years*			2000	2001	2002	2003	2004
5									
6	Inflation index	*Working_inflation_index*			1.000	1.050	1.103	1.158	1.180
7									
8	**CUSTOMERS**								
9									
10	Customers ('000)	*Working_customers*			250	300	360	432	518

Detailed attributes of the sheet

Row 1: Title of the model (linked back to what was entered on the input sheet).

Rows 3 and 4: Timelines to reference each column. Row 3 can be created on the sheet, but the value in E4 should be drawn for the input sheet to allow it to be changed. It can often be helpful to have this as a permanent header to the page. To do this select Row 5 and from the WINDOW menu select SPLIT. This will put a bar across the screen, allowing you to leave the top part fixed as you scroll down the working sheet. If you need to swap between the two halves of the sheet, press F6.

Row 6: It can be helpful to create common indexes at the top of the sheet that will be referred to on several occasions. An inflation index (created from data on the input sheet and in this example growing at 5%) saves repetitious creation on all cost and revenue lines when building models that use nominal values (including inflation).

Row 8: Subheading. It is worth having lots of subheadings to ensure that the build-up of logic is clear to the user.

Row 10: Calculation where a seed is used in column E (in this example 250) and behaviour trends it out over time (in this example 20% growth per annum). Note that the heading in column A includes details of the units that the numbers are based in.

Column B: The range names given to the rows so they can be used elsewhere on the working and output sheets.

When modelling on the working sheet it can be helpful to have two windows into the model to save having to continually refer back to the input sheet. To create this display, from the WINDOW menu select NEW WINDOW. This will create a second window of your spreadsheet. To see both windows, from the WINDOW menu select ARRANGE and check the "Horizontal" style. This puts the two windows one above the other. Select the input sheet for the top window and the working sheet for the bottom window. To move between the two windows press CTRL F6.

SHEET LAYOUT: OUTPUTS

The output sheet is to summarise workings for printing and should consist of the transfer of key lines from the working sheet as shown in Chart 8.5. Few calculations other than perhaps totalling should be required.

Chart 8.5 **Output sheet layout**

	A	B	C	D	E	F	G	H	I
1	Model title								
2									
3	Year number	Year_number			0	1	2	3	4
4	Years	Actual_years			2000	2001	2002	2003	2004
5									
6	PROFIT AND LOSS								
7					$'000	$'000	$'000	$'000	$'000
8	Revenue								
9									
10	Sales income	Output_sales_income			0	2,546	3,564	4,990	6,986

Detailed attributes of the sheet

Row 1: Title of the model (linked back to the input sheet).

Rows 3 and 4: Column titles created by using the range names from rows on the working sheet where these were set up. Note that all sheets should start with the first year in the same column. In this example, year 0 is set up in column E for both the working and output sheets.

Rows 6 to 8: Heading, subheading and display units. Although many models will be written and used in one country, it is important that the units of currency are clearly shown to make it obvious to the reader of any output. The main rule with currency is to be consistent throughout the model to avoid adding together financial values of mixed currencies.

Row 10: Data drawn from the working sheet with references rather than calculation.

Column B: Range names for use in other parts of the output sheet.

ALTERNATIVE MODEL LAYOUT

The methodology described above, using three styles of sheets (input, working and output), may not always be the most appropriate for all situations. Some modellers will develop complete components on one sheet, covering inputs at the top and then developing down through workings to create outputs. The benefit of this style is that when using the model the cause and effect of changing assumptions can be seen instantly without switching between sheets. It also enables modularisation, whereby completed components can be transferred and used in other models with little development and minimal adaptation.

Although this alternative layout mixes the three styles of sheets, the individual sections still comply with the principles of their particular style. This type of layout can create appearance difficulties because column widths have to stay constant in all sections, thus compromising visual presentation.

When starting out in modelling, it is recommended that separate input, working and output sheets are used to help apply a structural discipline to the model. Examples throughout this book use both styles to illustrate how they can be applied.

MAKING THE MODEL INTELLIGIBLE

Cells are free, so use them. When formulae become larger than one line of the screen, try to break up items into smaller components that are individually labelled. For example, instead of a large formula to work out revenue, break it down into a formula for number of customers, a formula for spend per customer and a third formula that multiplies the two former calculations. Time spent by the developer spreading out the model is more than compensated for by time saved by the users.

MAKING RANGE NAMES WORK

As discussed in Chapter 7, it is recommended that range names are used extensively when building the model. One of the clever results of applying range names to rows is that each number stays loyal to the column in which it was created. This is particularly useful on the working page. In Chart 8.6, for example, if a range name Working_staff_numbers is created for the row titled Staff, when the range name is applied in formulae the staff number showing in column F, which is a value of 280, will always be used in calculations in column F. Similarly, the staff number showing in column H, which is a value of 310, will always be used in calculations in column H, and so on.

Chart 8.6 **The use of range names**

	A	B	C	D	E	F	G	H	I
1	Model title								
2									
3	Year number	Year_number			0	1	2	3	4
4	Years	Actual_years			2000	2001	2002	2003	2004
34									
35	Employment								
36									
37	Staff	Working_staff_numbers			0	280	290	310	320
38	Cost per employee ($'000)	Working_cost_per_employee			0	12.2	12.6	13.0	13.5
39									
40	Total employment cost ($'000)	Working_total_employment_cost			0	3,416	3,654	4,030	4,320

In every year of row 40 the calculation is:

$$=Working\_staff\_numbers*Working\_cost\_per\_employee$$

The component elements stay loyal to the columns they originate from. Hence the need to ensure that every sheet of the model has its first year starting in the same column, in this example year o is in column E.

RETAINING CONSISTENT LOGIC BY HAVING THE SAME FORMULAE EVERY YEAR

In building a model that involves projections over a period of time, there will inevitably be events that occur in some years but not others. However, the model needs to retain its structure and flexibility. The way to handle these events is to trigger them with a year number, entered on the input sheet, that is tested using IF statements on the working sheet.

Take, for example, the introduction of a tax that is anticipated to become payable in 2002. Rather than coding the working sheet for 2000 and 2001 as two years of zeros followed by a tax formula for 2000 onwards, it would be better to put these details on the input sheet.

Year tax introduced   2002

Rate of tax   2%

On the working sheet the tax can be triggered by reference to the dates at the top of each column, for example:

$$=IF(Year\_number>=Year\_tax\_introduced,Rate\_of\_tax*Profit,0)$$

Changing the year on the input sheet allows the user to test what happens if the tax is brought in during 2001 or is delayed to 2003.

The objective on the working sheet is to have the same formula every year and any timed events being triggered by dates entered on the input sheet.

ROUNDING TO VISIBLE

Consider Chart 8.7.

Chart 8.7 **The effect of rounding**

	A	B	C	D	E	F	G	H
1		£m						
2	Sales of A	0						
3	Sales of B	0						
4	Sales of C	0						
5		1						
6								

If this were presented in a report, you might wonder whether there was an error. A first thought might be that the results would have been better presented in thousands and not millions.

To avoid rounding errors, it is helpful to choose a number of significant figures on the output sheet and consistently apply rounding to ensure that all the schedules add up. Although this could be seen as an accountant's desire for accuracy, it does help to validate the completeness of balance sheets as well as other audit tests.

The syntax is:

$$=ROUND(number, number\ of\ decimal\ places)$$

If the fraction is 0.5 or greater it will be rounded up; otherwise it will be rounded down. The number of decimal places can be negative and thus rounded to hundreds or thousands. To allow flexibility, it may be useful to set up the number of places of rounding on the input sheet and thus enable changes to be made quickly if the scale of the project should change.

For example, the number 123.456 rounded would be as shown in Chart 8.8.

Chart 8.8 **Rounding**

Number of places	Answer
0	123
1	123.5
−1	120

There are other derivations of rounding such as ROUNDUP, which always rounds up fractions to the next whole number, and ROUNDDOWN, which always ignores the fractional part.

SIGN CONVENTION

You need to have one. There are a few alternative conventions, but the most common is to have income, receipts and assets as positive and costs, expenditure and liabilities as negative. (One alternative is to have income as negative and costs as positive as this is then consistent with traditional debits and credits from book-keeping.)

As well as having a logical and consistent sign convention running through the workings and outputs, it is important to give users guidance with the sign for inputs. Normally, all inputs should be positive regardless of whether they are income, cost, asset or liability. The model can then convert the number to a negative for display or calculation. As explained earlier in this chapter (page 54), appropriate input validation can also be used to test that the correct signs are being used.

FORMATTING

With the modern spreadsheet there is a wide range of colours, fonts, tints and styles that with spare time can be used to liven up even the most unexciting of models. Although there is all this graphical power at your fingertips, there are several rules with formatting that will enhance the look and feel of the model.

Whatever selection you make for the design it is helpful to be consistent. So headings are always in capital letters and bold. Inputs are always shaded in the same colour. In this way the navigation round the model is made easy as well as looking professional.

Be aware that the model may be used on different types of hardware. Screen sizes vary so a visual impact may not be replicable on all machines. The amount of memory and the processing speed will also have an effect. Extra formatting takes up memory and time when recalculating. Thus on older, slower machines time can be at a premium.

Colours

Less is more. Restrict the spreadsheet colour scheme to three or four colours. Remember that any outputs are likely to be printed out and potentially photocopied. Most organisations need the output to look good in black and white.

A typical colour scheme might be as follows:

- Black text on a white background for the majority of the spreadsheet.
- A dark colour on a pale background to highlight input cells (shades of green or blue are typical).
- A dark red on a pale yellow background for warnings or error messages.

Fonts

Try to stick to one font throughout and use bold and larger font sizes only for titles and headings.

In printing out you may be eager to shrink the model to fit on one sheet of paper, but remember that it has to be read and that when severely shrunk minus signs and other vital details can disappear.

Lines

For subtotals and totals it is clearer to insert lines round the numbers, as shown in Chart 8.9.

Chart 8.9 **The use of lines in formatting output**

	A	B	C	D	E	F	G	H	I	J
1	**Model title**									
2										
3	Year number	*Year_number*			**0**	**1**	**2**	**3**	**4**	**5**
4	Years	*Actual_years*			2000	2001	2002	2003	2004	2005
5										
6	**PROFIT AND LOSS**									
23										
24	Revenue A				0	100	150	200	250	300
25	Revenue B				0	25	30	35	40	45
26	Total revenue	*Output_total_revenue*			0	125	180	235	290	345
27	Costs	*Output_total_costs*			0	(100)	(120)	(140)	(160)	(180)
28	Profit				0	25	60	95	130	165
29										

Subtotals (row 26) have a single line above them and totals (row 28) have a single line above them and a double line below them.

Number styles

Some basic rules in displaying numbers are as follows:

- ◪ Numbers should stay in black even if negative.
- ◪ Replace the minus sign with brackets as they are more enduring when photocopied.
- ◪ Put separators between thousands to enhance legibility.
- ◪ Choose an appropriate number of significant figures.

To set up a number style that meets these criteria complete the following:

- ◪ Select a cell and from the FORMAT menu select CELLS...
- ◪ Click on the "Number" tab and in the "Category:" box select CUSTOM.
- ◪ In the "Type:" box enter #,##0.00_);(#,##0.00).

The syntax works as follows:

- ◪ The format for positive numbers is on the left of the semicolon and negative is on the right.
- ◪ # means show a digit if there is one to show but ignore if not required.
- ◪ 0 means show the actual number, but show a zero if there is no digit to display. The benefit of this is that the user can see a calculation has been done and the answer is zero, rather than there being some potential numbers missing from the model if the cell is left blank.
- ◪ 00 after the decimal point gives two decimal places, but can be changed to none or many.
- ◪ By putting _) on a positive number, the _ means put a space after positive numbers the width of the next character, which in this case is a closed bracket. This will ensure that positive and negative numbers align vertically down the sheet when right justified.
- ◪ The () on the negative number means that negative numbers will have brackets round them.

Alternative formats that may be useful are as follows:

- ☑ Ignore .oo and show only whole numbers.
- ☑ Insert a comma after zero (eg, #,##0,) which will remove three significant figures such that 1234567 would be shown as 1,235. Be careful because arithmetic calculations will hold true to the full number and rounding errors may occur. It may be helpful to round to visible (see pages 58–9) when using this feature.

Column widths

Some modellers like to have all the columns of the model visible at once and hence use the zoom and column width features to create this.

At the end, it is aesthetically better to have identical column widths for all years, so check the maximum needed and set all the columns to this width (note that the largest numbers are often in the final year when the revenue and value has peaked).

SOME THINGS TO AVOID

Hiding information

The most common way to hide data is to use the functions that physically hide columns or rows. When this has been done it is obvious to the user as the column and row reference sequences have elements missing.

Another way to hide data is to convert the text to white so that the background is the same as the foreground and therefore invisible. Instances of this are hard for the user to find, particularly when located away from the main development area.

If you apply the principles described in this chapter and have a working sheet, there is no need to hide anything. The output sheet is used to tidy up workings for printing. It is recommended that for clarity everything used to generate the model output is visible.

Recalculation

The default setting in spreadsheets is that every time a cell is changed the whole workbook is recalculated. For most spreadsheet applications this occurs instantly. However, as a model grows the amount of calculation to be done can be huge and there will be an obvious pause for recalculation. At this stage it is tempting to switch from automatic to manual recalculation (from the TOOLS menu select OPTIONS→CALCULATION tab and check the manual box). Thereafter press F9 every time you want the model updated. This can be dangerous as some users may not be aware of this step in processing scenarios through the model and may not have pressed F9 before taking a decision on an output.

If auto-recalculation is turned off, make sure that warnings are clearly shown on the output sheet. Advanced modellers may write a short macro so that whenever the user moves to view an output sheet the model will automatically recalculate.

9 Macroeconomic factors

Macroeconomics is the study of the economy as a whole and focuses on the interaction of large-scale, aggregated variables. Microeconomics, in contrast, concentrates on the individual components within an economy. Examples of macroeconomic variables include inflation, exchange rates and interest rates. The definition can also be extended to include variables that are harder to measure and describe, such as the regulatory environment, company law, social trends and technological change.

This chapter looks at the forecasting of some of the variables commonly used in business models:

- Gross domestic product (GDP)
- Inflation
- Base interest rates
- Exchange rates
- Population

These five variables provide the building blocks from which many other macroeconomic variables can be derived. There is no consensus among economists over how best to forecast macroeconomic variables. Any technique that a business modeller employs will be a simplification of reality.

THIRD-PARTY FORECASTS

In large organisations there may already be a corporate view of the economy's growth rate, inflation and exchange rates, and the modeller may be obliged to use an existing set of assumptions. Small businesses may rely on forecasts from banks or brokers or reports by industry bodies and research agencies. In both cases, modelling macroeconomic variables is simply a matter of entering the relevant figures under the appropriate year headings in the spreadsheet.

Published reports usually do not extend far enough into the future to meet the needs of a ten-year cashflow forecast. In such cases the model must be flexible enough to accommodate the existing forecast and to generate the figures for the remaining years. On other occasions the model may have to be designed to produce a full forecast from year 1.

GROSS DOMESTIC PRODUCT

Definition and uses
Gross domestic product (GDP) is defined as the total value of goods produced and services provided in a country in one year. Numerous variables determine the growth of GDP, and to produce a formula that explains GDP growth is beyond the scope of this book. However,

many years of observation have revealed that GDP growth rates do not change dramatically from year to year and that they generally follow a cyclical pattern – sometimes described as the business cycle. These two observations can be used to produce a simple forecast for GDP growth and GDP.

The approach used assumes an average underlying GDP growth rate that has a linear trend in either a positive or a negative direction. The actual rate of growth in any one year, however, will depend on the position within the business cycle. The business cycle is modelled as a SINE curve where assumptions entered by the user determine the length and amplitude of the business cycle. The use of a SINE curve represents a simplifying assumption, as business cycles do not usually exhibit a constant cyclical pattern.

Forecasting GDP is useful as it provides a building block for forecasting imports and exports (which can be expressed as a percentage of GDP) and for providing an indicator of economic prosperity. Dividing total GDP by the total population gives GDP per head, which is a commonly used measure of an economy's economic health. GDP can also provide a useful starting point for forecasting market demand.

Seed

In Chapter 4 the current, actual level of a variable was defined as the seed, the starting point from which future values are forecast. When forecasting GDP the seed is the previous period's GDP, measured in units of the local currency. To develop a forecast for GDP, begin by creating a sheet name "GDP inputs" and enter the row and column headings from Chart 9.1 In Chart 9.1 the seed is entered as units 23,000 in cell E4 and this input is given the range name GDP_input_gross_domestic_product. This represents the value of GDP at year 0.

Behaviour

The term behaviour is used to describe the expected future path of a particular variable. In this example it is assumed that no alternative forecasts are available and that the modeller must forecast the behaviour of GDP for every year. The expected behaviour of GDP growth is modelled as a SINE curve and is defined by the user inputs below. This example assumes a five-year business cycle.

- ◪ The number of years for a complete business cycle (cell E5).
- ◪ The stage of the business cycle for the current level of GDP, that is, 23,000 (cell E6). A figure of 25% indicates a start point at the top of the cycle; a figure of 75% implies a start point at the bottom of the cycle. It is assumed that GDP of 23,000 is at the top of the cycle, which is represented by an assumption of 25%.
- ◪ The size of the variations during the cycle (cell E7). This represents the difference between the highest and lowest points of the cycle.
- ◪ The underlying growth rate of GDP (cell E8). This represents the average growth rate over the length of the business cycle.
- ◪ The amount each year by which the underlying growth rate changes (cell E9). Over time the underlying growth rate may change, and this is represented by the input in cell E9. The underlying growth rate may change over time if an economy is moving from being a developing economy into a modern state.

Chart 9.1 shows an input sheet containing all the inputs required to produce a GDP forecast. Each input has been given a range name, which is displayed in column B.

Chart 9.1 **Input assumptions for a GDP forecast**

	A	B	C	D	E
1	GDP Assumptions				
2					
3	Variable	Range name			Input
4	Gross domestic product – £	GDP_input_gross_domestic_product			23,000
5	Number of years for a complete cycle	GDP_input_length_of_cycle			5
6	Cycle start point	GDP_input_cycle_start_point			25%
7	Total amplitude	GDP_input_total_GDP_amplitude			1.0%
8	Average GDP growth rate	GDP_input_average_GDP_growth_rate			1.5%
9	Average GDP growth rate trend	GDP_input_average_GDP_growth_trend			0.05%

Modelling approach

Now create a separate workings sheet for the GDP forecast called "GDP workings", as shown in Chart 9.2. The example reveals the results of a ten-year forecast. The formulae in each column are identical. The workings have been broken down into a number of stages:

- ◪ Rows 4, 5 and 6 are intermediate steps in producing the GDP growth rate that is calculated in row 8.
- ◪ Row 4 determines the stage of the business cycle that will help determine the GDP growth rate.
- ◪ Row 5 divides the full amplitude of the business cycle in half.
- ◪ Row 6 adjusts the average growth rate for the trend in the average growth rate using a compounding calculation.
- ◪ Rows 4 to 6 are combined in row 8 to produce the GDP growth rate. The adjusted growth rate of row 6 is altered up or down by the multiplication of the position within the business cycle (row 4) and half of the amplitude (row 5).
- ◪ The resulting GDP growth rate is then used to generate the final result for GDP in absolute terms in row 9.

Chart 9.2 **GDP workings spreadsheet**

	A	B	C	D	E	F	G	H	I	J	K	L	M	N
1	GDP workings													
2														
3	Years				1	2	3	4	5	6	7	8	9	10
4	SINE curve position	Sine_curve_position			30.9%	-80.9%	-80.9%	30.9%	100.0%	30.9%	-80.9%	-80.9%	30.9%	100.0%
5	Half of amplitude	Half_of_amplitude			0.5%	0.5%	0.5%	0.5%	0.5%	0.5%	0.5%	0.5%	0.5%	0.5%
6	Adjusted growth rate	Adjusted_growth_rate			1.500%	1.501%	1.501%	1.502%	1.503%	1.504%	1.505%	1.505%	1.506%	1.507%
7														
8	GDP growth rate	GDP_growth_rate			1.660%	1.100%	1.100%	1.660%	2.010%	1.660%	1.100%	1.110%	1.670%	2.010%
9	GDP – £				23,381.8	23,639.0	23,899.0	24,295.8	24,784.1	25,196.6	25,472.7	25,755.4	26,185.5	26,711.9

The row headings in column A should be created first. A detailed explanation of each calculation in the working for year 1 is provided in Chart 9.3 and the same formula can be copied to every year. The forecast years 1–10 can be entered manually and given the range name *Year* for the range of cells E3 to N3. Before completing the code the additional range names described below must be created:

- ◪ *SINE_curve_position* for cells E4 to N4.
- ◪ *Half_of_amplitude* for cells E5 to N5.

☑ *Adjusted_growth_rate* for cells E6 to N6.
☑ *GDP_growth_rate* for cells E8 to N8.

Rows 4, 5 and 6 should be formatted as percentages, with rows 4 and 5 at one decimal place and the remaining rows at three decimal places.

Lastly, a relative range name must be created for the GDP of the previous period called *Previous_year_GDP* (see Chapter 7, page 43). In this example, select cell F9 and make cell E9 the relative cell.

Chart 9.3 **GDP workings code**

Row	Calculation	Actual calculation	Answer
SINE curve position	=SIN((PI()*2)/GDP_input_length_ of_cycle*(Year+GDP_input_length _of_cycle*GDP_input_cycle_start_ point))	=SIN((3.14*2)/5* (1+5*25%))	30.9%
Half of amplitude	=GDP_input_total_GDP_amplitude/2	=1.0%/2	0.5%
Adjusted growth rate	=(GDP_input_average_GDP_growth _rate*(1+GDP_input_average_ GDP_growth_trend)^(Year−1))	=(1.5%*(1+0.05%)^ (1−1))	1.500%
GDP growth rate	=ROUNDUP(SINE_curve_position* Half_of_amplitude+ Adjusted_growth_rate,4)	=ROUNDUP(30.9%* 0.5%+1.500%,4)	1.660%
GDP	=IF(Year=1, GDP_input_gross_domestic_ product*(1+GDP_growth_rate), Previous_year_GDP*(1+ GDP_growth_rate))	=IF(TRUE,23000* (1+1.660%))	23,381.8

The use of an IF statement in row 9 is required to ensure that the same formula can be used in each year. In the case of year 1 the model uses the initial input for GDP from the input section. In any other year the model simply looks at the level of GDP from the previous year.

Now assume that a forecast for GDP growth for the next two years has been obtained from an industry body. It would be useful to include this forecast for the first two years before reverting to the original forecasting approach. GDP is expected to grow by 1.8% in year 1 and 1.5% in year 2.

The input section has been expanded to include the manually entered GDP growth input assumptions and this extension is shown in Chart 9.4. The GDP growth input row is given the range name *GDP_input_GDP_growth_input*; the range should encompass cells E12 to N12.

Chart 9.4 Extended GDP input assumptions

	A	B	C	D	E	F	G	H	I	J	K	L	M	N
1	GDP assumptions													
2														
3	Variable	Range name			Input									
4	Gross domestic product - £	GDP_input_gross_domestic_product			23,000									
5	Number of years for a complete cycle	GDP_input_length_of_cycle			5									
6	Cycle start point	GDP_input_cycle_start_point			25%									
7	Total amplitude	GDP_input_total_GDP_amplitude			1.0%									
8	Average GDP growth rate	GDP_input_average_GDP_growth_rate			1.5%									
9	Average GDP growth rate trend	GDP_input_average_GDP_growth_trend			0.05%									
10														
11	Year				1	2	3	4	5	6	7	8	9	10
12	GDP growth input	GDP_input_GDP_growth_input			1.80%	1.50%								

Turning to the GDP workings sheet, a simple IF statement is added to the original GDP growth rate calculation to examine whether a manual entry has been made. If no entry has been made, GDP growth input = "" is TRUE, there is no entry, and the original calculation is performed. If an entry is present, then that entry is used.

Chart 9.5 shows the revised formula and provides the results for year 2 when the manual input of 1.50% is used.

Chart 9.5 Revised GDP growth rate calculation

Row	Calculation	Actual calculation	Answer
GDP growth rate	=IF(GDP_input_GDP_growth_ input="",ROUNDUP(SINE_curve_ position*Half_of_amplitude+ Adjusted_growth_rate,4),GDP_ input_GDP_growth_input)	=IF(FALSE,ROUNDUP (−80.9%×0.5%+1.501%, 4),1.500%)	1.500%

Chart 9.6 shows the revised GDP workings with manual entries for the first two years of the forecast. The remaining years are forecast by the model.

Chart 9.6 Revised GDP workings

	A	B	C	D	E	F	G	H	I	J	K	L	M	N
1	GDP workings													
2														
3	Years				1	2	3	4	5	6	7	8	9	10
4	SINE curve position	Sine_curve_position			30.9%	-80.9%	-80.9%	30.9%	100.0%	30.9%	-80.9%	-80.9%	30.9%	100.0%
5	Half of amplitude	Half_of_amplitude			0.5%	0.5%	0.5%	0.5%	0.5%	0.5%	0.5%	0.5%	0.5%	0.5%
6	Adjusted growth rate	Adjusted_growth_rate			1.500%	1.501%	1.502%	1.502%	1.503%	1.504%	1.505%	1.505%	1.506%	1.507%
7														
8	GDP growth rate	GDP_growth_rate			1.800%	1.500%	1.100%	1.660%	2.010%	1.660%	1.100%	1.110%	1.670%	2.010%
9	GDP - £				23,414.0	23,765.2	24,026.6	24,425.5	24,916.4	25,330.0	25,608.7	25,892.9	26,325.3	26,854.5

When an existing forecast for the first few years of the forecast period is used, the modeller must ensure that the transition from the manually entered figures and the results from the model are smooth. A simple approach is to plot the rates of GDP growth for the entire period and amend the assumptions describing the future behaviour of the growth rate to ensure that the existing forecast and those predicted by the model follow a consistent pattern. The results of the forecast from the above example, including the manual inputs, are shown in Chart 9.7 on the next page. The graph covers the entire forecast period (see page 49, Using graphs).

Chart 9.7 **GDP growth rate**

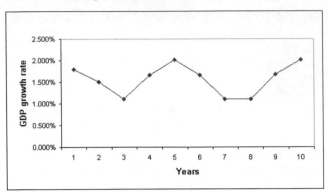

INFLATION RATE

Definition and uses

The inflation rate can be defined as the rate at which the price for a defined basket of goods changes over time. The absolute level of prices can be described by a price index. The annual percentage change in this index is the rate of inflation. There are many inflation indices. One of the most common measures is the retail price index, which attempts to represent the prices consumers have to pay each day. Definitions often vary – there was a protracted debate in the UK about whether mortgage interest costs on domestic properties should be included in or excluded from the retail price index. Economy-wide measures include the GDP deflator, and there are industry or sector specific measures as well. The ability to forecast inflation is useful for many aspects of modelling, including market size forecasts and predicting exchange rate movements.

Seed

The seed for inflation and price forecasts is the price index start point. In Chart 9.8 a figure of 100 is assumed and is entered on the inputs sheet with the range name *Inflation_input_inflation_index_start_point*.

Behaviour

There is considerable controversy over the determinants of inflation. Currently, many people see a relationship between the level of activity in the economy and inflation. As the economy grows, increased income levels generate an increase in demand for goods and services, and as a result prices are bid up as the supply of goods and services is assumed to respond more slowly to changes in demand. A simple approach, therefore, is to assume a comparatively stable trend for inflation, with variations around this trend that are related to the peaks and troughs of the business cycle, which was already captured in the modelling of GDP growth. However, a delay between demand increasing and suppliers recognising the increase in demand means that the cyclical movements in prices often lag the movements in GDP.

Chart 9.8 highlights some of the inputs required to develop a forecast for inflation. In addition to the inputs in Chart 9.8, some of the inputs from the modelling work done on GDP will be reused. These are:

- ☑ *GDP_input_length_of_cycle*
- ☑ *GDP_input_year*
- ☑ *GDP_input_cycle_start_point*

Chart 9.8 Inflation inputs

	A	B	C	D	E
1	Inflation inputs				
2					
3	**Variable**	**Range name**			**Input**
4	Index start point	*Inflation_input_inflation_index_start_point*			100
5	Average inflation rate	*Inflation_input_average_inflation_rate*			2.50%
6	Total amplitude	*Inflation_input_total_inflation_amplitude*			1.50%
7	Offset to GDP growth	*Inflation_input_inflation_offset_to_GDP*			1
8	Inflation rate trend	*Inflation_input_inflation_rate_trend*			0.50%

Modelling approach

It is suggested that users continue to use the workbook that contains the GDP workings. Additional inputs for inflation assumptions should be entered on a new sheet entitled "Inflation inputs".

The workings for the inflation forecast are presented in Chart 9.9. The initial inputs and the actual code are similar to those of the forecast for GDP. One significant change is the inclusion of an additional term in the SINE curve position calculation. A lag term has been introduced which offsets inflation from the stage of the business cycle calculated in the GDP working. The results in Chart 9.9 show that the SINE curve position results are always one period behind those of the GDP forecast.

Chart 9.9 Inflation workings

	A	B	C	D	E	F	G	H	I	J	K	L	M	N
1	Inflation workings													
2														
3	Years				1	2	3	4	5	6	7	8	9	10
4	SINE curve position	*Inflation_SINE_curve_position*			100.0%	30.9%	-80.9%	-80.9%	30.9%	100.0%	30.9%	-80.9%	-80.9%	30.9%
5	Half of amplitude	*Inflation_half_of_amplitude*			0.75%	0.75%	0.75%	0.75%	0.75%	0.75%	0.75%	0.75%	0.75%	0.75%
6	Adjusted growth rate	*Inflation_adjusted_growth_rate*			2.500%	2.513%	2.525%	2.538%	2.550%	2.563%	2.576%	2.589%	2.602%	2.615%
7														
8	Inflation rate	*Inflation_rate*			3.250%	2.750%	1.920%	1.940%	2.790%	3.320%	2.810%	1.990%	2.000%	2.850%
9	Inflation index	*UK_inflation_index*			103.3	106.1	108.1	110.2	113.3	117.1	120.4	122.7	125.2	128.8

To develop the code the following additional range names would be required:

- ☑ *Inflation_SINE_curve_position* for cells E4 to N4.
- ☑ *Inflation_half_of_amplitude* for cells E5 to N5.
- ☑ *Inflation_adjusted_growth_rate* for cells E6 to N6.
- ☑ *Inflation_rate* for cells E8 to N8.

A relative range name, *Previous_year_inflation_index*, must also be created in row 9. Chart 9.10 provides a detailed review of the inflation workings and a numerical example. The results relate to year 3.

Chart 9.10 **Inflation workings code**

Row	Calculation	Actual calculation	Answer
SINE curve position	=SIN((PI()*2)/GDP_input_length_of_cycle*(Year+(GDP_input_length_of_cycle*GDP_input_cycle_start_point)−Inflation_input_inflation_offset_to_GDP))	=SIN((3.14*2)/5*(3+(5*25%)−1))	(80.9%)
Half of amplitude	=Inflation_input_total_inflation_amplitude/2	=1.5%/2	0.75%
Adjusted growth rate	=(Inflation_input_average_inflation_rate*(1+Inflation_input_inflation_rate_trend)^(Year−1))	=(2.5%*(1+0.5%)^(3−1))	2.525%
Inflation growth rate	=ROUNDUP(Inflation_SINE_curve_position*Inflation_half_of_amplitude+Inflation_adjusted_growth_rate,4)	=ROUNDUP(−80.9%*0.75%+2.525%,4)	1.920%
Inflation index	=IF(Year=1,Inflation_input_inflation_index_start_point*(1+Inflation_rate),Previous_year_inflation_index*(1+Inflation_rate))	=IF(FALSE,100*(1+1.920%),106.1*(1+1.920%))	108.1

It would also have been possible to extend the code to include a manual override for the inflation rate in the same way that the GDP growth rate could have been overwritten. An additional input row would have been required in the input section where the user could enter the inflation rate directly. The calculation in row 8 would also have to be extended to include an IF statement, which would have an identical structure to the GDP example.

The graph in Chart 9.11 shows both the movements in the rate of inflation over the ten years of the forecast period and changes in GDP growth.

Chart 9.11 **Ten-year inflation forecast**

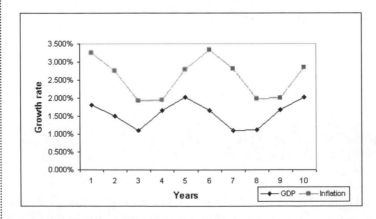

This inflation forecast will be used later in this chapter to produce an exchange rate forecast. To make easy reference to these workings, create the range name

UK_inflation_index for cells E9 to N9.

BASE INTEREST RATES

Definition and uses

The base rate is the rate of interest set by the central bank that provides the reference point for other banks within the banking system. In the UK the base rate is set by the Bank of England and in the United States by the Federal Reserve. The base rate is one of the main instruments for managing the economy.

The ability to forecast the base rate is useful, as it is essential for forecasting interest charges and income in the profit and loss account.

Seed

The seed is the current base rate expressed in percentage terms.

Behaviour

The base rate is often used as a tool for controlling inflation within an economy. When the central bank expects prices to rise it may raise interest rates in an attempt to reduce the level of demand in the economy. Increasing the base rate makes mortgages and consumer credit more expensive, which may reduce consumers' willingness to spend. The reduction in spend reduces demand and hence reduces the upward pressure on prices. An approach to forecasting base rates is to assume that inflation and interest rates move in roughly the same direction, but that there is a delay from when the central bank increases interest rates to when inflation increases. The somewhat counter-intuitive order of events is because it is assumed that the central bank can predict when inflationary pressures are building up in the economy and that it increases interest rates in anticipation of the rise in inflation. The code in this example could also be used in cases where inflation increases ahead of the base rate on the assumption that the central bank cannot foresee the build-up of inflationary pressure. The central bank reacts with an increase in the base rate only after the rate of inflation has been observed. This alternative description of the workings of the economy can be achieved by entering a negative rather than a positive offset to inflation.

Chart 9.12 indicates some of the inputs required to generate the base rate forecast. Once again some of the results from earlier workings will be reused, and it is suggested that users continue to use the workbook that contains the GDP and inflation examples. The variables common to this and earlier examples are:

- *GDP_input_length_of_cycle*
- *Year*
- *GDP_input_cycle_start_point*
- *Inflation_input_inflation_offset_to_GDP*

A base rate assumption sheet should be created, called "Base rate inputs", as illustrated in Chart 9.12.

Chart 9.12 **Base rate inputs**

	A	B	C	D	E
1	Base rate inputs				
2					
3	Variable	Range name			Input
4	Average base rate	Base_rate_input_average_base_rate			6.00%
5	Total amplitude	Base_rate_input_total_base_rate_amplitude			4.00%
6	Offset to inflation rate	Base_rate_input_base_rate_offset_to_inflation			-1
7	Base rate trend	Base_rate_input_base_rate_trend			0.50%

Modelling approach

The base rate calculation shown in Chart 9.13 has been performed in one single cell, although the calculation could have been broken down into stages in exactly the same way as the previous examples. The calculation is almost identical to the inflation calculation apart from the inclusion of an additional factor, the *Base_rate_input_ base_rate_offset_to_inflation*, which is set to −1 in this example.

Chart 9.13 **Base rate workings**

	A	B	C	D	E	F	G	H	I	J	K	L	M	N
1	Base rate workings													
2														
3	Years				1	2	3	4	5	6	7	8	9	10
4	Base rate				6.62%	4.42%	4.45%	6.71%	8.13%	6.77%	4.57%	4.60%	6.87%	8.28%

Chart 9.14 shows the single calculation used to derive the results above for year 3. Even with meaningful range names the formula is complex, and errors can easily be introduced and may be difficult to identify. As an exercise the user may attempt to produce the same results by breaking down the calculation into its constituent parts.

Chart 9.14 **Base rate workings code**

Row	Calculation	Actual calculation	Answer
Base rate	=ROUNDUP(SIN((PI()*2)/ GDP_input_length_of_cycle*(Year+ (GDP_input_length_of_cycle* GDP_input_cycle_start_point)− Base_rate_input_base_rate_offset_to_inflation− Inflation_input_inflation_offset_to_GDP))* Base_rate_input_total_base_rate_amplitude/2+ (Base_rate_input_average_base_rate* (1+Base_rate_input_base_rate_trend)^(Year−1)),4)	=ROUNDUP(SIN((3.14*2)/5* (3+(5*25%)−1))*4.0%/2+ (6.0%*(1+0.5%)^(3−1)),4)	4.45%

The graph in Chart 9.15 shows the trend in base rates over the forecast period.

Chart 9.15 **Base rate trend graph**

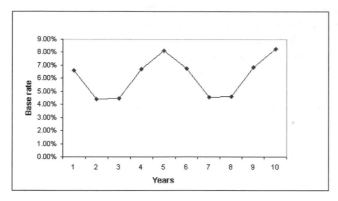

EXCHANGE RATES

Definition and uses

Like any other commodity, currencies can be brought and sold. The market where such transactions take place is called the foreign exchange market. The price at which two currencies exchange is called the exchange rate. When sterling is said to be "trading" on the foreign exchange market at $1.65 to £1 it implies that £1 will purchase $1.65.

Exchange rates are used throughout most models; for example, converting the cost of imported goods into the local currency and for foreign exchange gains and losses on debt denominated in the foreign currency.

Seed

To generate an average exchange rate for the first year of the forecast an inflation factor for both the start and end points of the year would be required. Many modellers, however, simply make an assumption for the average exchange rate for the first year and develop a forecast for the subsequent years. The initial assumption acts as the seed.

Behaviour

As with all the variables in this chapter there is no consensus among economists about the determinants of exchange rate movements. Furthermore, many economies and groups of economies actively manage their exchange rates. A simple theory of exchange rates is purchasing power parity (PPP), which argues that exchange rates move to ensure that the relative purchasing power of one currency against another remains constant. Exchange rates, therefore, are assumed to move in response to differential movements in inflation rates between the respective economies. If one country is experiencing more rapid inflation than another country, the cost of a basket of goods in the country with the higher rate of inflation will increase faster than the cost of the same goods in the other country. For a unit of the lower-inflation currency to retain the ability to purchase the same bundle of goods in the high-inflation country, the low-inflation currency will have to have the power to purchase more of the high-inflation currency. This effectively means that the low-inflation currency has appreciated against the high-inflation currency.

Chart 9.16 shows the inputs required to produce an exchange rate forecast. This example also uses the inflation index forecast produced on page 70. It is suggested that users continue to use the workbook that contains the earlier examples. A new sheet should be created for the exchange rate inputs, called "Exchange rate inputs", as shown in Chart 9.16. These are hypothetical figures and do not reflect actual UK data.

Chart 9.16 **Exchange rate inputs**

	A	B	C	D	E	F	G	H	I	J	K	L	M	N
1	Exchange rate inputs													
2														
3	Variable	Range name			Input									
4	Initial exchange rate - US$ / GB£	Exchange_rate_input_Initial_exchange_rate			1.60									
5	US inflation index start point	Exchange_rate_input_US_inflation_index_start_point			100.00									
6														
7	Year				1	2	3	4	5	6	7	8	9	10
8	US inflation rate	Exchange_rate_input_US_inflation_rate			2.00%	2.00%	2.00%	2.00%	2.00%	2.00%	2.00%	2.00%	2.00%	2.00%
9	Manual exchange rate entry	Exchange_rate_input_Manual_exchange_rate_entry						1.5900						

The inputs include the initial exchange rate as well as assumptions concerning annual dollar inflation. The dollar inflation figures could have been modelled using the techniques discussed earlier in this chapter, but for simplicity a manual input for these assumptions has been created. Exchange rates are often managed by governments or central banks. As a result, exchange rates, at least in the short term, may diverge from the levels suggested by the application of PPP. To accommodate managed exchange rate regimes, an input range has been included in row 9 where the user can manually enter an exchange rate or a broker's forecast. If no entry is made, the model will automatically revert to the PPP approach.

Range names have been created for the US inflation rate and the manual entry row. These names and their associated cells are:

- ☑ *Exchange_rate_input_US_inflation_rate* for cells E8 to N8;
- ☑ *Exchange_rate_input_manual_exchange_rate_entry* for cells E9 to N9.

Modelling approach

A separate sheet for the exchange rate workings should be created. Chart 9.17 shows the exchange rate workings and Chart 9.18 gives a detailed description of the formula for year 3. The US inflation index has been calculated by applying the US inflation forecast to the index of the previous period. In addition, row 5 links to the earlier inflation forecast in the range *UK_inflation_index*. It is assumed that the inflation forecast relates to the UK. Relative range names have been created for the previous period's inflation index and for the previous period's exchange rate:

- ☑ *Previous_US_inflation_index*
- ☑ *Previous_period_exchange_rate*

For example, in cell G4, the *Previous_US_inflation_index* is set equal to cell ='Exchange Rate Workings'!F4 in the "Refers to:" section of the Define Name dialog box and the $ signs have been removed. In cell G6, the *Previous_period_exchange_rate* is set equal to cell ='Exchange Rate Workings'!F6.

Chart 9.17 **Exchange rate workings**

	A	B	C	D	E	F	G	H	I	J	K	L	M	N
1	Exchange rate workings													
2														
3	Years				1	2	3	4	5	6	7	8	9	10
4	US$ inflation index				102.00	104.04	106.12	108.24	110.41	112.62	114.87	117.17	119.51	121.90
5	UK inflation index				103.25	106.09	108.13	110.22	113.30	117.06	120.35	122.75	125.20	128.77
6	Exchange rate - US$ / UK				1.6000	1.5883	1.5896	1.5900	1.5778	1.5576	1.5454	1.5455	1.5455	1.5327

The exchange rate calculation involves adjusting the previous period's exchange rate by the ratio of the proportionate change in the US inflation index and the proportionate change in the UK inflation index. The calculation is shown below:

$$\text{Previous period's exchange rate} \times \frac{\dfrac{\text{Current US inflation index}}{\text{Previous US inflation index}}}{\dfrac{\text{Current UK inflation index}}{\text{Previous UK inflation index}}}$$

Chart 9.18 **Exchange rate workings code**

Row	Calculation	Actual calculation	Answer
US$ inflation index	=IF(Year=1, Exchange_rate_input_US_ inflation_index_start_point*(1+ Exchange_rate_input_US_inflation _rate),Previous_US_inflation_index* (1+Exchange_rate_input_US_ inflation_rate))	=IF(FALSE,100*(1+2%), 104.04*(1+2%))	106.12
UK inflation index	=UK_inflation_index	108.13	108.13
Exchange rate US$/GBP	=IF(Year=1, Exchange_rate_input_initial_ exchange rate,IF(Exchange_Rate_ input_manual_exchange_rate_ entry="",Previous_period_ exchange_rate*((G4/F4)/(G5/F5)), Exchange_rate_input_manual_ exchange_rate_entry))	=IF(FALSE,1.6, IF(FALSE,1,5883× ((106.12/104.04)/ (108.13/106.09)), no entry))	1.5896

The results of the exchange rate forecast are presented in the graph in Chart 9.19 on the next page.

Chart 9.19 **$/£ exchange rate forecast**

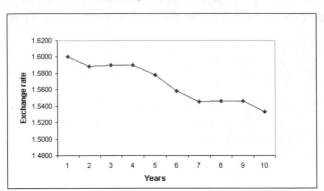

POPULATION

Definition and uses

The definition of population is usually straightforward – it is the number of people in a country. However, some care may need to be taken when a country has a large number of temporary residents or seasonal workers. Unfortunately, in some countries the quality of statistics is poor and population figures may be inaccurate.

The total population is often the starting point for forecasting market size, where the demand for goods and services is, in some way, related to the size of the population. It is also the starting point for detailed demographic analysis such as measuring the size of the working population, and for establishing age profiles and household structures.

Seed

The seed is the opening population at the start of the forecast period.

Behaviour

Patterns of population growth differ among countries, but a low rate of exponential growth can provide a reasonable forecast for many economies. In this simple example the population is assumed to grow by the same proportion each year. These two input assumptions are presented in Chart 9.20.

Chart 9.20 **Population inputs**

	A	B	C	D	E
1	Population inputs				
2					
3	Variable	Range name			Input
4	Opening population – millions	*Population_input_opening_population*			55.000
5	Population growth	*Population_input_population_growth*			1.02%

Modelling approach

Generating a forecast for the future population is straightforward and the workings are presented in Chart 9.21. A range name for the years, *Year*, will be required and should include the cells E3 to N3.

Chart 9.21 **Population workings**

	A	B	C	D	E	F	G	H	I	J	K	L	M	N
1	Population workings													
2														
3	Years				1	2	3	4	5	6	7	8	9	10
4	Population - millions				55.000	55.501	56.128	56.700	57.279	57.863	58.453	59.049	59.652	60.260

To generate the results a simple IF statement is used to ensure that the same formula can be used each year irrespective of whether the population of the previous period is being drawn from the initial assumptions or from the adjacent cell. In the latter case a relative reference is used to refer to *Previous_period_population*. The detailed code for year 3 is presented in Chart 9.22.

Chart 9.22 **Population workings code**

Row	Calculation	Actual calculation	Answer
Population	=IF(Year=1, Population_input_opening_ population,Previous_period_ population*(1+Population_input_ population_growth))	=IF(FALSE,55.0, 55.561*(1+1.02%))	56.128

OTHER MACROECONOMIC VARIABLES

When additional macroeconomic variables are required these can often be derived from the set of variables discussed in this chapter. For example, GDP per head, a useful measure of individual wealth, can be derived by dividing the total GDP forecast by the expected size of the population. Care must be taken to ensure that both the numerator and denominator of the calculation are in the same units, but otherwise the calculation is straightforward. The macroeconomic variables discussed in detail here will provide a solid basis for most business planning exercises.

10 Forecasting revenue

Forecasting revenue is one of the greatest challenges for the business modeller. The first problem is producing a meaningful and useful definition of the market place. In the telecommunications, information technology and media sectors, for example, there is such a high degree of convergence that it is becoming increasingly difficult to differentiate between the separate markets. Modellers may also have incomplete or inaccurate data as a basis for their forecasts. Even when an industry-wide revenue forecast has been produced, estimating a business's market share of that revenue can be even more difficult. Market share has many determinants and some important factors, such as brand strength, are difficult to measure and model.

APPROACHES TO REVENUE FORECASTING

Classification of forecasting methodologies

The different approaches to forecasting can be classified in many ways. A useful classification is as follows:

- **Extrapolation techniques**, such as time series analysis, implicitly assume that the past will be a reasonable predictor of the future. This assumption may be valid for mature and stable businesses, such as the water and gas utilities. However, many industry sectors are experiencing increasing levels of structural change. The use of extrapolative techniques for these sectors may generate poor results.
- **Causative techniques**, such as multiple regression, attempt to understand the fundamental relationships that determine the dynamics of a market. This understanding, combined with a set of assumptions about the future, provides the basis for the forecast. Because the underlying relationships are often estimated from historical data, these techniques are useful when only small, incremental changes in assumptions are expected in the future.
- **Judgmental techniques.** Modellers may often be asked to produce a forecast for a new product or market where there is no available historic data. In these cases, forecasting can become judgmental and highly subjective. Although the forecasts can be refined through studying the results of market research and by examining the experiences of similar or related products in other markets and countries, the task of forecasting becomes more like an art than a science.

In practice, most modellers rely on a mixture of all three techniques. They may establish the current market trends through time series analysis, and attempt to understand market dynamics through multiple regression techniques. This understanding will then be combined with their belief of how these relationships might develop in the future to produce a forecast.

Decomposition of revenue

The modeller's ultimate objective is to develop a forecast for the total revenue of a business. This can be decomposed into a number of elements. The individual elements that comprise the total revenue for a business will depend on the industry in which it operates. In many industries total revenue can be calculated from an estimate of the number of customers who demand a product or service; the quantity of that product or service that they demand; and the price charged per unit of that product or service. The exact definitions of customers, products and services, and prices may differ, but the general approach will usually prove valid. Decomposing a forecast into the individual elements allows the modeller to examine to what extent a change in total revenue is a result of changes in quantities (sometimes referred to as volume changes) and changes in price.

Historically, in the case of the mobile communications industry, a major proportion of the total revenue was generated by voice traffic. This voice revenue could be decomposed into a number of readily identifiable elements:

- The number of customers using the network.
- The average number of minutes of voice calls made by each customer.
- The average price charged for each minute of use.

The total voice revenue for a mobile business could be calculated using the following equation:

$$\text{Average number of customers} \times \text{Average number of voice minutes} \times \\ \text{Average price per minute}$$

To produce the most accurate forecast and to gain the greatest insight into the economics of a business, it is often necessary to generate a forecast for total revenue through a combination of forecasts of the individual elements.

Price elasticity of demand

Once a revenue forecast is broken down into volume and price effects, the modeller must consider the relationship between changes in price and changes in demand or volume. In many markets, an inverse relationship exists between the price of a product or service and the quantity of that good or service demanded by the customer. This inverse relationship can be seen in the downward-sloping demand curve in Chart 10.1.

Chart 10.1 **A downward-sloping demand curve**

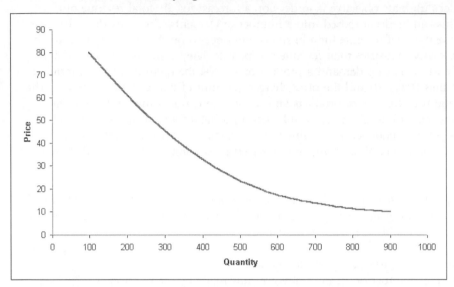

The price elasticity of demand is a measure of how sensitive the changes in the quantity demanded by a customer are to changes in price. Price elasticity can be expressed mathematically as:

$$\text{Price elasticity of demand} = \frac{\dfrac{Q2 - Q1}{Q1}}{\dfrac{P2 - P1}{P1}}$$

Price elasticities are usually negative, reflecting the inverse relationship between price and quantities. Elasticities also vary depending on the position along the demand curve. The slope of the demand curve at a particular point provides an estimate of the price elasticity of demand. Measuring elasticities is a complex subject and a range of techniques can be employed. A detailed discussion of this topic is beyond the scope of this book. However, if price elasticity estimates are available these can be incorporated into the revenue forecast (an example is given on page 108).

Bottom-up versus top-down forecasting

Total revenue forecasts created from a combination of individual elements are sometimes called "bottom-up" forecasts. The forecasting methodologies best suited to bottom-up forecasts include multiple-regression techniques.

An alternative to creating bottom-up models is to forecast total revenue directly, without examining the individual elements that comprise total revenue. A forecast based on this approach is sometime referred to as a "top-down" forecast. Useful techniques for producing top-down forecasts include time series analysis and, once again, multiple-regression techniques.

In practice, many modellers adopt both top-down and bottom-up approaches when faced with an uncertain future market. To add confidence to a forecast, it is often advisable to use a number of different approaches.

In the case of third-generation mobile data services, modellers may be forced to adopt both approaches. In the case of long-term, ten-year revenue forecasts, uncertainties about the capabilities of the new technologies prohibit the use of bottom-up models. Modellers simply cannot envisage the individual services and products that may be offered over a third-generation network in ten years' time. Consequently, the forecasts have to be derived from an analysis of customer spending patterns. Assumptions have to be made, for example, concerning the level of current entertainment expenditure on music and video that will one day be delivered over the airwaves to a mobile device. However, there is a reasonable level of certainty about the services that can be offered over the next 2–3 years, and these could be forecast using the bottom-up method. The final forecast, however, is a combination of both approaches.

Time frame

The time frame and the number of periods within each unit of time should be determined at the beginning of the modelling project. In the case of a short-term forecast (6–18 months), the modeller may be able to rely on extrapolative and causative techniques, as the structure of the market is unlikely to change dramatically in this period. The modeller must also consider the impact of seasonal factors if the requirement is to produce a monthly forecast. Seasonal variations and the relevance of past trends and relationships diminish as the forecast extends further into the future.

TIME SERIES ANALYSIS

Time series data

A considerable amount of information is presented in time series such as the retail price index, GDP and interest and exchange rates. A time series is a sequence of values relating to a repeating sequence of points in time. This chapter demonstrates how to isolate the trend from a time series and use that trend and the associated seasonal factors to produce a forecast. A more detailed theoretical understanding of time series analysis techniques can be obtained from any elementary text on statistics.

Chart 10.2 contains a time series of new customers, sometimes called gross connections, who subscribe to a mobile network. The data cover four years on a quarterly basis.

Chart 10.2 **Gross connections by quarter**

	1995	1996	1997	1998
Spring	24	48	68	107
Summer	44	66	85	125
Autumn	61	91	100	138
Winter	79	105	125	159

Components of a time series

Each data point, or observation, within a time series can be thought of as containing a number of different components:

- ◪ The trend (T) is the long-term, underlying movement of the data.
- ◪ The evolution of the trend will reflect the booms and slumps of the business cycle. This wave-like pattern, observed in much economic data, is represented by the cyclical component (C).
- ◪ The observation will also comprise a seasonal component (S), reflecting the influences of seasonal events such as Christmas and summer holidays.
- ◪ The last element of any observation will be the residual or "disturbance" component (R), that is, a random, non-systematic element caused by unpredictable factors such as delays in shipments and industrial strikes.

A long data series is required to estimate the cyclical component. In the case of a short series, as in the example above, the cyclical component is usually ignored.

To develop a forecast the time series must be broken down into its constituent parts. The forecast should reflect not only the underlying trend for the data but also the seasonal factors. It is also important to understand how these factors interrelate.

Additive and multiplicative models

The components described above can relate in a number of ways. They may have an additive relationship, where the observation (Y) is the sum of all the components. This additive model is written algebraically as:

$$Y=T+S+R$$

Alternatively, the observation (Y) may be the result of the product, or multiplication, of all the components. This is described as a multiplicative model:

$$Y=T*S*R$$

A plot of the data can be useful for determining which is the most appropriate model to use. If the seasonal variations appear to increase with an upward trend or decrease with a downward trend with time, the multiplicative model may be best. A comparatively constant level of seasonal variation suggests the use of the additive model. The graph in Chart 10.3 contains the data from Chart 10.2. The graph reveals that sales increase during the year with the peak sales period during the fourth quarter, probably at Christmas.

There is also a strong upward trend. The level of variation appears relatively constant, suggesting the use of the additive model.

Chart 10.3 **Gross connections per quarter**

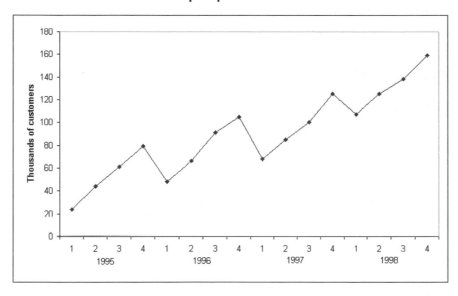

An alternative approach for selecting the best model is to examine the difference between the largest and smallest observations in each year. If the differences are increasing with time for an upward trend or decreasing with time for a downward trend, the multiplicative model should be used. If the differences remain reasonably stable, the additive model would be better.

The differences between the largest and smallest values for the above time series data are:

1995 = 79 − 24 = 55
1996 = 105 − 48 = 57
1997 = 125 − 68 = 57
1998 = 159 − 107 = 52

These differences are reasonably stable, which confirms the choice of the additive model.

Estimating the trend using the built-in moving average function

A simple and common technique for estimating the trend is to calculate a moving average. A four-month moving average, for example, involves calculating the average of the first four observations and then moving the calculation along one month, so that the oldest observation is dropped from the average and the next observation in the series is included. This average calculation moves through the entire time series until all the observations have been included. A spreadsheet package, such as Excel, can be used to calculate a moving average and plot it on the graph containing the original data.

Adding a moving average trendline using Excel
- ☑ Click in the graph.
- ☑ Click a point on the series.
- ☑ Right click and select ADD TRENDLINE.
- ☑ On the TYPE tab select MOVING AVERAGE.
- ☑ Under "Period:" select 4, to represent quarters.
- ☑ Click OK.

The results of adding a trendline are shown in Chart 10.4.

Chart 10.4 **Trend in gross connections per quarter**

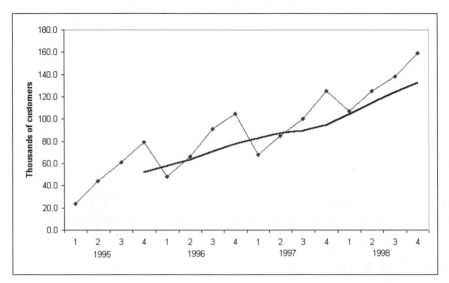

The choice of the number of months is important for producing a good trendline. If the data has been plotted, as in this example, it is often possible to determine, by eye, the number of months for each season. In the example there is clearly a repeating four-month pattern in the data, which implies that a four-month moving average should be used. If the pattern is not obvious, then alternative numbers of months should be used until the straightest trendline is produced.

If numerical results are required, Excel's Analysis Toolpak can be used. The moving average results can be computed by following the appropriate prompts in the Analysis Toolpak dialog boxes. Alternatively, the approach described below can be used to generate a moving average that is correctly centred, which is essential when the data are presented quarterly or monthly.

Estimating the trend and seasonal factors manually
Producing the trend and the accompanying seasonal factors requires two stages.

- ☑ A correctly centred moving average must be calculated.
- ☑ The seasonal factors must be derived.

Estimating the trend

The moving average should be centred on the middle of the quarter. Based on the data in the example, the first term of a four-period moving average would be centred on the middle of the year, June 30th, and the next term on September 30th. However, if the average of these two terms is taken the result is a correctly centred average, midway between these dates and the mid-point of the quarter. The process can be repeated for subsequent months to produce a correctly centred moving average.

The set-up of this spreadsheet is column-based rather than row-based. The raw data – year, quarter, observation number and data values – are set up in columns A, B, C and D respectively. The layout is shown in Chart 10.5. The moving average figures can be calculated easily, as demonstrated in Chart 10.5, by first adding in 4s then adding in 2s and dividing by 8 to give a correctly centred trend in column G. In the case of monthly data, add in 12s then add in 2s and divide by 24. The code for this task is shown in Chart 10.6 and relates to row 13. The spaces are deliberate and are the result of centring the moving average calculation.

Chart 10.5 Calculating the trend

	A	B	C	D	E	F	G
1	Quarterly data						
2							
3	Year	Quarter	Observation number	Data	Add in fours	Add in twos	Trend
4							
5	1995	1	1	24			
6		2	2	44	208		
7		3	3	61	232	440	55.00
8		4	4	79	254	486	60.75
9	1996	1	5	48	284	538	67.25
10		2	6	66	310	594	74.25
11		3	7	91	330	640	80.00
12		4	8	105	349	679	84.88
13	1997	1	9	68	358	707	88.38
14		2	10	85	378	736	92.00
15		3	11	100	417	795	99.38
16		4	12	125	457	874	109.25
17	1998	1	13	107	495	952	119.00
18		2	14	125	529	1,024	128.00
19		3	15	138			
20		4	16	159			

Chart 10.6 Code for calculating the trend (row 13)

Column	Calculation	Actual calculation	Answer
Year	Input	Input	1997
Quarter	Input	Input	1
Observation number	Input	Input	9
Data	Input	Input	68
Add in 4s	=SUM(D12:D15)	=105+68+85+100	358
Add in 2s	=SUM(E12:E13)	=349+358	707
Trend	=F13/8	=707/8	88.38

If the results from column G are plotted on a graph, they produce a correctly centred trendline that is identical in shape to the line produced by the graph function. The graph of the trendline is shown in Chart 10.7.

Chart 10.7 **Trendline for gross additions**

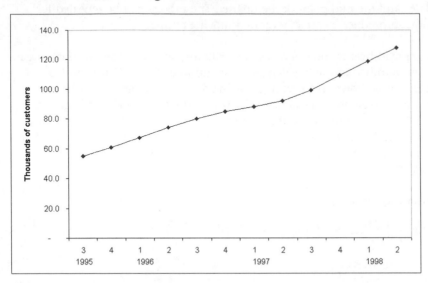

Chart 10.8 **Seasonal factors**

	A	B	C	D	E	F	G	H	I
1	**Quarterly data**								
2									
3	Year	Quarter	Observation number	Data	Add in fours	Add in twos	Trend	Difference	Seasonally adjusted data
4									
5	1995	1	1	24					41
6		2	2	44	208				50
7		3	3	61	232	440	55.00	6.00	55
8		4	4	79	254	486	60.75	18.25	61
9	1996	1	5	48	284	538	67.25	(19.25)	65
10		2	6	66	310	594	74.25	(8.25)	72
11		3	7	91	330	640	80.00	11.00	85
12		4	8	105	349	679	84.88	20.13	87
13	1997	1	9	68	358	707	88.38	(20.38)	85
14		2	10	85	378	736	92.00	(7.00)	91
15		3	11	100	417	795	99.38	0.63	94
16		4	12	125	457	874	109.25	15.75	107
17	1998	1	13	107	495	952	119.00	(12.00)	124
18		2	14	125	529	1,024	128.00	(3.00)	131
19		3	15	138					132
20		4	16	159					141
21									
22	**Seasonal factors**						Quarter		
23	Year				1	2	3	4	
24	1995						6.0	18.3	
25	1996				(19.3)	(8.3)	11.0	20.1	
26	1997				(20.4)	(7.0)	0.6	15.8	
27	1998				(12.0)	(3.0)			
28									
29	Total				(51.6)	(18.3)	17.6	54.1	
30	Average				(17.2)	(6.1)	5.9	18.0	
31									
32	Adjustment			(0.6)	(0.2)	(0.2)	(0.2)	(0.2)	
33									
34	Seasonal factor				(17.4)	(6.2)	5.7	17.9	

Calculating the seasonal factors

The calculation of the seasonal factors in Chart 10.8 is a little more involved. The code for the calculation of the seasonal factors is presented on a cell-by-cell basis in Chart 10.9. The differences between the actual data and the trend must be computed in column H of Chart 10.8 and placed in the seasonal factor table in Chart 10.9 under the appropriate season. The additive model described on page 82 shows that the actual observation (Y) minus the trend (T) is equal to the seasonal factor plus the residual. As the residual is random, it is assumed that the average of all the residuals is zero. Therefore averaging the differences in each quarter gives the average seasonal factor as the average of the residuals is assumed to be zero. The average for each season has been calculated in row 30.

Seasonal factors, however, must add to zero, so the sum of all the averages is computed and divided by 4 to give the adjustment factor in row 32. This adjustment is then added to each of the averages to give the seasonal factors in columns E to H of row 34.

Chart 10.9 **Calculating the seasonal factors**

	A	B	C	D	E	F	G	H
21								
22	Seasonal factors						Quarter	
23	Year				=B5	=B6	=B7	=B8
24	=A5						=H7	=H8
25	=A9				=H9	=H10	=H11	=H12
26	=A13				=H13	=H14	=H15	=H16
27	=A17				=H17	=H18		
28								
29	Total				=SUM(E24:E27)	=SUM(F24:F27)	=SUM(G24:G27)	=SUM(H24:H27)
30	Average				=E29/3	=F29/3	=G29/3	=H29/3
31								
32	Adjustment			=-SUM(E30:H30)	=$D$32/4	=$D$32/4	=$D$32/4	=$D$32/4
33								
34	Seasonal factor				=E30+E32	=F30+F32	=G30+G32	=H30+H32

Lastly, to derive the seasonally adjusted series in column I of Chart 10.8, the appropriate seasonal factor is algebraically subtracted from the original data. Examples of the formulae for doing this are as follows:

$$\text{Cell I5} = D5 - \$E\$34$$
$$\text{Cell I6} = D6 - \$F\$34$$
$$\text{Cell I7} = D7 - \$G\$34$$
$$\text{Cell I8} = D8 - \$H\$34$$

and then the pattern is repeated so that:

$$\text{Cell I9} = D9 - \$E\$34$$
$$\text{Cell I10} = D10 - \$F\$34$$

and so on to cell I20.

Forecasting using the trend, seasonal factors and the additive model

Once the trend and seasonal factors have been estimated, the information can be used to extrapolate the trend and, after adjusting for the seasonal factors, produce a forecast. From the graph it is clear that the trend is reasonably linear, so one of the many linear forecasting worksheet functions that are discussed in more detail later can be used. The FORECAST function estimates the equation of the straight line that best fits the trend data and then uses the equation of the line to produce a forecast for the required months in the future. An example of a forecast based on the calculated trendline is shown in Chart 10.10.

Chart 10.10 **Forecasting using the FORECAST function**

	A	B	C	D	E	F	G	H	I
1	Quarterly data								
2									
3	Year	Quarter	Observation number	Data	Add in fours	Add in twos	Trend	Difference	Seasonally adjusted data
4									
5	1995	1	1	24					41
6		2	2	44	208				50
7		3	3	61	232	440	55.00	6.00	55
8		4	4	79	254	486	60.75	18.25	61
9	1996	1	5	48	284	538	67.25	(19.25)	65
10		2	6	66	310	594	74.25	(8.25)	72
11		3	7	91	330	640	80.00	11.00	85
12		4	8	105	349	679	84.88	20.13	87
13	1997	1	9	68	358	707	88.38	(20.38)	85
14		2	10	85	378	736	92.00	(7.00)	91
15		3	11	100	417	795	99.38	0.63	94
16		4	12	125	457	874	109.25	15.75	107
17	1998	1	13	107	495	952	119.00	(12.00)	124
18		2	14	125	529	1,024	128.00	(3.00)	131
19		3	15	138					132
20		4	16	159					141
21									
22	Seasonal factors						Quarter		
23	Year				1	2	3	4	
24	1995						6.0	18.3	
25	1996				(19.3)	(8.3)	11.0	20.1	
26	1997				(20.4)	(7.0)	0.6	15.8	
27	1998				(12.0)	(3.0)			
28									
29	Total				(51.6)	(18.3)	17.6	54.1	
30	Average				(17.2)	(6.1)	5.9	18.0	
31									
32	Adjustment			(0.6)	(0.2)	(0.2)	(0.2)	(0.2)	
33									
34	Seasonal factor				(17.4)	(6.2)	5.7	17.9	
35									
36	Forecast								
37									
38	Period				17	18	19	20	
39	Trend				141.3	147.5	153.8	160.0	
40	Seasonal Factor				(17.4)	(6.2)	5.7	17.9	
41	Forecast				123.9	141.3	159.5	177.9	

The code that generates these results from row 36, for column F, is shown in Chart 10.11.

Chart 10.11 **Code for forecasting based on the trend and using FORECAST function**

Row	Calculation	Actual calculation	Answer
Period	Manual Input	18	18
Trend	=FORECAST(F38,$G$7:$G$18,$C$7:$C$18)	Forecast by fitting a straight line and extrapolating	147.5
Seasonal factor	=F34	=−6.2	(6.2)
Forecast	=F39+F40	=147.5−6.2	141.3

The multiplicative model

Where a multiplicative model is deemed more appropriate a small modification of the approach is required. The trend should be estimated in the usual way, but the modeller should remember that the multiplicative model is written as follows:

$$Y = T*S*R$$

So to isolate the seasonal factors (S) and the residual (R), the actual observation must be divided by the trend:

$$Y/T = S*R$$

In column H, rather than subtract, the actual number is divided by the trend to give a seasonal factor and residual ratio. Through the process of averaging, these residual factors are eliminated and the same calculations for producing the seasonal factors can be performed. Forecasting involves the same line-fitting exercise as the trend, but rather than adding the seasonal factors, the forecast trend figure should be multiplied by the seasonal factor.

Limitations of time series analysis

Despite being a useful and simple technique, this approach has a number of limitations. Forecasts based on time series analysis assume that the future will be similar to the past and that the trend of the data will be linear. This technique also assumes that the same seasonal pattern is expected in the future and that either the additive or the multiplicative model will remain the most appropriate representation of the data. More sophisticated procedures can be used for time series analysis, such as Holt Winter's exponential smoothing and Box-Jenkins procedures. These, however, are beyond the scope of this book and the reader should to refer to a statistical text to explore such techniques.

REGRESSION TECHNIQUES

As mentioned earlier, projecting forward, or extrapolating the trends in historic data, can often form the basis for a forecast. Forecasting based on fitting a straight line to the data was introduced in the discussion of time series analysis. The technique for estimating the equation of the best-fitting straight line is usually called regression analysis. The FORECAST function used earlier employs regression analysis. The equation of the straight line can be used to forecast any point in the future for which the same relationship is expected to hold. Later this chapter explores fitting curves to data that do not fit a straight line.

Regression analysis

The statistical technique for estimating the best-fitting straight line is that of ordinary least squares regression. Regression analysis examines the relationship between a dependent variable and one or more independent or explanatory variables. The dependent variable is the one the modeller is trying to explain or forecast, whereas the explanatory or independent variables are those believed to influence or explain the movements in the dependent variable. For example, in a mobile phone business the number of gross connections in a month (Y), the dependent variable, may be influenced by the following explanatory variables: time (X1), the cost of a handset (X2) and the connection commission paid to dealers (X3). This could be written algebraically as follows:

$$Y=m1*X1+m2*X2+m3*X3+a$$

The variables m1 to m3 are the coefficients estimated by ordinary least squares regression and a represents the intersection with the y-axis. The larger, or more statistically significant, the coefficients, the more important a determinant they are of the dependent variable. The coefficient of determination R^2 (which is calculated automatically by most spreadsheet packages) indicates how much of the variation in Y is explained by the explanatory variables. The greater the value of R^2, the more the variation in the dependent variable is explained by the selected independent variables.

The square root of the coefficient of determination is the product moment correlation coefficient in the case of linear regression of a straight line. The product moment correlation is a number between 1 and −1. If r = 1 then there is a perfect, positive relationship between the dependent and explanatory variable. A perfect relation implies that every data point lies on a straight line. If r = −1 then a perfect negative relationship exists, and if r = 0 there is no relationship.

Estimating the coefficients

To demonstrate a number of linear regression estimation techniques, it is necessary to develop a forecast for gross connections based on the historical data set out in Chart 10.12. The example starts with a single independent variable, time, and is then extended to include other independent variables.

Chart 10.12 **Gross connections and independent variables**

Month	Gross connections	Connection bonus	Handset selling price	Time period
January	400	200	50	1
February	287	150	70	2
March	196	100	90	3
April	355	150	90	4
May	387	170	90	5
June	300	150	90	6
July	234	100	90	7
August	325	120	70	8
September	295	120	60	9
October	430	150	50	10
November	497	170	40	11
December	551	200	30	12

Chart 10.13 shows how data for the month, month number or time period and gross connections have been set out in a spreadsheet.

Chart 10.13 **Historic gross connections**

	A	B	C	D	E	F	G	H	I	J	K	L	M	N	O	P
1	Historic gross connections															
2																
3	Month	Month			Jan	Feb	Mar	Apr	May	Jun	Jul	Aug	Sep	Oct	Nov	Dec
4	Month number	Month_number			1	2	3	4	5	6	7	8	9	10	11	12
5	Gross connections	Gross_connections			400	287	196	355	387	300	234	325	295	430	497	551

It is often useful to plot the data and this has been done. A regression line and equation has also been added by following the procedure described below.

Adding a regression trendline
- Click in the graph.
- Click a point on the series.
- Right click and select ADD TRENDLINE.
- On the TYPE tab select LINEAR.
- On the OPTIONS tab check the boxes "Display equation on chart" and "Display R-squared on chart".
- Click OK.

The resulting graph, the regression line and the regression equation and R^2 value are shown in Chart 10.14.

Chart 10.14 **Regression equation for monthly gross connections against time**

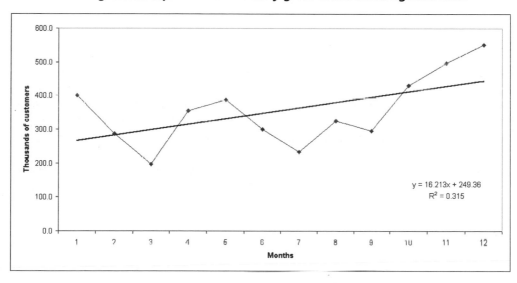

The R^2 value is very low at 0.315. This implies that only 31.5% of the variation in gross connections is explained by time, so any forecast based on this regression equation will be liable to considerable error. The correlation coefficient is the square root of $R^2=SQR(0.315)=0.561$. Although this value is low it is possible to show, using significance testing, that time is still a significant determinant of gross connections.

This procedure is quick and simple to use. However, to develop a forecast it is necessary to use the equation of the straight line. The use of the graphical procedure does not allow this unless the formula is reproduced manually by extrapolating the coefficients by hand and entering them in a spreadsheet. But this would not update dynamically if any of the underlying data were to be changed.

The TREND function

The TREND function can be used for linear regression when there is only one explanatory variable. Chart 10.15 uses the TREND function to generate the predicted values, which can then be compared with the actual values to gauge how good a fit the estimated straight line is to the historic data.

Chart 10.15 **Generating predicted values using the TREND function**

	A	B	C	D	E	F	G	H	I	J	K	L	M	N	O	P
1	Historic gross connections															
2																
3	Month	Month			Jan	Feb	Mar	Apr	May	Jun	Jul	Aug	Sep	Oct	Nov	Dec
4	Month number	Month_number			1	2	3	4	5	6	7	8	9	10	11	12
5	Gross connections	Gross_connections			400	287	196	355	387	300	234	325	295	430	497	551
6																
7																
8																
9	Using the trend function															
10																
11	Month				1	2	3	4	5	6	7	8	9	10	11	12
12	Actual gross connections				400	287	196	355	387	300	234	325	295	430	497	551
13	Predicted values				266	282	298	314	330	347	363	379	395	411	428	444
14	Absolute error				134	5	102	41	57	47	129	54	100	19	69	107
15	Error squared				18,070	27	10,405	1,663	3,200	2,176	16,604	2,924	10,057	342	4,801	11,465
16																
17	Mean square error				6,811											

When a number of alternative methods of forecasting are being used it is useful to be able to measure the quality of the different forecasts to help select the most effective forecasting methodology. The mean square error (MSE) can be used to identify the best-fitting model. The MSE examines the sum of the square of the differences between the actual data from the forecast and the predicted values based on the equation of the straight line. A straight line has been fitted to the data, but it could have been a curve. If the MSE for each alternative were to be computed, the model that generated the smallest value would be chosen.

The supporting code is shown in Chart 10.16 and the analysis relates to year 1. To generate the code it is necessary to create the following range names in rows 4 and 5 of Chart 10.15.

- *Month_number* for cells E4 to P4
- *Gross_connections* for cells E5 to P5

Chart 10.16 **Supporting code for the TREND function**

Row	Calculation	Actual calculation	Answer
Month	=Month_number	=1	1
Actual gross connections	=Gross_connections	=400	400
Predicted values	=TREND(Gross_connections, Month_number,E11)	=Application of ordinary least squares with the explanatory variable=1	266
Absolute error	=ABS(E12−E13)	=Absolute(400−266)	134
Error squared	=E14^2	=134*134	18,070
Mean square error	=SUM(E15:P15)/12	=(18070+27+...+11465)/12	6,811

Forecasting using the TREND function

The TREND function can also be used to generate predicted values. Chart 10.17 shows the results of a forecast using this function for months 13, 14 and 15.

Chart 10.17 **Forecasting using the TREND function**

	A	B	C	D	E	F	G
19	Forecast						
20							
21	Month				13	14	15
22	Sales forecast				460	476	493
23	Actuals				515	475	506
24	Difference				-55	1	-13

The formula for sales forecast is identical except for the inclusion of future values of the explanatory variables instead of historic figures in the TREND function. It is assumed that once the forecast has been made it is possible to compare the forecast values with those that were actually observed. The code for column E is shown in Chart 10.18.

Chart 10.18 **Code for forecasting using the TREND function**

Row	Calculation	Actual calculation	Answer
Month	Input	13	13
Sales forecast	=TREND(Gross_connections, Month_number,E21)	=Application of ordinary least squares with the explantory variable=13	460
Actuals	Input	515	515
Difference	=E22−E23	=460−515	(55)

The LINEST function

The TREND function discussed above does not produce the estimates of the coefficients that would be required to write the equation of the straight line. The use of the TREND function also limits forecasting to the use of just one explanatory variable. The LINEST function, in contrast, provides the values of the coefficients and also allows multiple explanatory variables. It can also generate a number of statistical results that can be used to test the significance, or the strength, of the explanatory variables and the quality of the forecast. It is, however, more complex to use than the TREND function. The results are presented in Chart 10.19.

Chart 10.19 **Using the LINEST function**

	A	B	C	D	E	F	G
27	Using the LINEST function						
28							
29	Slope	Slope			16.21		
30	Intercept	Intercept			249.36		
31							
32	Predicted values from the regression line				460	476	493

LINEST is an array function, which means that a single formula contains a number of different results. There are two ways of using the formula:

- ☑ It can be entered as an array formula.
- ☑ The INDEX function can be combined with the LINEST function to extract the appropriate elements from the array into a single cell.

The code to produce the results is shown in Chart 10.20. The range names "Slope" and "Intercept" have been created to generate the results. The detailed working relates to month 13 or column E.

Chart 10.20 **Supporting code for the use of the LINEST function**

Row	Calculation	Actual Calculation	Answer
Slope	=INDEX(LINEST (Gross_connections,Month_ number),1)	=Application of ordinary least squares regression	16.21
Intercept	=INDEX(LINEST(Gross_connections, Month_number),2)	=Application of ordinary least squares regression	249.36
Forecast	=Intercept+Slope*E21	=249.63+16.21*13	460

The INDEX function requires modellers to enter which element of the array they wish the spreadsheet to report. The indices to produce the results above are:

- ☑ 1 for the slope coefficient
- ☑ 2 for the intercept

The results of using the LINEST function are identical to those of the TREND function, but the equation of the best-fitting straight line ($y=a+bx$, where a is the intercept and b is the slope coefficient) can now be written:

$$Y=249.36+16.21X$$

This is the same equation that was produced by Excel in Chart 10.14 (see page 91).

Multiple regression

There are many factors other than time that determine the level of gross connections. If additional explanatory variables can be included, the quality of the forecast might be improved. The R^2 value implies that only 31.5% of the variation in gross connections has been explained using time as the explanatory variable. By introducing additional explanatory variables the R^2 value may be increased.

Suppose that bonuses paid to dealers for connecting customers and handset prices are possible additional explanatory variables. The data on these two additional explanatory variables were presented earlier in Chart 10.12 (see page 90) and have now been set up in Chart 10.21. As all the data in this section are inputs, no supporting code has been provided. The only task is to set up the range names in italics for the range of cells between columns E and P.

Chart 10.21 **Actual data for multiple regression analysis**

	A	B	C	D	E	F	G	H	I	J	K	L	M	N	O	P
1	Multiple regression															
2																
3	Month	Month			Jan	Feb	Mar	Apr	May	Jun	Jul	Aug	Sep	Oct	Nov	Dec
4	Gross connections	Gross_connections			400	287	196	355	387	300	234	325	295	430	497	551
5																
6	Connection bonuses	Connection_bonus			200	150	100	150	170	150	100	120	120	150	170	200
7	Handset selling price	Selling_price			50	70	90	90	90	90	90	70	60	50	40	30
8	Time	Time			1	2	3	4	5	6	7	8	9	10	11	12

The LINEST function has been used as an array to obtain all the additional information about the equation of the estimated line, and the results are shown in Chart 10.22 on the next page.

Using the array function

☑ Highlight the empty block of cells D14 to G16.
☑ Without clicking anywhere else on the spreadsheet, type the formula:

$$=LINEST(Gross\_connections,E6:P8,,TRUE)$$

The formula will appear in the top left-hand corner of the highlighted cells.

☑ Rather than simply pressing ENTER, depress CTRL and SHIFT simultaneously before pressing ENTER.

The array formula will appear as

$$\{=LINEST(Gross\_connections,E6:P8,,TRUE)\}$$

in cells D14 to G16. The format of the cells can be changed to three decimal places to improve the presentation.

Chart 10.22 **Using LINEST as an array function**

	A	B	C	D	E	F	G
12	Regression results using the array feature						
13				Time	Price	Bonus	Intercept
14	Value			13.622	(0.327)	2.338	(58.329)
15	Standard error			2.987	0.609	0.330	95.754
16	R squared, standard error of Y estimate			0.951	27.066	#N/A	#N/A

If the word TRUE had been placed in between the first two commas, the intercept would have been forced to zero. The inclusion of the word TRUE at the end of the statement requires that the supporting statistics are computed and presented.

The second row of information contained in the array can be used to test the significance of the explanatory variables. The estimates of the coefficients can be divided by the standard error to produce the t-statistic that can then be used for significance testing. If a set of t-tables is used, both the months and the bonuses are shown to be significant but handset selling prices are not. The fact that gross connections are more sensitive to changes in bonuses than handset selling prices is a useful commercial insight for the business. Reducing handset prices reduces revenue for the business but does not have a significant impact on the number of gross connections.

The first row of results in the array provides the information required to derive the equation of the multiple regression line. It is important to note that the order of the coefficients is reversed when compared with the order of the data. An alternative is to use the INDEX function introduced above. Exactly the same results are achieved as shown in Chart 10.23.

Chart 10.23 **Combining the INDEX and LINEST functions**

	A	B	C	D	E
18	Regression results using the INDEX function				
19					
20	Value of time coefficient	*Time_coefficient*			13.622
21	Value of price coefficient	*Price_coefficient*			(0.327)
22	Value of bonus coefficient	*Bonus_coefficient*			2.338
23	Intercept	*Intercept*			(58.329)

The supporting code is presented in Chart 10.24. The formulae are identical except for the index number, which runs from 1 to 4 and relates to different values within the array.

Chart 10.24 **Code for INDEX and LINEST functions**

Row	Calculation	Actual calculation	Answer
Value of time coefficient	=INDEX(LINEST (Gross_connections,E6:P8),1)	Application of ordinary least squares regression	13.622
Value of price coefficient	=INDEX(LINEST (Gross_connections,E6:P8),2)	Application of ordinary least squares regression	(0.327)
Value of bonus coefficient	=INDEX(LINEST (Gross_connections,E6:P8),3)	Application of ordinary least squares regression	2.338
Intercept	=INDEX(LINEST (Gross_connections,E6:P8),4)	Application of ordinary least squares regression	(58.329)

The equation of the straight line can now be written as:

$$Y = -58.329 + 13.622 \times Time - 0.327 \times Handset\ selling\ price + 2.338 \times Bonus$$

The results appear intuitively correct:

- Gross connections would be expected to increase over time and therefore time would have a positive coefficient.
- An increase in the handset selling price to the customer would make buying a phone less attractive, so a negative coefficient would be expected.
- The more incentive dealers have to sell connections the greater are the likely number of connections, so a positive coefficient for the connection bonus would be expected.

The third row of the array contains the R^2 value, which has now increased to 95.1% compared with 31.5%. This indicates that considerably more of the variation in gross connections can be explained compared with using time alone.

Chart 10.25 **Forecasting using the multiple regression equation**

	A	B	C	D	E
25	Forecast				
26					
27	Time period	Time			13
28	Price	Price			90
29	Bonus	Bonus			100
30					
31	Forecast gross connections				323.2

The results can now be used to forecast the future levels for gross connections depending on different time periods and different combinations of handset selling prices and connection commission bonuses. The code to support the forecast of 323 gross connections in period 13 with a handset selling price of 90 and a connection bonus of 100 is presented in Chart 10.26.

Chart 10.26 **Forecasting using the results of multiple regression**

Forecast Gross connections	=Intercept+Time_coefficient*Time	=−58.329+13.622	323.2
	+Price_coefficient*Price	*13−0.327*90+	
	+Bonus_coefficient*Bonus	2.338*100	

Limitations of regression analysis

Although regression analysis is a useful and powerful technique, it has a number of limitations. The key assumption of regression analysis is that of linearity, but this is not always an appropriate model for forecasting purposes. Even when a relationship has demonstrated linearity in the past, there is an implicit assumption that the linear relationship will be continued into the future and this may not be realistic. Regression analysis also assumes that the estimated coefficients are stable and that it is possible to obtain forecasts for future values of the explanatory variables.

To avoid drawing erroneous assumptions from the results of multiple regression analysis, it is important to ensure that the model used is appropriate. For the results of the regression analysis to be useful the model must be correctly specified, which implies that it should include all relevant explanatory variables. But it is important to avoid including a pair of explanatory variables that are themselves highly correlated. When two highly correlated explanatory variables are included significance testing of the complete model can generate non-significant results. However, when one of the closely correlated variables is removed from the equation the coefficients may then be found to be significant. The problem of two explanatory variables being closely related is known as collinearity. Unfortunately, a detailed discussion of this topic is beyond the scope of this book.

LONG-TERM FORECASTING

Chart 10.27 contains data representing the penetration of mobile phones in the UK since their launch in 1985. Penetration is defined as the number of mobile phone users divided by the total size of the population. The data are also presented graphically in Chart 10.28. The TREND function has been used to add a regression line, and its equation to the graph has been used as a starting point for producing a long-term forecast for subscribers.

Chart 10.27 **Historic UK mobile penetration**

Year	Subscribers ('000)	Population ('000)	Population penetration %
1985	48.2	56,685	0.1
1986	122.0	56,852	0.2
1987	260.0	57,009	0.5
1988	498.0	57,158	0.9
1989	870.0	57,358	1.5
1990	1,140.0	57,561	2.0
1991	1,225.0	57,808	2.1
1992	1,391.0	58,006	2.4
1993	2,002.0	58,191	3.4
1994	3,529.4	58,395	6.0
1995	5,355.0	58,606	9.1
1996	6,810.0	58,801	11.6
1997	8,462.0	59,009	14.3
1998	13,001.0	59,237	21.9
1999	23,944.0	59,501	40.2

Source: Coleago Consulting Ltd, *Annual Abstract of Statistics 2000; Monthly Digest of Statistics*, October 2000.

Chart 10.28 **Mobile customers regression analysis**

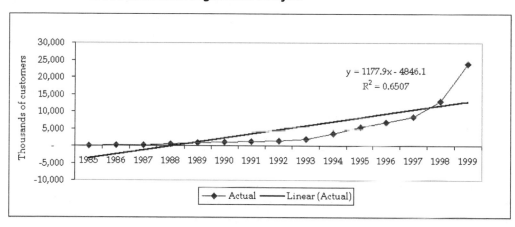

$$y = 1177.9x - 4846.1$$
$$R^2 = 0.6507$$

The use of a linear-based forecast fails to capture the acceleration in growth since 1997. It is clear from an inspection of the graph that a linear model is not appropriate.

The modeller may feel that an exponential growth model would provide a better basis for a forecast. Unfortunately, the use of Excel's Exponential GROWTH function, for example, would result in penetration forecasts of more than 100% after two years, which is not realistic. To produce a more meaningful long-term forecast it is necessary to have a more detailed understanding of market behaviour.

The product life cycle

Many products and services, once launched, follow what is often called the product life cycle (PLC). The PLC is the profile of a product's sales over time and it usually has five distinct phases:

- Product development (not shown in Chart 10.29) – research and development work is carried out to create and prepare the product for launch.
- Introduction – sales and sales growth are usually low as only the early adopters within the market acquire the product.
- Growth – the product becomes much more widely accepted and begins to penetrate the mass market.
- Maturity – as the market saturates the product reaches maturity and sales growth slows.
- Decline – unless action is taken to rejuvenate the product, it will go into decline and sales will begin to fall.

Four stages of the PLC are shown in Chart 10.29.

Chart 10.29 **Stages of the product life cycle**

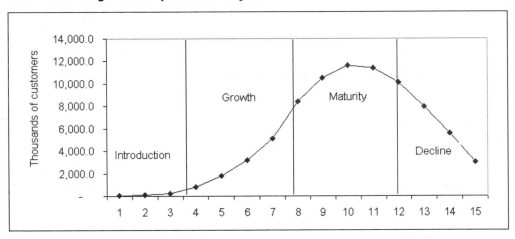

The mobile market in the UK has passed through the introduction phase and is now experiencing a period of rapid growth. To produce a robust long-term forecast for future mobile penetration it is necessary to develop a technique for producing a non-linear forecast that captures the features of the PLC.

Fitting a product life cycle curve

In many industries, new technological developments ensure that the market continues to develop, or the underlying demand remains but the means by which that demand is met alter. Both these alternatives allow the decline phase of the PLC to be ignored for market forecasting purposes. It is therefore assumed that the PLC has an upper asymptote (a level to which the curve approaches but never quite reaches), as shown by the horizontal line in Chart 10.30.

Chart 10.30 **Product life cycle with an upper asymptote**

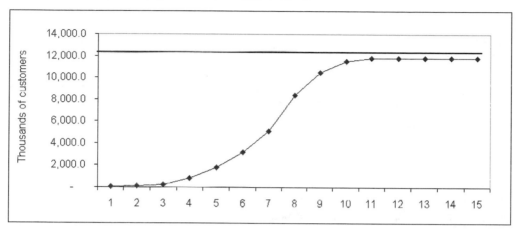

The horizontal line that runs parallel to the upper asymptote is the maximum level of penetration that would be expected in the market. For the purposes of this example a maximum penetration level of 75% is assumed which, when applied to the population, generates a customer base equal to the 12m customers in Chart 10.30.

There are various trend curves that fit these types of data, such as simple modified exponential, Gompertz and Logistic. However, fitting these curves to the dataset using a spreadsheet would be difficult. An alternative curve that fits these types of data and that, after suitable transformations described below, can be used on a spreadsheet to forecast a PLC can be written as:

$$d = \frac{\text{Maximum penetration}}{(e^{\alpha + \beta t} + 1)}$$

where d is the actual penetration after t years and α and β are parameters to be estimated from the actual data. By using the log transformation shown below the equation can be written in the form of a straight line. This allows estimates for α and β to be derived using the ordinary least squares regression techniques described above. To arrive at a formula that can be used in a spreadsheet, the equation must be rearranged to give:

$$\frac{\text{Maximum penetration}}{d} - 1 = e^{\alpha + \beta t}$$

Taking logarithms to base e gives:

$$\text{Ln} \left[\frac{\text{Maximum penetration}}{d} - 1 \right] = \alpha + \beta t$$

Regressing the expression on the left against time (t) gives estimates for both α and β. An assumption has been made about the level of maximum penetration; in the example this is 75%. The example shows how the curve would be fitted to the original dataset using a combination of the INDEX and LINEST functions before producing a forecast for the next ten years. Chart 10.31 shows the actual data and also the estimated curve for the same time period.

Chart 10.31 **Unadjusted fitted product life cycle curve**

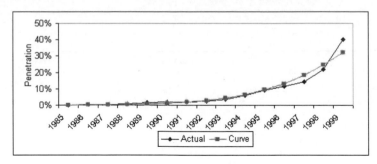

The spreadsheet required to produce the curve in Chart 10.31 is presented in Chart 10.32. The data used to generate the curves can be found in row 17 (for the actual penetration rates) and row 27 (for the historic fitted penetration rates).

Chart 10.32 **Mobile penetration forecast**

	A	B	C/D	E	F	G	H	I	J	K	L	M	N	O	P	Q	R	S
1	Mobile penetration forecast																	
3	Historic penetration and maximum expected penetration																	
5	Year	*Historic_years*		1985	1986	1987	1988	1989	1990	1991	1992	1993	1994	1995	1996	1997	1998	1999
7	Reference	*Historic_reference*		1	2	3	4	5	6	7	8	9	10	11	12	13	14	15
9	Population	*Historic_population*		56,685	56,852	57,009	57,158	57,358	57,561	57,808	58,006	58,191	58,395	58,606	58,801	59,009	59,237	59,501
11	Actual subscribers	*Actual_subscribers*		48.2	122.0	260.0	498.0	870.0	1,140.0	1,225.0	1,391.0	2,002.0	3,529.4	5,355.0	6,810.0	8,462.0	13,001.0	23,944.0
13	Maximum expected penetration	*Maximum_penetration*		75%														
15	Curve estimation																	
17	Actual penetration	*Actual_penetration*		0.1%	0.2%	0.5%	0.9%	1.5%	2.0%	2.1%	2.4%	3.4%	6.0%	9.1%	11.6%	14.3%	21.9%	40.2%
18	Log transformation of actual pene	*Transformed_penetration*		6.781	5.854	5.097	4.444	3.880	3.607	3.538	3.410	3.035	2.434	1.975	1.700	1.442	0.883	-0.146
19					Adjustment													
20	Estimated alpha	*Alpha*		6.5														
21	Estimated beta	*Beta*		(0.4)														
23	Exponential of estimated alpha	*Exponential_alpha*		674.2														
25	Goodness of fit																	
27	Historic forecast penetration			0.2%	0.3%	0.4%	0.6%	0.9%	1.3%	2.0%	2.9%	4.4%	6.4%	9.3%	13.3%	18.4%	24.8%	32.1%
29	Penetration and subscriber forecast																	
30	Year			2000	2001	2002	2003	2004	2005	2006	2007	2008	2009	2010	2011	2012	2013	2014
31	Reference	*Future_reference*		16	17	18	19	20	21	22	23	24	25	26	27	28	29	30
32	Penetration forecast	*Penetration_forecast*		39.8%	47.3%	54.1%	59.8%	64.2%	67.5%	69.9%	71.5%	72.7%	73.4%	74.0%	74.3%	74.5%	74.7%	74.8%
33	Forecast population	*Future_population*		59,718	59,935	60,153	60,373	60,592	60,813	61,035	61,257	61,480	61,704	61,929	62,154	62,380	62,608	62,836
34	Forecast subscribers			23,762	28,370	32,549	36,080	38,894	41,044	42,643	43,816	44,678	45,318	45,806	46,189	46,501	46,768	47,002

All range names relate to rows of data from column E to column S, apart from *Maximum_penetration*, *Alpha* and *Beta*, which are single cell ranges names.

The calculations in Chart 10.33 refer to the year 1986 or column F unless stated otherwise.

Chart 10.33 **Code for calculating the product life cycle curve**

Row	Calculation	Actual calculation	Answer
Year	=Last_year+1	=1985+1	1986
Reference	=Last_year+1	=1+1	2
Population	Input	56852	56,852
Actual subscribers	Input	122	122
Maximum expected penetration (column E)	Input	75%	75%
Actual penetration	=Actual_subscribers/ Historic_population	=122/56852	0.2%
Log transformation	=LN(Maximum_penetration/ Actual_penetration 1)	=LOG(75%/0.2%−1)	5.85
Estimated alpha (column E)	=INDEX(LINEST (Transformed_penetration, Historic_reference),2)+F20	=Result of ordinary least squares regression+0	6.5
Estimated beta (column E)	=INDEX(LINEST (Transformed_penetration, Historic_reference),1)+F21	=Result of ordinary least squares regression+0	(0.4)
Exponential of alpha (column E)	=EXP(Alpha)	=EXP(6.5)	674.2
Historic forecast penetration	=Maximum_penetration/(1+ Exponential_alpha*EXP(Beta* Historic_reference))	=75%/(1+674.2 *EXP(−0.4*2))	0.3%
Year (column E)	=S5+1	=1999+1	2000
Year (column F)	=E30+1	=2000+1	2001
Reference (column E)	=S7+1	=15+1	16
Reference (column E)	=Last_year+1	=16+1	17
Penetration forecast	=Maximum_penetration/(1+ Exponential_alpha*EXP(Beta* Future_reference))	=75%/(1+674.2 *EXP(−0.4*17))	47.3%
Forecast population	Input	59935	59,935
Forecast subscribers	=Penetration_forecast*Future _population	=47.3%*59935	28,370

The curve fitting does not always produce a smooth and reasonable PLC curve. It is usually necessary to make adjustments to both α and β so that the fitted curve fits closer to the most recent observations. A better fit to the most recent years' actual data will often result in a better forecast. The modeller can use cells F20 and F21 to adjust the α and β values to produce a better fit. The formulae in Chart 10.33 were produced with reference to these adjustment cells. The curve in Chart 10.34 has been adjusted to provide a better fit to the penetration figures of the later years 1997, 1998 and 1999, compared with the unadjusted graph in Figure 10.31. The adjustments used were 6.05 for α in cell F20 and −0.43 for β in cell F21.

Chart 10.34 **Adjusted product life cycle curve**

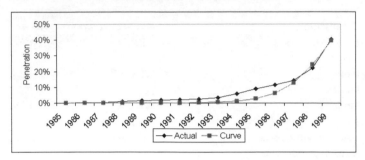

When the adjusted values for α and β are used to forecast the future levels of mobile penetration the curve in Chart 10.35 is obtained. The graph captures both the actual data and the forecast values, and shows how mobile penetration continues to accelerate during the first few years of 2000 before the rate of growth slows as the industry reaches a degree of maturity.

Chart 10.35 **Actual and forecast penetration**

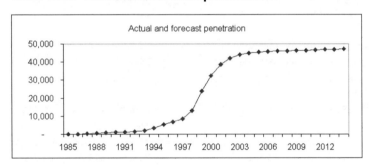

If the level of maximum penetration were changed the shape of the curve would alter accordingly and the penetration curve would have a different profile. The maximum penetration level is a crucial input into the forecasting process. To obtain a better forecast for the maximum level of penetration, the modeller can use market segmentation techniques to refine the forecast for this important input.

SEGMENTATION

Individual customers within a market will have a range of needs, desires, interests, incomes and demands for a particular product or service. A perfect market forecast would be created from a series of individual customer-by-customer forecasts. Such an approach is clearly impractical for all but a few rare exceptions. A practical approach that still improves forecasting accuracy is to produce individual forecasts for groups of customers with similar needs, preferences, incomes and demands. These groups of customers with similar needs are referred to as customer segments.

The basis on which a market segments depends on a great many factors that will be specific to that particular market but may include income, age, location, industry, sex and education. In the case of long-term mobile customer forecasts, the customer base is often broken down into two broad segments: business and consumer. The business segment is defined as mobile users whose employers pay the bill. The consumer segment is defined as customers who pay for their mobile calls themselves.

Segmentation can be used to produce a more accurate assumption for the expected maximum penetration of mobile communications used in the example above. In this example, a maximum penetration level of 75% was assumed.

Consumer segment

It is necessary to determine the size of the segments. In the case of the consumer segment, it is assumed that it is a subset of the total population. For consumer customers, age might be considered an important determinant of the propensity to use mobile telephones. The total population is therefore broken down into age bands and a maximum penetration level is applied to each band. Very young and very old people will have much lower maximum levels of penetration than those in the 20–25 age band. A number of different classifications could have been used to analyse the total population, but age is a useful indicator and data on age distribution are usually readily available.

In Chart 10.36 the calculation is broken down into three sections:

- The first section analyses the total population across all the age bands. The sum of all the inputs must add to 100%.
- In the second section the maximum potential penetration of the demographic bands must be entered. The very young and the very old have much lower assumptions compared with the middle age bands. These are all inputs.
- The third section calculates the maximum addressable market for each of the age bands by multiplying the total population by the age band proportion by the maximum penetration assumption. The population figure in row 39 is an input.

Chart 10.36 **Consumer segment**

	A	B	C	D	E
1	Consumer segment				
2					
3	Year				1999
4					
5	Demographic description				
6	0 - 14				5.0%
7	15 - 19				9.0%
8	20 - 24				14.0%
9	25 - 29				22.0%
10	30 - 34				15.0%
11	35 - 39				12.0%
12	40 - 44				10.0%
13	45 - 49				7.0%
14	50 - 54				2.5%
15	55 - 59				1.5%
16	60 - 64				1.0%
17	65 - 69				0.6%
18	70 and over				0.4%
19					
20	Total				100.0%
21					
22	Maximum potential penetration of demographic bands				
23	0 - 14				38.0%
24	15 - 19				77.0%
25	20 - 24				78.0%
26	25 - 29				74.0%
27	30 - 34				73.0%
28	35 - 39				72.0%
29	40 - 44				70.0%
30	45 - 49				63.0%
31	50 - 54				38.0%
32	55 - 59				30.0%
33	60 - 64				22.0%
34	65 - 69				3.0%
35	70 and over				1.0%
36					
37	Maximum potential addressable market				
38					
39	Population				59,501
40					
41	0 - 14				1,131
42	15 - 19				4,123
43	20 - 24				6,498
44	25 - 29				9,687
45	30 - 34				6,515
46	35 - 39				5,141
47	40 - 44				4,165
48	45 - 49				2,624
49	50 - 54				565
50	55 - 59				268
51	60 - 64				131
52	65 - 69				11
53	70 and over				2
54					
55	Total addressable market				40,861
56	Maximum penetration of the population				69%

The calculations are presented in Chart 10.37. The total addressable market is a sum of all the age band calculations. Lastly, the maximum size of the consumer segment is expressed as a proportion of the total population to give a result of 69%.

Chart 10.37 **Code for calculating consumer segment**

Row	Calculation	Actual calculation	Answer
Row 41, column E	=E$39*E6*E23	=59501*5%*38%	1,131
Total addressable market	=SUM(E41:E53)	=1131+4123+...+2	37,770
Maximum penetration of the population	=E55/E39	=40861/59501	69%

Cell E41 can be copied to cell E53.

Business segment

For the business segment we will assume that it represents a subset of the total working population. In the case of business customers we might examine only the working population and then analyse the working population by the size of the company they work for in terms of number of staff. We can then apply individual maximum penetration assumptions to each firm size band.

Chart 10.38 **Business segment**

	A	B	C	D	E
59	Business segment				
60					
61	Year				2000
62					
63	**Staff size**				
64	1 - 75 staff				60.0%
65	Greater than 75 staff				40.0%
66					
67	Total				100.0%
68					
69	**Maximum potential penetration**				
70	1 - 75 staff				44.0%
71	Greater than 75 staff				22.0%
72					
73					
74	**Maximum potential addressable market**				
75					
76	Working population				24,750
77					
78	1 - 75 staff				6,534
79	Greater than 75 staff				2,178
80					
81	Total addressable business market				8,712
82	Maximum penetration of the working population				35%
83	Maximum penetration of the population				15%

The calculations for the business segment are similar to those for the consumer segment. The differences are the use of staff size instead of age, and the use of the working population instead of the total population. All the other calculations are identical in approach. The last difference is converting the maximum penetration of the working population into the maximum penetration of the population. This is important, as the penetration rates from the two segments will need to be combined to establish a revised figure for the total penetration of the population. The calculations are shown in Chart 10.39. The analysis of staff size in rows 64 and 65 are inputs as is the working population assumption.

Chart 10.39 **Code for calculating the business segment**

Row	Calculation	Actual calculation	Answer
Row 78, column E	=E$76*E64*E70	=24750*60% *44%	6,534
Total addressable market	=SUM(E78:E79)	=6534+2178	8,712
Maximum penetration of the working population	=E81/E76	=8712/24750	35%
Maximum penetration of the population	=E81/E39	=8712/59501	15%

The total penetration calculation is a simple sum so a detailed description has not been provided. Chart 10.40 shows the combined consumer and business maximum penetration levels, which can then be used as a revised input into the product life cycle curve example. The use of a segmented approach has resulted in a more accurate forecast of the total maximum penetration.

Chart 10.40 **Total penetration**

	A	B	C	D	E
86	Total penetration of the population				
87	Consumer segment				68.7%
88	Business segment				14.6%
89					
90	Total penetration				83.3%

Total revenue

Returning to the results of Chart 10.32 (see page 102), row 34 shows a forecast for the total number of mobile customers in the market. This forecast does not include the adjustments to alpha (α) and beta (β). This example can now be extended to derive a forecast for revenue for an individual business within the market. Begin by calculating the average number of customers in the market for each period. Then apply a market share percentage (an input assumption) to calculate the average number of customers for each period for the business. Then assume that these customers use their mobile phones for a certain number of minutes each year. The number of minutes per customer per year is derived from a combination of the minutes from the previous period, the reduction in price during the period (an input assumption) and a price elasticity of demand (PED) assumption. The formula is a rearranged version of the formula introduced earlier (see page 80), and can be written as:

$$= \frac{-PED \times Previous\ Usage \times (Previous\ Price - Current\ Price)+Previous\ Usage}{Previous\ Price}$$

Total revenue is then calculated by multiplying the average number of customers by average annual usage and lastly by the price per minute. The final result is expressed in thousands. Chart 10.41 shows the workings.

To achieve the results, relative range names need to be created for:

- *Previous_usage*, for example, cell H43 references cell G43
- *Previous_price*, for example, cell H43 references cell G41
- *Current_price*, for example, cell H43 references cell H41

Chart 10.41 **Calculating total revenue**

	A	B	C	D	E	F	G	H	I	J	K	L	M	N	O	P	Q	R	S
37	Revenue forecast																		
38	Average market customers	Average_market_customers				26,066	30,460	34,315	37,487	39,969	41,843	43,230	44,247	44,998	45,562	45,997	46,345	46,634	46,885
39	Market share	Market_share				30%	32%	34%	36%	36%	36%	36%	36%	36%	36%	36%	36%	36%	36%
40	Average business customers	Average_business_customers				7,820	9,747	11,667	13,495	14,389	15,064	15,563	15,929	16,199	16,402	16,559	16,684	16,788	16,878
41	Price per minute	Price_per_minute				0.25	0.24	0.23	0.22	0.21	0.21	0.21	0.21	0.21	0.21	0.21	0.21	0.21	0.21
42	Price elasticity of demand	Price_elasticity_of_demand				-0.47	-0.47	-0.47	-0.47	-0.47	-0.47	-0.47	-0.47	-0.47	-0.47	-0.47	-0.47	-0.47	-0.47
43	Average usage per year per cust	Average_usage_per_year				1,570	1,600	1,631	1,664	1,700	1,700	1,700	1,700	1,700	1,700	1,700	1,700	1,700
44	Total revenue - thousands					3,069	3,742	4,376	4,941	5,136	5,377	5,555	5,686	5,782	5,955	5,911	5,955	5,992	6,025

The detailed calculations are shown in Chart 10.42 and relate to column H.

Chart 10.42 **Code for calculating total revenue**

Row	Calculation	Actual calculation	Answer
Average market customers	=AVERAGE(G34,H34)	=(32550 + 36080)/2	34,315
Market share	Input assumption	=34%	34%
Average business customers	=Average_market_customers *Market_share	=34315*34%	11,667
Price per minute	Input assumption	=0.23	0.23
Price elasticity of demand	Input assumption	=-0.47	(0.47)
Average usage per year per customer	= -Price_elasticity_of_demand *((Previous_usage*(Previous_ price-Current_price))/Previous_ price)+Previous_usage	=0.47*((1600*(0.25 -0.24))/0.25)+1600	1,631
Total revenue (thousands)	=Average_business_customers *Average_usage_per_year* Price_per_minute/1000	=11667*1631*0.23 /1,000	4,376

Mix effects

The example above examined the average usage levels for consumer and business customers as a whole. Another approach would be to do the calculations for consumer customers and business customers individually and then combine the two forecasts to give total revenue. This would allow the modeller to examine the effects on total revenue of changes in the mix of the customer base between business and consumer.

This chapter has explored a number of forecasting approaches and how they can be applied to a spreadsheet model. There are many other forecasting tools that have not been discussed, but these approaches will allow the modeller to generate at least an initial forecast in most cases.

11 Operating costs

INTRODUCTION

The group of operating cost assumptions covers the non-revenue parts of a profit and loss account and includes the elements of cost of sales and overheads (interest and tax are covered in Chapters 13 and 14). This is perhaps the easiest area of the three assumption groups of revenue, operating costs and capital costs. So much of it is dependent on the scale of business defined by the revenue and capital assumptions.

In developing a truly dynamic model, where a change in the revenue assumption will automatically change the underlying costs, the dependence relationship between revenue and each cost needs to be identified and used to drive the cost assumption. This chapter will explore the ways to manage these relationships and build up a detailed cost base for the model.

Completeness of operating costs

The first stage of building the cost base for the model is to identify the set of costs that will be included. Although omission will yield a positive impact on the model, it requires discipline and thoroughness to ensure completeness. Often a good place to start is to obtain a printout of cost ledger codes from a finance department. This will provide a list of all the headings and subheadings, under which the costs incurred by a business are currently categorised, for recording transactions in a company's accounts.

The difficulty is to provide guidance or a checklist, as the list of costs is entirely dependent on the situation being modelled and will differ from one type of business to another. In the absence of a set of ledger codes, Chart 11.1 provides guidance on core headings and typical errors or omissions.

Chart 11.1 **Examples of core headings and common errors or omissions**

Section	Headings	Common errors or omissions
Cost of sales	Materials	Allow for waste or rework at all stages, raw materials, work in progress and finished goods.
	Packaging	Prepare for new designs, particularly on pack promotions that may need to be printed. Products sold abroad will need multi-language packaging and compliance with local regulations on product description and content. Allow for wastage in use.
	Labour	Ensure there are sufficient staff to cover both sickness and holidays. There will inevitably be leavers requiring an allowance for recruitment and training costs.
	Distribution	Outsourcing is easier to estimate as delivery sizes and distances are difficult to predict for a fleet operation. Allowance needs to be made for time, damage and even theft. Products sold abroad may be subject to additional taxes/duties and time delays.

Section	Headings	Common errors or omissions
	Maintenance	All equipment will need maintenance and allowance should be made for both the cost and lost production. Appropriate insurance may cover some of the risk.
	Warranty	There will be a cost of non-performance of product and service and some allowance should be made to cover this. Only experience over time will show the level required.
Overheads	Advertising and marketing	Difficult to manage on a project level and more easily controlled by an annual budget.
	Premises and accommodation	Although the rent of a property is fairly predictable, the other costs such as repairs, security, grounds, rates, insurance can add a significant extra cost.
	Salaries	This should cover the board, indirect staff (finance, human resources, IT, marketing and sales) as well as support staff (secretarial, post and cleaning). As with labour, there will be leavers from the business incurring recruitment and retraining costs for replacement. With all payroll the salary cost needs to be adjusted for employment taxes, pensions and bonus payments. Staff expenses should also be identified at this stage including travel and subsistence costs. It may even be appropriate to include round sum amounts for items such as the Christmas party and other social costs.
	Depreciation and amortisation	Although the management of fixed assets is dealt with in Chapter 12, this list would be incomplete without the inclusion of depreciation. (Note that the depreciation of production equipment could be included under cost of sales as a direct cost of the business.)
	Utilities	The cost of the utilities will include power (machine running, light, heat and air conditioning) and communication (telephone and postage). Although the unit costs of most communication costs are falling around the world, the growth in volume use is typically underestimated by most business plans (particularly telephone/data transmission).
	Other office costs	This can include a wide variety of costs covering stationery, computer enhancements, photocopying and insurance. These costs are often best summarised into a total cost rather than separated out into a plethora of tiny amounts that individually are immaterial to the project being modelled.

Cost behaviour

In building seed and behaviour assumptions for costs the aim is to link them directly to revenue to enable changes in revenue to change the underlying costs automatically and create a dynamic model. These links are often in the form of ratios relating a cost to sales units or value. However, each of the operating costs will behave differently in relation to sales and require careful coding in the model. Initially, it can be useful to distinguish the two broad categories of cost behaviours – variable costs and fixed costs.

Variable costs

For every extra unit produced by a business it will need to incur additional costs of items such as raw materials and packaging. These costs will vary directly with the volume of sales and are known as variable costs. Thus any change in sales volume will have a consequential effect on variable costs. Chart 11.2 shows what a graph of this would look like.

Chart 11.2 **A typical variable costs graph**

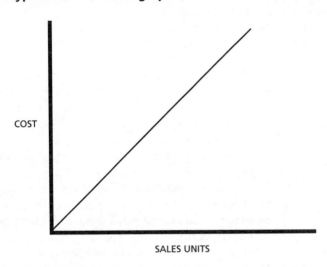

For low volumes of sales this is a linear relationship, but as volumes rise economy of scale effects in bulk buying can trigger volume discounts and cause the cost to rise more slowly. Many modellers ignore the economy of scale effect and base their assumptions on a simple linear relationship, which can be built up from:

- ◪ Number of units of output
- ◪ Quantity of variable item per unit of output
- ◪ Cost per unit of variable item

Creating the code to evaluate a variable cost such as material costs is shown in Chart 11.3. Rows 5 to 20 of the input page are omitted as they show revenue assumptions.

Chart 11.3 **Evaluating materials' costs**

Input page

	A	B	C	D	E	F	G	H
1	**Model title**							
2						Scenarios		
3	Dataset	1	*Dataset*		1	2	3	4
4								
21	**Operating costs**							
22	Quantity per unit	2	*Input_quantity_per_unit*		2	2	2.2	2.2
23	Cost per unit	0.72	*Input_cost_per_unit*		0.72	0.75	0.7	0.72

This sheet is originated using the OFFSET function as described in Chart 7.7 on page 46.

Working page

	A	B	C	D	E	F	G	H	I
1	**Model title**								
2									
3	Year number	Year_number			0	1	2	3	4
4	Years	Actual_years			2000	2001	2002	2003	2004
5									
6	**Material cost**								
7	Production units	Working_production_units			0	1,200	1,500	1,800	2,100
8	Material usage	Working_material_usage			0	2,400	3,000	3,600	4,200
9	Material cost	Working_material_cost			0	1,728	2,160	2,592	3,024

The calculations for scenario 1 in year 2 are shown in Chart 11.4.

Chart 11.4 **Code for evaluating material costs**

Row	Calculation	Actual calculation	Answer
Production units	From production workings		1,500
Material usage	=Working_production_units* Input_quantity_per_unit	=1500*2	3,000
Material cost	=Working_material_usage* Input_cost_per_unit	=3000*0.72	2,160

To make this more sophisticated and bring in economy of scale effects, the price profile can be created with a stepped linear graph, as shown in Chart 11.5.

Chart 11.5 **Variable costs with economy of scale effect**

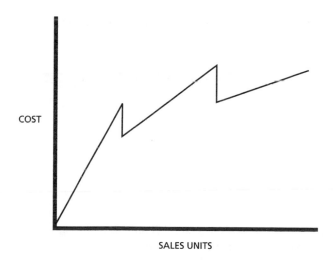

This graph would represent a situation such as a unit cost of £1 for the first 2,000 units, 85p for the next 2,000 and 80p thereafter. To model this effect can give rise to nested IF statements that can become complex with a wide range of discount levels.

The easiest way to manage this is through a look-up table that can be set up on the input page, as shown in Chart 11.6.

Chart 11.6 **Raw material costs with volume discounts**

	A	B	C	D	E	F	G	H
1	**Model title**							
2						Scenarios		
3	Dataset	1	*Dataset*		1	2	3	4
4								
13								
14	Raw material costs		*Input_raw_material_costs*					
15								
16	Price per unit							
17	0	1.00			1.00	1.05	1.10	1.15
18	2,000	0.85			0.85	0.87	0.88	0.89
19	4,000	0.80			0.80	0.81	0.82	0.83
20			Name this range of cells as:					
21			*Input_raw_material_costs*					
22								
23								

On the working or output sheet, this table of prices can be accessed by using the command VLOOKUP.

The syntax of this function is:

=VLOOKUP(look up value,data table,column number to be returned,exact or near match)

So in the example the data table is the range A17:B19 containing units and prices, named *Input_raw_materials_costs*. The look-up value will depend on volume and the column to be returned will be the price (which is the second column).

Chart 11.7 **Evaluating material costs with economy of scale effects**

Working page

	A	B	C	D	E	F	G	H	I
1	**Model title**								
2									
3	Year number	*Year_number*			**0**	**1**	**2**	**3**	**4**
4	Years	*Actual_years*			2000	2001	2002	2003	2004
5									
6	**Material cost**								
7	Production units	*Working_production_units*			0	1,200	1,500	1,900	2,100
8	Material usage	*Working_material_usage*			0	2,400	3,000	3,800	4,200
9	Material cost per unit	*Working_material_cost_per_unit*			0	0.85	0.85	0.85	0.80
10	Material cost	*Working_material_cost*			0	2,040	2,550	3,230	3,360

The production units and material usage are taken from Chart 11.4 on the previous page. The new calculations in year 2 are shown in Chart 11.8

Chart 11.8 **Code for evaluating material costs with economy of scale effects**

Row	Calculation	Actual calculation	Answer
Material cost per unit	=VLOOKUP (Working_material_usage, Input_raw_material_costs,2)	=VLOOKUP(3000, Input_raw_material_costs,2)	0.85
Material cost	=Working_material_usage* Working_material_cost_per_unit	=3000*0.85	2,550

In the VLOOKUP function no value has been put into the "exact or near match" field as the default is "near match". The function works on the principle that if no exact match can be found it will return the nearest value that is lower than the look up value. Hence the table in Chart 11.6 should be set up with the quantities at the lowest end of the price ranges.

Fixed costs

With small changes in volume through the business the cost of some items, such as property rent or security, generally stay constant and hence they are known as fixed costs. However, for significant changes in volume it is likely that the property would not be big enough and additional property will be required, thus the cost will have a step change at certain levels of volume. Chart 11.9 shows what a graph of a fixed cost would look like.

Chart 11.9 **A typical fixed cost graph**

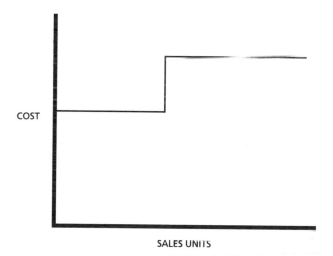

COST

SALES UNITS

It is often difficult for the business to be efficient when operating at maximum capacity (in the region just before a step change in cost). This is because resources become stretched and cause prioritisation conflicts.

It is also inefficient to operate at levels where additional resources are hardly justified because of their low utilisation. In these circumstances, it can be useful to use price increases or decreases as a means of influencing demand and thus maintaining costs at an optimal level. To code these effects it is crucial to understand the relationship between fixed costs and sales and when the trigger points for the step changes will arise (see also Drivers of costs below). For example, a credit controller might be able to handle 500 customer accounts, so as the number of customers rises the number of credit controllers will also need to rise.

The calculation can be done by using either simple division or the ROUNDUP function. The difficulty arises in managing fractions. If 1.2 credit controllers are required, should the business employ one or two staff? A prudent model will round up these fractions and use two, perhaps allowing for the recruitment and training time. The calculation should also be based on the maximum number of accounts in the year (the higher of the opening and closing values).

For example, on an input sheet, data can be set up with 500 as the number of customer accounts per credit controller. This is range named *Input_customer_accounts_per_credit_ controller*. The working page could operate as shown in Chart 11.10.

Chart 11.10 **Determining the number of credit controllers required**

	A	B	C	D	E	F	G	H	I	J
1	Model title									
2										
3	Year number	Year_number			0	1	2	3	4	5
4	Years	Actual_years			2000	2001	2002	2003	2004	2005
5										
21										
22	Credit controllers									
23	Customer accounts	Working_customer_accounts			0	240	380	580	890	1,050
24	Credit controllers	Working_credit_controllers			0	1	1	2	2	3

The calculations in year 4 are as shown in Chart 11.11. Rows 6 to 20 are not shown as they are the revenue calculations from which the number of customer accounts is derived.

Chart 11.11 **Code for determining the number of credit controllers required**

Row	Calculation	Actual calculation	Answer
Customer accounts	From sales workings		890
Credit controllers	=ROUNDUP(MAX(H23:I23)/ Input_customer_accounts_per_ credit_controller,0)	=ROUNDUP(MAX (580,890)/500,0)	2

DRIVERS OF COSTS

Having identified the types of costs and their variable or fixed behaviour, the next stage is to understand the driver of the costs incurred. The "driver" is the factor that determines the amount spent. For example, the cost of light and heat might be driven by the size of property to be used by the business, the number of units of power required per unit of property in an average year and the expected cost per unit of power.

These drivers can be hard to find and may rely on researching assumptions in a logical order. Continuing the example, the size of property will not be known until the number of people and amount of equipment are identified. Therefore it is helpful to build a cost driver dependency map. By starting with revenue and the number of units of output, the links can be built up to cover the entire cost base.

This map can then be used to build up the set of input assumptions that are needed to drive the model and create the outputs. At this stage it is important not to over-engineer a model such that there are detailed assumptions on non-critical values. As mentioned above, office costs can be consolidated and set up as either a cost heading for the business as "other overheads" or one heading per employee as "overheads per person".

An example cost driver map for property space is shown in Chart 11.12.

Chart 11.12 **Cost driver map for calculating property space requirement**

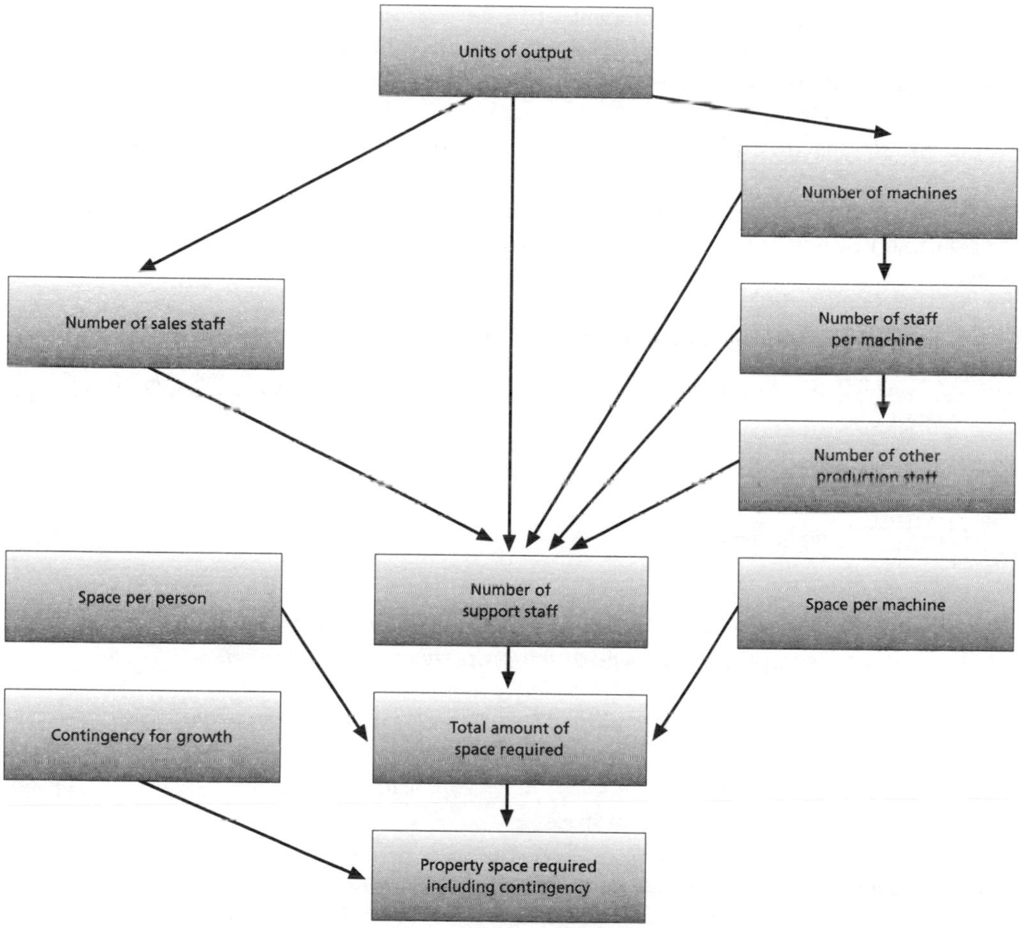

All these assumptions link back to units of output and thus help retain the dynamic nature of the model. A change in sales will trigger changes in staff levels that will also ultimately trigger changes in property requirements.

Inflexible costs

There are some fixed costs, such as property, that are inflexible. This means that they cannot be purchased in ideal unit sizes and extra units cannot be bought and sold quickly. In these circumstances two assumptions are needed.

- ☑ Define a unit size that can be a purchasable block, such as 5,000 sq ft, and use the technique shown in fixed costs to calculate the number of property blocks that are needed for the number of staff or amount of equipment required.
- ☑ Define a period of time over which property blocks are to be held, such as five years. This means that any property transaction (purchase, reserve or option) must be right for five years, taking account of forecast needs.

To achieve this second assumption and retain the controllable nature of the model the following three functions are required:

- ☑ MOD to trigger the period interval;
- ☑ MAX to find the highest amount of space required in the period;
- ☑ OFFSET to define a variable range of data.

All these functions are explained in Chapter 7 and their application is illustrated below.

On the input page define the period over which a property block can be purchased. For the example in Chart 11.13 assume this is called *Input_property_period* and set at five years.

Chart 11.13 **Anticipating future property requirements**

	A	B	C	D	E	F	G	H	I	J	K	L	M	N	O	P	Q
1	Model title																
2																	
3	Year number	Year_number			0	1	2	3	4	5	6	7	8	9	10	11	12
4	Years	Actual_years			2000	2001	2002	2003	2004	2005	2006	2007	2008	2009	2010	2011	2012
5																	
21	Property costs																
22	Property units	Working_property_units			1	3	5	6	6	6	7	7	9	9	10	10	11
23	Property required	Working_property_purchase			6	0	0	0	0	9	0	0	0	0	11	0	0

The calculations in year 0 are as shown in Chart 11.14. Rows 6 to 20 are not shown as they are the revenue assumptions from which the property units are derived.

Chart 11.14 **Calculation for anticipating future property requirements**

Row	Calculation	Actual calculation	Answer
Property units	From workings of space required		1
Property required	=IF(MOD(*Year_number*, *Input_property_period*)=0, MAX(OFFSET(D22,0,0,1, *Input_property_period*)),0)	IF(MOD(0,5)=0, MAX(OFFSET(D22,0,0,1,5)),0)	6

Once the property unit is purchased the annual rental can be charged in each year of the model until the next calculation is performed.

Triangulation

For some costs the annual amount will be based on neither a value at the start of the year nor a value at the end of the year, but an average of the two. An example might be payroll cost. If there are 10 employees at the start of the year and 16 at the end, the payroll cost should be calculated on the average of 13. This assumes that there is an even distribution of new hires joining and leavers departing. Should the business start a project or department then the hires may be clustered towards one point and the maximum value for the year should be taken as the basis for the payroll cost calculation.

To calculate the triangulation effect use the average function:

=Average(Start year head count,End year head count)

Chart 11.15 **The triangulation effect on average value for some costs**

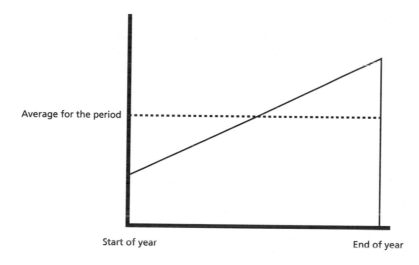

Average for the period

Start of year

End of year

Inflation

In developing cost profiles for the model, it is often easier to generate code that builds up in real values (excluding inflation). This not only makes the differentiation of fixed and variable costs more obvious (because the fixed costs stay constant), but it can also help at the debugging stage when the nominal values (including inflation) can be more difficult to interpret.

Once the real values are generated, it is then a simple step to adjust them by inflation factors and generate nominal values. Chapter 9 illustrates methods of modelling inflation assumptions. The key to generating realistic data is to understand the nature of the inflationary impact on the costs. For example, wages and salaries typically inflate faster than average prices and utilities have experienced considerable deflationary effects in the last few years (particularly in telecommunications). The modeller needs to link the correct inflation factor to each cost profile and remember that some costs may not inflate, such as property rent that is negotiated and fixed for a set period of years.

As the cost section is developed, it is helpful to document in the row heading whether a row of data is in nominal or real values and to show beside the nominal rows which inflation factor has been applied. This will enable users of the model to understand the impact of changes in assumptions.

Tax

Chapter 14 covers the calculation and modelling of tax on profits. However, in this chapter on costs it is relevant to cover the impact of purchase, sales or value-added tax. For most businesses this type of tax is levied on all sales and recovered when incurred on purchases. Effectively, the business operates as a collection agent. The impact on a model is therefore normally in cashflow – the timing difference between collection and paying over to the government. Many models ignore this tax as the timing difference is usually marginal to the business.

If the tax is ignored in the model, the operating cost assumptions should exclude any tax that can be recovered from the government. However, in some countries there are categories of cost where the tax is irrecoverable, such as luxury items that are not necessary for the continuance of business like entertaining and expensive cars. For these types of costs the cost assumptions should include the irrecoverable purchase tax.

12 Capital expenditure and working capital

Any model that has a balance sheet as one of its outputs will almost certainly require code to build the lines for capital expenditure on fixed assets and working capital (items of stock, debtors and creditors). This chapter looks at the nature of these items and some of the practical coding that can be used.

FIXED ASSETS

What are fixed assets?

Fixed assets are items that are purchased with the intention of being used in the business rather than resold, such as a car for a sales representative. The item will typically provide the business with a benefit over a period of time.

There are two distinct types of fixed assets:

- ◾ Tangible, such as buildings, machines, vehicles and office equipment
- ◾ Intangible, such as patents, licences, goodwill and brands

The principles and code for handling the two types of fixed assets in a model are broadly similar. However, the precise treatment of goodwill and brands can vary from country to country as the accounting for this type of item is a hot topic for most accounting bodies around the world.

How should fixed assets be treated?

One way to treat an asset would be the same as an expense, the full cost being written off on purchase. However, this would cause considerable fluctuations in profit whenever assets were acquired. An alternative method might be to track the market value of the asset over time. But this ignores the fact that the benefit of most assets is more likely to be derived over time rather than moving with market values.

The method used is to spread the cost of the asset over an estimated period of benefit or useful economic life. This spreading concept, or matching of cost against the years that derive benefit, is known as "depreciation" for tangible assets and "amortisation" for intangible assets. A common exception to this principle is land, which, unless the business is in mining, need not be depreciated.

In most companies, the administration required for capitalising and depreciating assets means small assets are often written off on purchase. This is sometimes known as the *de minimis* level for fixed assets, typically £500 or £1,000. The *de minimis* rule can become difficult to apply when buying an item like a computer. The total cost is over the limit, but if the computer is separated into screen, keyboard, modem, processor and so on then each individual item is below the limit. Each company has its own policy on dealing with these issues and related items are usually grouped into one asset for the purpose of fixed asset accounting.

Take, for example, a van that is purchased for £10,000. The company plans to keep it for three years and then sell it. It estimates the market value of the three-year-old van will be 40% of the purchase price. Therefore the van will lose £6,000 in value over the three years.

The market value of the van is likely to drop steeply at the outset and flatten out over time. The graph in Chart 12.1 illustrates this exponential type of profile.

Chart 12.1 **Estimated market value of a van over time**

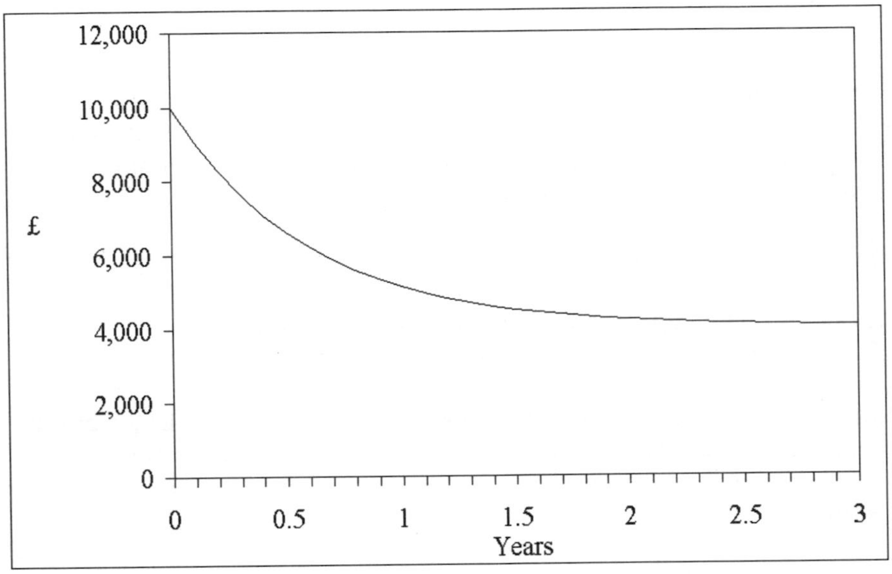

For modelling purposes, the market value during the asset's life is largely irrelevant. Depreciation will be used to spread the estimated fall in value over the three-year period of ownership. The question is how?

Straight line depreciation

The most common method of depreciation is "straight line", which spreads the estimated loss evenly over the period of ownership. To calculate the annual cost use the formula:

(Purchase price–Estimated disposal proceeds)/Estimated period of ownership

For the van example this will be:

(£10,000–£4,000)/3=£2,000 per year

The balance sheet will show the cost of the asset, the accumulated depreciation and the net book value, and the profit and loss account will record the annual cost of depreciation, as shown in Chart 12.2.

Chart 12.2 **Depreciation of an asset**

Year	0	1	2	3	4
Balance sheet					
Cost	10,000	10,000	10,000	10,000	0
Accumulated depreciation	–	(2,000)	(4,000)	(6,000)	0
Net book value	10,000	8,000	6,000	4,000	0
Profit & loss					
Depreciation	0	2,000	2,000	2,000	0

At the point of sale it is unlikely that the asset will realise exactly the net book value (unless it is part of a prearranged buy-back deal). Therefore there will be a small profit or loss on disposal.

The treatment of this asset for cashflow purposes is shown in Chart 12.3.

Chart 12.3 **Cashflow from purchase and sale of an asset**

Year	0	1	2	3	4
Cashflow	(10,000)	0	0	0	4,000

Reducing balance depreciation

Another method of depreciation that is used by some companies is "reducing balance", which tries to approximate the typical curved behaviour of the market value graph by taking a proportion of the previous year's net book value.

Some companies use a set percentage, such as 25%, or it can be calculated using the formula:

$$1-((\text{Estimated disposal proceeds/Purchase price})^{(1/\text{Estimated period of ownership})})$$

Applying this to the van example the reducing balance rate would be:

$$1-((4000/10000)^{(1/3)})=26.3194\%$$

Chart 12.4 **Reducing balance depreciation of an asset**

Year	0	1	2	3	4
Balance sheet					
Cost	10,000	10,000	10,000	10,000	0
Accumulated depreciation	0	(2,632)	(4,571)	(6,000)	0
Net book value	10,000	7,368	5,429	4,000	0
Profit & loss					
Depreciation	0	2,632	1,939	1,429	0

Although the cashflow will be the same as for the straight line method, the cost impact is higher in the early years.

Other depreciation methods

Other depreciation methods can be used such as "sum of the digits" and "consumption proportion". These are rarely applied in practice except in the mining industry, where the consumption method can sometimes be found. In this case the cost of a mine is allocated across the recoverable reserves it contains. The depreciation is a function of the amount of the reserves extracted during the period.

Purchase cost

For all these depreciation methods the purchase cost of an asset must be defined. For most items, this is simply the cash paid. However, there can be complications such as when the asset is imported, where duties and shipping are paid or when there are some sizeable installation costs. In these circumstances, it would be harsh to charge these costs to the profits in the year of purchase. Therefore it is common for the costs of getting an asset to its "location and condition of use" to be added to the purchase price and the total depreciated over the useful life.

Some companies construct their own assets, such as a retailer building an out-of-town superstore. In these cases the cost of the asset is the total of all the individual contractor invoices for building the asset. It is also possible to include a proportion of the company's own labour costs for those employees involved in the construction. More controversial can be the inclusion of interest costs in funding the asset during the course of construction. Accounting standards prevent this in some countries.

Useful economic life

The start point for useful economic life and hence for charging depreciation is usually the purchase date for an item. However, for a constructed asset this is usually set as the date it is brought into service.

How long is the asset expected to be of benefit? In many companies this will be set by a standard policy (for example, cars are replaced every three or four years) or a standard depreciation term (for example, machines are depreciated to zero over eight years). For other assets a judgment will have to be made on what is credible while taking into account the potential impact of technical obsolescence. Personal computers may physically last ten years or more, but for a business to keep up with technology and remain competitive it may need to buy new computers every three years.

Estimated proceeds of sale/residual value

Compared with the purchase cost, it is far more difficult to identify the future value that can be realised at the end of an asset's useful life or on disposal.

There are a few general principles:

- ▨ **Cars.** There are widely available guide prices that make it reasonable to assume a second-hand value which, after four years, is around 25% of purchase cost.
- ▨ **Plant.** Most companies do not buy equipment and machinery with an intention of resale. This is partly because there will be a limited second-hand market, but often

because technology changes will cause obsolescence (for example, computers). In these situations no residual value should be assumed, except for scrap values for material.

- ▨ **Buildings.** For special-purpose buildings it would be prudent to assume no residual value. For office buildings that have alternative uses a residual value is appropriate depending upon location.
- ▨ **Land.** In evaluating the residual value of land there are four key considerations:
  - Will the activity on the land contaminate or change its value? (For example, a nuclear power station)
  - Is the purchase price affected by its surroundings, which may be subject to change? (For example, a shop reliant on passing trade when a bypass could be built)
  - Can the land be used for more than one purpose? (For example, could it be sold for housing)
  - How will inflation and market conditions change its value?

It should be noted that if the disposal proceeds of an asset is the critical factor that determines whether a project goes ahead, the company should consider whether its trading activities are viable and whether it should focus more on asset management.

As well as identifying disposal proceeds, it is helpful to identify exit options during the life of the project. Should a 25-year project not deliver the desired benefits, what is the cost of exit after 5, 10, 15 and 20 years? Based on the difference between a straight line depreciation graph and a market value graph, it is likely that most assets will realise less than book value during their early years of ownership.

Abandonment

Some assets will not only end their useful life with no value, but also create a significant liability for the disposal costs; for example, decommissioning and decontaminating a nuclear power station or abandoning an oil platform. In these circumstances, it is normal to depreciate an asset to zero over its life and to create an abandonment provision over the same period. For example, a $250m installation may be depreciated over 25 years at the rate of $10m a year plus a $2m abandonment provision. This will create a fund of $50 at the end of its life to pay for the dismantling and abandonment.

Timing of purchase

Most models are set up with yearly time intervals; thus it is a normal assumption to purchase an asset at the end of a preceding year so it can be ready for use during that year. This may not always coincide with reality, but it is the most prudent approach. The main effect will be to accelerate slightly the depreciation costs and funding requirements. More sophisticated assumptions are possible, but these will require a lot of code to allow for uneven first and last years. The benefit in business valuation terms can be minimal.

Coding in the spreadsheet

The scenario being modelled is likely to comprise a wide range of fixed assets, including buildings, technical equipment, office equipment and vehicles. Each of these is likely to have a different asset life and hence depreciation rate. For simplicity, it is helpful to group similar items together as each category will have to have its own set of cost, depreciation and net book value calculations. The addition of all the categories results in the total fixed asset numbers.

Buying assets

In producing a dynamic model, there are three triggers that will prompt a fixed asset purchase:

- ◪ The start of trade, such as buying an accounting system.
- ◪ The activity level in the business, such as the number of desktop computers needed.
- ◪ The life of the asset and hence the need for replacement; for example, desktop computers may last only three years.

In triggering the purchase (or construction) of an asset, it is important to ensure that the expenditure is timed to occur before its forecast use. For example, time should be allowed for activities like installation, testing and staff training before operational use.

Ideally, the business should spread its investment in assets as evenly as possible over time. This prevents a huge crescendo of investment at the outset and then replacement of all the assets at the same time some years later. The most effective way to achieve a smoothing of investment is to combine asset rental with a replacement programme. A replacement programme should commence before assets become obsolete and then carry on for some period after obsolescence. By keeping the assets that were replaced early they can be standbys for those that will be replaced late.

Start of trade

In a model of a new venture, several events will be triggered in the first year. Therefore one of the model's inputs could be set to this point in time and range named *Start_year*. Use a simple IF statement to purchase the required items at the right time:

$$=\text{IF}(\textit{Year\_number}=\textit{Start\_year},\textit{Input\_van\_cost},0)$$

Activity level

One of the key modelling principles is to be able to change any one input and still have a valid model with a valid answer. Thus the ability to trigger asset purchases based on activity level is fundamental to maintaining this principle. To implement this a business must identify the activity that needs new assets to be purchased.

Take, for example, a distribution business that needs vans for deliveries. The key assumption will be the volume of sales that can be distributed by a van each year. A ROUNDUP function can be used to calculate the number of vans needed.

If a van can distribute $100,000 of sales a year, the formula would be:

$$=\text{ROUNDUP}(\textit{Sales}/100000,0)$$

This method will ensure that there are enough vans when sales do not fall in complete units of 100,000. For example, if there were sales of $420,000 the answer would be 5. These vans should be purchased at the end of the preceding year so they are ready for use in the following year.

Replacement of assets

For replacement of assets, the model needs to trigger a repurchase at the end of the life of an asset. The code therefore needs to look back a definable number of years to find the original purchases. There are two ways to achieve this, using MOD or OFFSET.

1. MOD

The way to use this function for replacing assets is to buy them every time the MOD of the year number divided by the asset life is zero. For example, if a van had a four-year life set up as an input and range named *Input_life_of_asset*:

$$=IF(MOD(Year\_number, Input\_life\_of\_asset)=0, Input\_van\_cost, 0)$$

This would buy assets in years 0, 4, 8, 12 and so on.

2. OFFSET

This function is a way of picking up a number that is a definable distance away, as explained in Chapter 7. The syntax is:

$$=OFFSET(start\ point, rows\ away, columns\ away)$$

The benefit of this function is the "definable distance away". This can be set as the asset life and become a changeable input.

Using the example above, if vans have a four-year life the model might look like Chart 12.5 on the next page.

To run this example two inputs are set up as follows:

- ☑ *Input_volume_per_van* $100,000
- ☑ *Input_life_of_asset*   4

Chart 12.5 **Automating replacement of assets**

	A	B	C	D	E	F	G	H	I	J	K
1	**Model title**										
2											
3	Year number	Year_number			0	1	2	3	4	5	6
4	Years	Actual_years			2000	2001	2002	2003	2004	2005	2006
5											
36	**Revenue**										
37	Sales	Working_sales			0	40,000	80,000	120,000	180,000	240,000	310,000
38											
39	**Fixed assets**										
40	Vans needed	Working_vans_needed			1	1	2	2	3	4	
41											
42	Vans b/fwd	Working_vans_b_fwd			0	1	1	2	2	3	
43	Vans disposed	Working_vans_disposed			0	0	0	0	(1)	0	
44	Vans purchased	Working_vans_purchased			1	0	1	0	2	1	
45	Vans c/fwd				1	1	2	2	3	4	
46											

The arrows show the effect of the OFFSET function reversing out the purchases four years previously.

The calculations for year 4 in column I are shown in Chart 12.6. Rows 6 to 35 are omitted as they cover revenue workings, the result of which is the sales line in row 37.

Chart 12.6 **Code for automating replacement of assets**

Row	*Calculation*	*Actual calculation*	*Answer*
Vans needed	=ROUNDUP(J37/ Input_volume_per_van,0)	=ROUNDUP(240000, 100000,0)	3
Vans brought forward	H45	2	2
Vans disposed	=IF(Year_number<Input_life_of_asset,0, −OFFSET(I44,0,−Input_life_of_asset))	=IF(4<4,0,−OFFSET (I44,0,−4))	(1)
Vans purchased	=MAX(0,Working_vans_needed− Working_vans_b_fwd− Working_vans_disposed)	=MAX(0,3−2−1)	2
Vans carried forward	=SUM(I42:I44)	=SUM(2−1+2)	3

The vans needed in row 40 is based on the sales in the subsequent year, and so the assets are purchased at the end of the year prior to their use.

The disposal of vans in row 43 uses the OFFSET statement. This is set to look back four years and reverse the purchases. The code is set within an IF statement to ensure it does not look back before the beginning of the model and cause reference errors.

The van purchases in row 44 use a MAX statement to check whether the number of vans needed this year is greater than those already held. Using a zero in the MAX statement will ensure the answer is never negative and that vans will not be sold or replaced if demand falls.

Coding in the spreadsheet to depreciate assets

Once the asset is purchased the cost of ownership should be spread over the years of use.

The examples used in this chapter have an input on the model so that the asset life can be changed (it is currently set at four years). The depreciation period is set as the same as the asset life. As this period changes both the replacement of assets and the depreciation rate will change.

Straight line depreciation

Straight line depreciation is illustrated in Chart 12.7 using the van example, with the cost as $10,000 and the disposal value as $4,000 after four years. Rows 5 to 22 are omitted as they contain revenue workings.

This example builds on Charts 12.5 and 12.6 with additional inputs set up for:

- ▪ Input_van_cost $10,000
- ▪ Input_disposal_value $4,000

Chart 12.7 **Straight line depreciation**

	A	B	C	D	E	F	G	H	I
1	**Model title**								
2									
3	Year number	Year_number			0	1	2	3	4
4	Years	Actual_years			2000	2001	2002	2003	2004
23									
24	**Fixed assets**								
25	Cost b/fwd				0	10,000	10,000	20,000	20,000
26	Additions	Working_FA_addition			10,000	0	10,000	0	20,000
27	Disposals	Working_FA_disposal			0	0	0	0	(10,000)
28	Cost c/fwd				10,000	10,000	20,000	20,000	30,000
29									
30	**Depreciation**								
31	Depn b/fwd				0	0	1,500	3,000	6,000
32	Charge for year	Working_depn_charge			0	1,500	1,500	3,000	3,000
33	Disposals	Working_depn_disposal			0	0	0	0	(6,000)
34	Depn c/fwd				0	1,500	3,000	6,000	3,000
35									
36	**Net book value**	Working_net_book_value			10,000	8,500	17,000	14,000	27,000

The calculation of the number of vans needed is shown in the asset purchase and replacement examples above. The lines of code for the fixed assets and depreciation for year 4 are shown in Chart 12.8.

In both the fixed assets and the depreciation sections there are lines for disposal of assets. This ensures that assets that are either disposed of or fully written off are eliminated. Where assets are replaced they show up as both an addition and disposal. This is important for the cashflow part of the model.

Note that assets that have a zero book value should not be used to artificially inflate the cost and depreciation figures in a business and hence should be removed.

Chart 12.8 **Code for straight line depreciation**

Row	Calculation	Actual calculation	Answer
Fixed asset cost b/fwd	=H28		20,000
Additions	=Working_vans_purchased*Input_van_cost	=2*10000	20,000
Disposals	=Working_vans_disposed*Input_van_cost	=−1*10000	(10,000)
Fixed asset cost c/fwd	=SUM(I25:I27)	=20000+20000− 10000	30,000
Depreciation b/fwd	=H34		6,000
Charge for year	=(Input_van_cost−Input_disposal_value)/ Input_life_of_asset/Input_van_cost*I25	=(10000−4000)/4 /10000*20000	3,000
Disposals	=Working_vans_disposed*(Input_van_cost− Input_disposal_value)	=−1*(10000−4000)	(6,000)
Depreciation c/fwd	=SUM(I31:I33)	=6000+3000−6000	3,000
Net book value	=I28−I34	=30000−3000	27,000

If inflation is used in the model, then the code needs to account for the change in prices from the date of purchase to the date of sale. The necessary additions to the code are shown in Chart 12.9.

Chart 12.9 **Code for straight line depreciation with inflation on assets**

Row	Calculation
Fixed asset additions	Multiply the asset cost by an inflation factor for the relevant year such as: cost*((1+Input_inflation)^Year_number)
Fixed asset disposals	Use OFFSET to multiply the asset cost by the inflation factor for the year of original purchase
Depreciation charge	The code will already handle inflation if it is included
Depreciation disposals	Use OFFSET to multiply the depreciated amount by the inflation factor for the year of original purchase

Reducing balance depreciation

If the business is using a reducing balance method, the amendments to the above straight line code are as shown in Chart 12.10.

Chart 12.10 **Code for reducing balance depreciation**

Row	Calculation
Depreciation charge for year	Apply the reducing balance depreciation rate to the net book value of the previous year
Depreciation disposals	Multiply the number of vans by the net book value on disposal. This calculated as: asset cost*((1−reducing balance percentage)^asset life)

Assets already on the books

For models built around activities other than new ventures it is likely that the business will start with a portfolio of fixed assets that are already being used. These will have a variety of ages and need to be included in the calculations.

For each category of assets two attributes are required for each historic year of purchase, as illustrated in Chart 12.11.

Chart 12.11 **Managing existing assets**

	A	B	C	D	E	F	G	H	I	J
1	Model title									
2										
3	Historic years				-5	-4	-3	-2	-1	0
4										
5	Vehicles									
6	Original cost				8,750	0	9,250	0	0	10,000
7	Number of units				2	0	1	0	0	2

Chart 12.11 is a data table and therefore should be either on the input sheet or on a special "Existing asset" sheet, which should be treated as an input sheet. No scenarios are used, however, as this is factual, unchangeable data.

Using assumptions for asset life and estimated proceeds of sale, this information can be used to create the first year asset values.

Coding in the spreadsheet to sell assets

The above coding covered the purchase of assets and the replacement of assets. Asset sales can take place before the asset is obsolete. However, in many business plans and models such occurrences are rare. They usually optimistically assume growth and not decline.

Automating asset sales to match rises and falls in revenue can cause some problems. The order of asset sales needs to be defined. This is usually set as the oldest is sold first, but this may not be the most appropriate if cash is required in the business. Also code can cause an asset to be sold one year only to be repurchased the next. Ideally, the code needs to look ahead to ensure a sale is justifiable. This can be achieved by using the OFFSET function set to check whether there is a purchase required in the following year.

The proceeds of sale are difficult to predict. On the market value graph for an asset in Chart 12.1 (see page 122), the net book value on a straight line depreciation basis is likely to overstate the actual value of the asset. (An exception is property, which may have risen, depending on the market). If the reason the business is shedding assets is a downturn in revenue, then this might imply that the economy is weak. The realisable price in a weak economy could be particularly low, causing a significant loss to be made.

Calculating the current net book value of each asset requires a large block of coding. This is needed to keep track of the acquisition date of each year's asset purchases. Therefore it is worth establishing whether the model really needs the functionality of selling assets during their life before embarking on this piece of code.

The coding in Chart 12.12 allows for a user defined asset life.

Chart 12.12 **Setting up a sheet to manage the net book value of each year's assets**

	A	B	C	D	E	F	G	H	I	J
1	**Model title**									
2										
3	Year number	*Year_number*			**0**	**1**	**2**	**3**	**4**	**5**
4	Years	*Actual_years*			2000	2001	2002	2003	2004	2005
5										
6	**Vans**									
7	Vans b/fwd				0	1	1	2	2	3
8	Purchases	*Working_vans_purchased*			1	0	1	0	2	1
9	Disposals	*Working_vans_disposed*			0	0	0	0	(1)	0
10	Vans c/fwd				1	1	2	2	3	4
11										
12	**Purchase year**									
13	Year 0				1	1	1	1	0	0
14	Year 1					0	0	0	0	0
15	Year 2						1	1	1	1
16	Year 3							0	0	0
17	Year 4								2	2
18	Year 5									1
19	Total				1	1	2	2	3	4
20										

The data table of asset ages is created from the data in Chart 12.5 (see page 128) and repeated here as the van analysis in rows 7 to 10. The total of vans c/fwd is used to calculate which vans are still owned on a FIFO (first in first out) basis.

Taking column I, the code for the age of assets boxes is shown in Chart 12.13.

Chart 12.13 **Code for managing the net book value of each year's assets**

Row	Calculation	Actual calculation	Answer
17 (Year 4)	=MIN(vans bought year 4[I8],vans c/fwd year 4[I10])	=MIN(2,3)	2
16 (Year 3)	=MIN(vans bought year 3[H16],vans c/fwd year 4[I10]−vans bought in year 4[G17])	=MIN(0,3−2)	0
15 (Year 2)	=MIN(vans bought year 2 and in use year 3[H15], vans c/fwd year 4[I10]−SUM(I16:I17))	=MIN(1,3−SUM(0+2))	1
14 (Year 1)	=MIN(vans bought year 1 and in use year 3[H14], vans c/fwd year 4[I10]−SUM(I15:I17))	=MIN(0,3−SUM(1+0+2))	0
13 (Year 0)	=MIN(vans bought year 0 and in use year 3[H13], vans c/fwd year 4[I10]−SUM(I14:I17))	=MIN(0,3−SUM(0+1+0+2))	0

For other years, it is not a matter of copying the formulae horizontally across. Always start at the highest required row in the column (for example, in column G it would be row 15 and in column J it would be row 18). In this cell put a MIN formula for vans bought that year and vans carried forward that year. In the rows above put a MIN formula for vans bought in the column to the left and total vans carried forward less those accounted for in the rows below. For example, in I15 the formula is:

=MIN(vans one column to the left[H15],vans c/fwd[I10]−
vans accounted for in rows below[sum(I16:I17)])

This triangular data table can now be used to control the asset base. Two key uses are to calculate the asset cost total and net book value of any sales (see Chart 12.14).

Chart 12.14 **Evaluating asset costs and net book value on disposal**

Row	Calculation
Asset cost	Take the number of assets in each column and multiply it by the purchase price for the year of acquisition
Net book value of sales	Identify when an asset is no longer carried forward from one column to the next. For example, the asset purchased in year 0 (row 13) is removed in year 3 (column H) as it is no longer carried forward to year 4 (column I). By reference to the year of the row and the year of the column, the age of the asset at sale can be calculated and hence the net book value on disposal. For example, the asset disappears in year 4 and was purchased in year 0, hence it was four years old at sale and by knowing the depreciation value its net book value can be calculated.

This data table will need to be repeated for each type of asset.

WORKING CAPITAL

What is working capital?

Working capital has several definitions, but in modelling terms it is most easily thought of as the place where cash is "held" between being spent on purchases and received on sales. It mainly comprises stock (inventory), debtors (receivables) and creditors (payables). There is often dispute about whether working capital includes cash. For the purposes of this chapter the coding for cash is excluded as it is covered in Chapter 14.

A typical transaction cycle might be as shown in Chart 12.15.

Chart 12.15 **Cashflow cycle**

For example, take £100 of stock purchased and sold on credit with the selling price being £120, as shown in Chart 12.16.

Chart 12.16 **Illustration of cashflow cycle**

Stage	Item	Impact on accounts
1	Stock purchased	Stock increases by £100 and the creditor is owed £100
2	Creditor is paid	The creditor is reduced to zero and cash is reduced by £100
3	Stock sold	All the stock is cleared, the debtor owes £120 and £20 profit is recognised
4	Cash received from debtor	The debtor is reduced to zero and cash is increased by £120

Overall cash was reduced by £100 in stage 2 and increased by £120 in stage 4. The cash was held in working capital between those points.

The cycle is not always perfect and particular treatment is required for the items listed in Chart 12.17.

Chart 12.17 **Considerations for the cashflow cycle**

Item	Event
Creditor	When taking advantage of volume or settlement discounts
Stock	When stock is stolen or discarded
Debtor	When a bad debt is recognised

There are two special types of debtor and creditor to allow for the timing difference between the purchase and sale of goods or services and their use in the business. These are prepayments and accruals. For example, when insurance is purchased in advance for a year, the benefit of the premium is derived evenly throughout the year. At any point, the unused period of benefit can be calculated and shown as a prepayment.

Chart 12.18 **Illustration of prepayments and accruals**

	Prepayments	Accruals
Debtors	Prepaid costs (invoices paid in advance of benefit)	Accrued revenue (work completed but not yet invoiced)
Creditors	Prepaid revenue (customers pay in advance for their product or service)	Accrued costs (costs incurred for which an invoice will be received in the future)

How should working capital be treated?

The importance of the working capital items depends on the nature of the model being built. Working capital needs to be included to record transactions at the correct time. Sales arise in the profit and loss account when products or services are delivered. In the cashflow sales arise when the cash is received. Confusing these two events can create some serious errors in a model.

The best way to control working capital is by using day ratios that measure the number of days a transaction will be held as a working capital item, as shown in Chart 12.19.

Chart 12.19 **Defining working capital day ratios**

	Start point	End point
Stock days	Goods arrive through gate	Goods depart out of gate
Debtor days	Invoice despatched to customer	Cash received from customer
Creditor days	Invoice received from supplier	Cash paid to supplier

For simplicity, one ratio can be used for each working capital item; for example, debtor days set at 45. If more sophisticated data is available, a payment profile can be used, as shown in Chart 12.20.

Chart 12.20 **Aged debt profile**

Average number of days	% of sales
30	50
60	25
90	15
120	5
Bad debts	5
Total	100

For more information on the handling of bad debts, see Chapter 14 (pages 153–6).

The use of accruals and prepayments will depend on the type of business being modelled. For example, a tour operator receives almost all its cash in advance of conveying its customers. The money will be held as prepaid revenue in creditors until the customers travel. Once the service is delivered it will be recognised as sales.

For many models accruals and prepayments are an unnecessary detail. The accuracy to which other assumptions can be forecast should be considered before spending too long on fine-tuning these items. It is common to assume that for a cost such as insurance, the annual period of cover is the same as the company year and hence no prepayment will arise.

Coding in the spreadsheet
The following examples show how to code the effects of working capital in models. They assume that the business earns revenues evenly through a year and there are no seasonal effects.

One continuous example is used to illustrate each item of working capital. A wholesale business sets up and achieves sales in year 1 of £1,200,000, created as *Input_initial_sales* on the input sheet. Sales grow at £120,000 a year, created as *Input_annual_sales_increase* on the input sheet, for four years. The business ceases at the end of the fourth year.

Debtors
The impact of debtors in a business is a time delay between a sale and the receipt of cash. Taking the example and focusing on debtors, assume customers take an average of two months to pay their invoices. This is created as *Input_debtor_period* on the input sheet

and set to 2. *Input_year_length* is set up as 12 (representing 12 months).

Chart 12.21 **The financial impact of debtors**

	A	B	C	D	E	F	G	H	I	J	K
1	**Model title**										
2											
3	Year number	Year_number			0	1	2	3	4	5	Total
4	Years	Actual_years			2000	2001	2002	2003	2004	2005	
5											
6	**Profit and loss**										
7	Sales	Output_sales			0	1,200	1,320	1,440	1,560	0	5,520
8											
9	**Balance sheet**										
10	Debtors	Output_debtors			0	200	220	240	260	0	
11											
12	**Cash flow**										
13	Receipts	Output_receipts			0	1,000	1,300	1,420	1,540	260	5,520

The example in Chart 12.21 assumes no bad debts and that all customers pay on the due date. The total recognised in the profit and loss account equals the total recognised in the cashflow.

Because of the timing difference caused by debtors an extra year in the model is required, year 5, to collect the debtors left at the end of year 4. Some companies use a 10-year plan for all models of investment evaluations but show an 11th year to sweep up items like working capital and tax.

The calculations in year 3 of the example are as shown in Chart 12.22.

Chart 12.22 **Code for calculating the financial impact of debtors**

Row	Calculation	Actual calculation	Answer
Sales	=Last_year+Input_annual_sales_increase	=1320+120	1,440
Debtors	=Output_sales*(Input_debtor_period/ Input_year_length)	=1440*(2/12)	240
Receipts	=G10+Output_sales−Output_debtors	=220+1440−240	1,420

In the example in Chart 12.22 the debtor measure is calculated in whole months. An alternative method is to base it on days and use 61/365. This would give the model more flexibility.

Stock
Holding stock will tie up cash until it can be sold and the cash collected from customers. Using the measure of stock days will ensure that the stock levels are kept in line with sales. In building a dynamic model, stock days are best driven by sales to ensure the business model does not become production oriented.

Using the example, assume the company charges a 20% mark-up on bought-in goods, set up as an input for *Input_mark_up*, and stock levels need to be enough for three months' sales, set up as an input for *Input_stock_period* of 3.

Chart 12.23 **The financial impact of stock**

	A	B	C	D	E	F	G	H	I
1	**Model title**								
2									
3	Year number	Year_number			0	1	2	3	4
4	Years	Actual_years			2000	2001	2002	2003	2004
5									
6	**Profit and loss**								
7	Sales	Output_sales			0	1,200	1,320	1,440	1,560
8	Cost of sales	Output_cost_of_sales			0	1,000	1,100	1,200	1,300
9	Gross profit				0	200	220	240	260
10									
11	**Stock working**								
12	Stock b/fwd				0	250	275	300	325
13	Stock sold				0	1,000	1,100	1,200	1,300
14	Stock c/fwd				250	275	300	325	0
15	Stock bought				250	1,025	1,125	1,225	975
16									

The example in Chart 12.23 assumes that:

- no stock is written off or stolen;
- when the business ceases at the end of year 4 there is exactly the right amount of the right type of stock to satisfy the customers.

Adjustments would be needed to correct for the above items. The detail will depend on the nature of the business being modelled.

The calculations in year 3 are as shown in Chart 12.24.

Chart 12.24 **Code for calculating the financial impact of stock**

Row	Calculation	Actual calculation	Answer
Sales	As debtors example		1,440
Cost of sales	−Output_sales/(1+Input_mark_up)	=1440/(1+0.2)	1,200
Gross profit	=Output_sales−Output_cost_of_sales	=1440−1200	240
Stock b/fwd	=G14		300
Stock sold	=Output_cost_of_sales		1,200
Stock c/fwd	=I8*(Input_stock_period/Input_year_length)	=1300*(3/12)	325
Stock bought	=H13+H4−H12	=1200+325−300	1,225

Depending on how the rest of the model is structured, this method of calculating closing stock, by using next year's sales, could cause a circular reference. If this happens, use the current year's sales. Using next year's sales is more prudent, as it gears up the business in advance of increased activity.

A manufacturing business would need to have three categories of stock: raw materials, work in progress and finished goods. The coding for this would be similar to the example in Chart 12.23, with rows 12 to 15 being repeated for each of the three categories. A "stock days" measure would link the sales to the amount of finished goods. A production time would control the work in progress level to achieve the demand for finished goods. A second stock days measure would control the amount of raw material that is needed for smooth production.

Creditors

Creditors will delay the payment of cash until after the goods or services have been received. Using the measure of creditor days will ensure that the creditors rise and fall in line with purchases.

Continuing the example, assume suppliers require payment in one month, which has been set up as *Input_creditor_period* and set to 1.

Chart 12.25 **The financial impact of creditors**

	A	B	C	D	E	F	G	H	I	J
1	Model title									
2										
3	Year number	Year_number			0	1	2	3	4	Total
4	Years	Actual_years			2000	2001	2002	2003	2004	
5										
6										
7	Stock working									
8	Stock bought	Output_stock_bought			250	1,025	1,125	1,225	975	4,600
9										
10	Balance sheet									
11	Creditors	Output_creditors			250	85	94	102	0	
12										
13	Cash flow									
14	Payments				0	1,190	1,116	1,217	1,077	4,600

The example in Chart 12.25 assumes a bulk delivery of stock at year 0 ready to start the business. This will be paid for in year 1. In the final year there will be no creditors as the business is unlikely to continue buying stock in the last month of existence.

The calculations in year 3 are shown in Chart 12.26.

Chart 12.26 **Code for calculating the financial impact of creditors**

Row	Calculation	Actual calculation	Answer
Stock bought	As stock example		1,225
Creditors	=Output_stock_bought*(Input_creditor_period/ Input_year_length)	=1225*(1/12)	102
Payments	=G11+Output_stock_bought−Output_creditors	=94+1225−102	1,217

To achieve the effects in year 0 and the final year, use IF statements for identifying which year of the model the calculation is being performed for. In year 0 the creditor should equal the stock bought. In the final year the creditors should equal zero.

Creditors can also arise from overhead and fixed asset purchases. Only include this level of detail if the purchases of these items are significant.

13 Modelling funding issues

INTRODUCTION

Previous chapters have concentrated on the operational cashflow generated by a project covering revenue, operating costs and capital costs. This chapter looks at how to fund the project. Typically, a project will require cash investment in the early years to pay for the purchase of assets and the set-up costs in advance of the revenue. In later years the project should move through the cash breakeven point and the model will need to handle cash surpluses.

The cumulative net cashflow position of a project will typically show a J curve.

Chart 13.1 **Cumulative project cashflow**

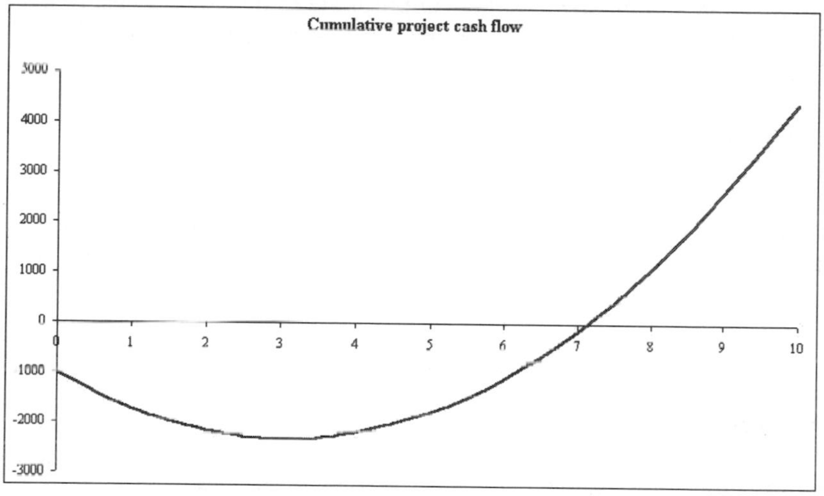

In the example in Chart 13.1, the project runs at a cashflow deficit for just over seven years, with the peak funding requirement being over £2m in year 3. The data is shown in Chart 13.2. This is only illustrative for the purposes of the J curve and there is no formula for its derivation.

Chart 13.2 **Data table for J curve**

	A	B	C	D	E	F	G	H	I	J	K	L	M	N	O
1	£'000														
2															
3	Year number	Year_number			0	1	2	3	4	5	6	7	8	9	10
4															
5	Opening cashflow				0	(1,000)	(1,720)	(2,160)	(2,320)	(2,200)	(1,800)	(1,120)	(160)	1,080	2,600
6	Net change in year				(1,000)	(720)	(440)	(160)	120	400	680	960	1,240	1,520	1,800
7	Closing cashflow				(1,000)	(1,720)	(2,160)	(2,320)	(2,200)	(1,800)	(1,120)	(160)	1,080	2,600	4,400

For projects such as company acquisitions, the investment at time 0 can be so large that the surplus may not be realised unless the investment itself is sold. In this case it will need a level of permanent funding.

IDENTIFYING THE CASHFLOW TO BE FUNDED

To identify the funding requirement, a robust model of the operational cashflow needs to be built. The operational cashflow should include revenue, costs, purchase and sale of fixed assets, movements in current assets (such as debtors and creditors) and movements in non-interest bearing current liabilities (such as creditors). All debt, equity, interest and dividends should be excluded. This is explained in detail in Chapter 15 (see page 176).

Falling between operating cashflow and funding cashflow are leases. The most common ways to treat these are as follows.

- ☑ Operating leases (or rents) should be treated as an operating cashflow. These leases are generally short-term and usually represent the hire of an asset. The asset may be used by several lessees during its life.
- ☑ Finance leases are typically a means of obtaining the long-term use of an asset with payment by instalment. The choice of a finance lease or asset purchase is typically a funding issue. Therefore in a model it is more appropriate to include the cost of the asset in the cashflow and then look at the leasing decision as part of the overall project funding.

Having calculated and modelled the operating cashflow, the net cashflow of all the operating items will give a project its funding requirement and any potential cash surplus.

Sensitivity analysis (as described in Chapter 19) should be applied to all the key variables to ensure that deviations from the plan will still leave a worthwhile project and that it is worth moving to this stage.

TYPES OF FUNDING

A wide range of funding sources is available for projects. Some of the most commonly used are shown in Chart 13.3.

Chart 13.3 **Funding sources**

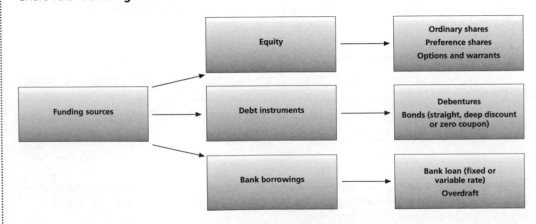

Details of each type are given in Chart 13.4, including cost implications, risk and their typical purpose.

Chart 13.4 **Details of funding sources**

Duration	Cost	Risk of repayment to investor	Purpose
Ordinary shares			
Permanent finance, although there are complex legal processes available to allow some repayment	Usually serviced by dividends paid out of profit, once all other costs have been met	Ordinary shares are the last to be paid in event of a winding up and therefore have highest risk of repayment	Ordinary shareholders own the company and provide the core long-term funding for corporate infrastructure
Preference shares			
Sometimes given a repayment date otherwise like ordinary shares	Usually a fixed percentage dividend. This is sometimes cumulative, should the company be unable to afford payment	Paid before ordinary shares	Usually issued to raise share capital without diluting control. Preference shareholders are not normally able to vote at meetings
Options and warrants			
These are the right to buy ordinary shares on a future date at a predetermined price	No cost until the option or warrant is exercised. At this point they become ordinary shares that attract dividends	No cost at issue and therefore if the exercise price at the due date is not attractive they lapse	Often used as an incentive. Either issued with ordinary shares as an incentive to purchase the ordinary shares or used as part of remuneration as an incentive for executives to perform
Debentures			
Fixed with a predetermined repayment date	Fixed rate of interest	Secured on the property of the company, usually freehold buildings	Long-term loan finance

Duration	Cost	Risk of repayment to investor	Purpose
Bonds			
Fixed with a predetermined repayment date	Fixed rate interest rate return. Varieties of straight, deep discount and zero-coupon. All offer varying timings for the payment of interest: during the life of the bond, at the end or a mixture of the two	The loan is issued in certificate form that can be traded like shares. Repayment ranks before all equity	Long-term loan finance with a cashflow profile to match the cash profile of a project
Convertibles			
Permanent capital first as debt then as equity. There can be a repayment option if the share price at conversion is not attractive	A low interest rate return for a set period, followed by conversion into ordinary shares providing the share price has achieved a specified level	While the convertible is in the form of debt it usually ranks after other debt. Once converted to ordinary shares then the risk is as per other shares	Long-term finance that with a low initial cost
Loans			
Often fixed with a predetermined repayment date and sometimes interim repayments	A percentage return that can be fixed or variable. The variable rate is usually linked to a base rate plus an increment	Ranks before all shareholders and will sometimes be secured on assets	Funding for projects which will generate sufficient funds to allow repayment
Overdrafts			
A rolling facility that normally has a fixed time period	Usually a variable rate at a significant increment over a base rate	Depends on security arrangements but can rank behind other forms of debt	Meeting day-to-day working capital timing differences
Leasing			
For the life of the asset being leased	Normally a fixed interest rate cost	Secured on the asset being leased	To fund specific asset purchases with potential tax and replacement benefits

The most appropriate source for a project will depend on a range of factors, including investment control, operating environment, cost of raising and servicing the funding, amount required, duration and risk. All these aspects will be explored in this chapter.

PROJECT CONTROL

Before choosing the funding source it is important to clarify how the project is to be controlled. For example, a small-scale fixed asset purchase will clearly be controlled by the investing business, but for new products or entry into new markets there may be joint-venture opportunities to share the initial cost and project risk. The type of control required may dictate the most appropriate type of funding. The choices are either internal, from surpluses within the investing companies, or external, from investors and lending institutions.

For a clear separation of a company's activities or for joint ownership, it may be preferable to set up the project within a newly formed company. Thus the success or failure of the new project can be isolated from investors' other activities. In setting up the company it is important to consider how its results will affect the financial statements of any investing company. Structuring the proportion of equity owned and control exercised will define which of three types of accounting treatment it will receive.

- **Subsidiary.** Where the investing company owns at least 50% of the equity and controls the board of directors. In this situation the results of the subsidiary in total will be consolidated (added together) with those of the investing company.
- **Associated company.** Where the investing company has significant influence by owning at least 20% of the shares, but less than 50%. This is accounted for by the "equity method" – only the investing company's proportion of the results of the associated company are included in the investing company's accounts.
- **Investment.** Where the investing company owns less than 20% of the equity of the investment it is shown as a fixed asset investment. The value is at original cost or subsequent revaluation.

For high-risk or speculative projects, major companies will often choose to have their investment as an associate to minimise the impact of any early losses on the results of the holding company. Options will sometimes be used to secure greater control at a later date when the business should have reached profitability.

For an overseas investment, the governments of some countries impose a limit on the amount of overseas control in an investment. In these situations the investor has no option but to find a local joint-venture partner and share control.

OPERATING ENVIRONMENT

The operating environment is how the project fits in with other investments for funding purposes. In large organisations lots of projects are usually pooled so the company can have access to a wider range of funding sources. The funding for a particular project is drawn from the central Treasury department, often with little indication of the origin of the funds being used. However, the small projects will typically be part of the capital budget, which may be funded from the cash generated by the current year's profits.

For most projects a form of debt is the most common source of funding. It is generally cheap to raise and flexible in duration. The raising of equity for projects is rare except for major corporate acquisitions. Care should be taken as the amount of debt raised could distort the mix of debt and equity funding and raise the overall risk and funding cost of the whole business (see page 148).

For overseas projects, the funding issues can become more complex as exchange rates provide additional project volatility. Hedging techniques can be used to mitigate some of the foreign exchange risk. A common hedging technique is to borrow money in the same currency as the investment and try to match the amount of borrowing to the value of the net investment. Thus as exchange rates move the exchange gains made on the net investment are matched by an equal exchange loss on the borrowing, and vice versa.

For example, take the following investment in the United States by a UK company. It has invested £500,000 and borrowed in dollars when the rate was 2:1. This gives an initial investment and borrowing of $1,000,000.

	£	Exchange rate	$
Net investment	500,000	2:1	1,000,000
Borrowing	500,000	2:1	1,000,000

One year later the exchange rate has moved to 1.6:1. The US investment has changed its UK value from £500,000 to £625,000.

	$	Exchange rate	£
Net investment	1,000,000	1.6:1	625,000
Borrowing	1,000,000	1.6:1	625,000

There are no foreign exchange gains or losses as the gain on the investment is exactly matched by the loss on the borrowing.

With overseas investment some governments impose tight operating constraints by, for example:

- not allowing profits to be remitted out of the country so any surpluses have to be reinvested back in the business;
- encouraging further inward investment of the profits by levying withholding tax on any remittance out of the country. The rates of tax vary, with some being quite punitive.

Care is needed to explore the project and funding environment before identifying the funding source. Even with careful planning it is impossible to predict the actions of future governments on investment in their country. For more information on completing foreign exchange calculations, see Chapter 14 (pages 160–5).

COST OF FUNDING

There is a simple rule for the cost of funding: the greater the perceived risk of the project the greater the return required by the investor and hence the greater is the cost. International credit agencies assess the risk of companies and allocate them a credit rating. A rating of AAA is very low risk, and these companies pay comparatively low rates for their funding. However, a speculative business will be a much greater risk and will expect to pay a premium for its funding.

For individual projects, investors make their own judgment on the risk involved and whether the anticipated cashflow in the opportunity provides a sufficient return.

Equity is commonly more expensive than debt because of the order in which investors are repaid should the company cease trading (debt is usually repaid before equity). Furthermore, the cost of issuing equity is usually much greater than debt because of stock exchange procedures that have to be complied with and the management of a potentially large number of investors.

The cost of debt funding can vary as governments and central banks raise and lower their country's principal lending rates. However, this volatility can be avoided in projects by taking a fixed rate loan that gives a predictable cost to the project.

WEIGHTED AVERAGE COST OF CAPITAL

For many projects the funding will come from a company's central funds. The weighted average cost of capital (WACC) is the average funding rate for all the sources of finance. The "weighted" part refers to the way it is calculated with reference to the amount that each source of finance contributes to the total. This is explained in more detail in Chapter 15.

FUNDING STRIPS

In funding a project, the operational cashflow identifies the cash requirement. This profile excludes the cost of funding the investment. Therefore greater funding is required to allow for the servicing of finance with payment of dividends and interest until cash breakeven.

To identify the overall funding requirement, the operational cashflow needs to be adjusted by the expected cost of servicing the funding. This can be delivered by using a specific funding rate for the project or the WACC to inflate the cashflow (remember that if the operational cashflow is after tax then the funding cost should also be after tax).

From the earlier J curve example, with a WACC of 10% entered on the input page as Input_WACC, the servicing adjustment would be as shown in Chart 13.5.

Chart 13.5 **Adjusting cashflow for the cost of funding**

	A	B	C	D	E	F	G	H	I	J	K	L	M	N	O
1	**Model title**														
2	£'000														
3	Year number	Year_number			0	1	2	3	4	5	6	7	8	9	10
4															
5	Cash b/fwd				0	(1,000)	(1,856)	(2,504)	(2,922)	(3,088)	(2,977)	(2,561)	(1,809)	(688)	839
6	Net change in year				(1,000)	(720)	(440)	(160)	120	400	680	960	1,240	1,520	1,800
7	Total				(1,000)	(1,720)	(2,296)	(2,664)	(2,802)	(2,688)	(2,297)	(1,601)	(569)	832	2,639
8															
9	Average funding in year	Working_average_funding_in_year			0	(1,360)	(2,076)	(2,584)	(2,862)	(2,888)	(2,637)	(2,081)	(1,189)	72	1,739
10															
11	WACC (10%)				0	(136)	(208)	(258)	(286)	(289)	(264)	(208)	(119)	7	174
12															
13	Cash c/fwd	Working_cash_cfwd			(1,000)	(1,856)	(2,504)	(2,922)	(3,088)	(2,977)	(2,561)	(1,809)	(688)	839	2,813
14															

Row 6 is the operational cashflow for the model, with rows 5 and 7 being the cumulative cash balance.

Row 9 is used to find the average amount of cash needed during the year.

Row 11 is the funding cost (at 10%) for borrowing the average amount of cash required. This interest cost is added into the cumulative cashflow for the project.

The calculations in year 3 are shown in Chart 13.6.

Chart 13.6 **Code for adjusting cashflow for the cost of funding**

Row	Calculation	Actual calculation	Answer
Cash b/fwd	G13		(2,504)
Net change in year	From operating cashflow		(160)
Total	=SUM(H5:H6)	=−2504−160	(2,664)
Average funding in year	=AVERAGE(H5,H7)	=AVERAGE(−2504,−2664)	(2,584)
WACC	=ROUND(*Working_average_ funding_in_year** Input_WACC,0)	=ROUND(−2584*10%,0)	(258)
Cash c/fwd	=H7+H11	=−2664−258	(2,922)

The cash c/fwd is the profile that requires funding.

For specific funding, it is unlikely that one sum for a defined period will be sufficient to cover the funding requirement of a project. Amounts will be unused at the start and again at the end. A combination of several smaller sums, each of different duration, will more closely match the profile of the project. These are sometimes known as "funding strips". From the example above, adjusted for funding cost, the funding strips might look like the graph in Chart 13.7.

Chart 13.7 **Funding strips**

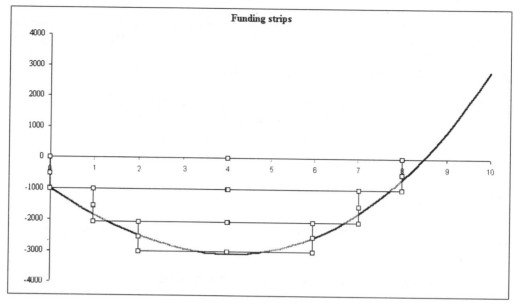

The three strips are:

- ◪ £1m for eight years starting at time 0;
- ◪ £1m for six years starting at time 1;
- ◪ £1m for four years starting at time 2.

Funding strips will never exactly match the cashflow profile, nor should they. The variations when running the project compared with the model will always give rise to some differences. The uncovered cash requirements may be taken from an overdraft facility to enable the cash to be available.

For the model to calculate the funding strips use the ROUND function. The number of decimal places that the model should round to is determined by the funding units. In this example the funding is in units of £1,000,000 where the data is shown in thousands. Therefore the function =ROUND (number, decimal places) will be set with decimal places as −3.

Chart 13.8 **Data table for J curve**

	A	B	C	D	E	F	G	H	I	J	K	L	M	N	O
1	Model title														
2	£'000														
3	Year number	Year_number			0	1	2	3	4	5	6	7	8	9	10
4	Cash c/fwd	Working_cash_cfwd			(1,000)	(1,856)	(2,504)	(2,922)	(3,088)	(2,977)	(2,561)	(1,809)	(688)	839	2,813
5															
6	Funding	Working_funding			(1,000)	(2,000)	(3,000)	(3,000)	(3,000)	(3,000)	(3,000)	(2,000)	(1,000)	0	0

The calculations in year 3 are as shown in Chart 13.9.

Chart 13.9 **Code for calculating data table for J curve**

Row	Calculation	Actual calculation	Answer
Funding	=MIN(ROUND(*Working_cash_ cfwd,*−3),0)	=MIN(ROUND(−2922,−3),0)	(3,000)

The function MIN is used to ensure no positive funding strips are identified.

The benefit of using funding strips is that there are no large amounts of surplus cash being unutilised by the project. This method also enables the capital repayments to be made in stages rather than all at once.

TIME PERIODS

When choosing the most appropriate funding source the duration of the funding will affect the decision.

Chart 13.10 **Appropriate funding for different time periods**

Over 15 years	Use a form of equity funding (providing the amount is over £25m)
Between 5 and 15 years	Consider a debt instrument (providing the amount is over (£10m)
Under 5 years	Bank loans usually provide the cheapest and most flexible source (potentially fixed rate to remove the uncertainty of interest rate movements)
Under 1 year	Bank overdraft

If the example above were to be specifically funded, the most appropriate method would be to commit to three fixed-rate loans for the periods shown in the strip funding. The interest rate for the second and third tranche can be fixed at the outset but may not always be at the same rate as the initial tranche. The business would also need to agree an overdraft facility for up £500,000 to meet the need of the unfunded parts of the cashflow profile and allow for variations in the plans.

DEBT TO EQUITY RATIOS

The relationship between debt and equity is referred to as gearing or leverage. As part of managing the funding of projects it is vital to ensure the debt to equity ratio of the business as a whole is appropriate. If there is too much debt, the company is highly geared. The implications of this are that the interest cost must be met before any dividends can be paid to the shareholders. When interest cannot be paid, there is a serious risk of the business not being able to repay the debt funders, and the debt funders will exercise their rights in the loan agreements to take control of the company. If there is too little debt, shareholders lose out through the dilution of earnings.

Sometimes funding instruments, such as convertibles, are difficult to classify as either debt or equity. The normal rule is to include these items as debt up to the point of conversion.

There are many methods of calculating gearing, leverage and debt to equity ratios. The options concern whether to include or exclude items such as creditors and cash.

One of the best methods is to compare interest-bearing debt to equity. This focuses on pure funding and excludes the operational aspects of creditors. The calculation is debt divided by equity.

Take, for example, three companies that all have the same total funds and the same operating profit, as shown in Chart 13.11. Their difference is the mix of debt and equity in each business.

Chart 13.11 **Illustration of debt to equity ratio**

Business	A	B	C
Debt	750	500	250
Equity	250	500	750
Total funding	1,000	1,000	1,000
Operating profit	200	200	200
Interest (10%)	(75)	(50)	(25)
Profit before tax	125	150	175
Tax (30%)	38	45	53
Earnings	87	105	122
Rate of return for equity investors	87/250=34.8%	105/500=21%	122/750=16.3%
Debt to equity	750/250=300%	500/500=100%	250/750=33.3%

- ▨ Business A is highly geared and should profits fall the earning will be quickly eroded and potentially jeopardise the company's ability to service its interest obligations.
- ▨ Business B has what is generally accepted as the maximum proportion of debt before funders impose constraints. This is 50% of the business being funded by debt.
- ▨ In Business C the low debt has greatly reduced the rate of return for shareholders.

Note that the example is not strictly true, because as the proportion of debt rises the debt funders typically perceive more risk and therefore increase their interest rate. To prevent businesses from borrowing too much there are often covenants in a loan agreement that constrain the debt to equity level of a business. A common covenant requires that a loan becomes immediately repayable if a certain debt to equity ratio is exceeded.

In choosing the appropriate funding source it is necessary to consider not only the impact that the additional funding will have on the debt to equity ratio, but also the constraints on being able to take on more projects in subsequent years.

PUTTING THE FUNDING COST BACK IN THE MODEL

Once the funding source and cost have been identified, they need to be put back into the model to complete the construction of the profit and loss account, balance sheet and cashflow statement.

Profit and loss account

In this statement the cost of servicing the funding will be shown. The most important issue is that the funding cost must be calculated on an accruals basis with reference to the period for which the funding was taken. It is not simply recording when the physical payments are made.

Take, for example, a loan taken one month before the end of a year with interest paid quarterly. Although no physical interest payment has been made, the profit and loss account should show that there is a one-month interest cost.

For more complex debt instruments that defer the payment of interest until the end of the funding period, the calculation of the interest cost each year is more complex. In these situations the interest should be allocated at a constant rate on the carrying value amount of net investment.

For example, a $100m zero coupon five-year bond is redeemed at a premium of 61%. The true yield of the bond is 10%, calculated using the formulae:

$$\text{Yield} = (\text{Redemption price}/\text{Purchase price})\hat{}(1/\text{Period of ownership}) - 1$$
$$\text{Yield} = (161/100)\hat{}(1/5) - 1$$
$$\text{Yield} = 10\%$$

The profit and loss and cashflow would be as shown in Chart 13.12.

Chart 13.12 **Calculating funding costs of debt instruments**

Year	Interest charge in profit and loss account ($m)	Cashflow ($m)	Carrying value ($m)	Yield on opening carrying value (%)
0	0.00	+100.00	100.00	0
1	10.00	0.00	110.00	10
2	11.00	0.00	121.00	10
3	12.00	0.00	133.10	10
4	13.10	0.00	146.41	10
5	15.41	−161.00	0.00	10

Balance sheet

The balance sheet will show the amount of debt or equity as separate amounts for each type of funding instrument. The amount will be the value of the funding. There may also be an accrual shown under creditors for the interest charged to the profit and loss account but not paid in the cashflow.

Cashflow statement

The cashflow statement will show the cash received from and paid to the funder. This will include the cashflow of both the principle and the interest and dividends. Chapter 14 covers small cash surpluses and deficits.

14 Further financial statement development

This chapter examines the remaining areas necessary to complete a full financial model. Interest income and charges, bad debt, taxation, and foreign exchange gains and losses are normally the last elements of the financial statements to be modelled, as they rely on results developed elsewhere in the model. For each of the four elements there is a brief discussion of some of the relevant accounting principles and a generic approach to modelling, then a specific example is examined in detail.

INTEREST INCOME AND CHARGES

Issues in modelling interest income and charges

When modelling interest, it is assumed that the movement between the opening and closing positions occurs smoothly throughout the period. This allows the average debt for the period to be calculated based on the average of the opening and closing balances. The appropriate interest rate can then be applied to this average to calculate the interest income or expense for the period. It is possible to use an identical modelling approach for both interest income and interest expenses. In this chapter the focus is on interest income. The interest rate assumption must correspond with the length of the period. A model based on six-month periods would obviously produce incorrect forecasts if a 12-month interest rate assumption were used.

In developing the interest forecasts, the business modeller should ensure that any interest rate assumptions are consistent with the underlying model. If all the cashflows have been forecast in nominal terms, for example, then the interest rate used should be a nominal rate. If a real forecast has been prepared, then a real interest rate would be required.

Interest rate assumptions

Modelling interest income requires interest rate assumptions for the entire forecast period. The appropriate rate can be entered directly by the user. Alternatively, a premium or discount to the base rate can be entered, which is applied to the base rate forecast described in Chapter 9. Whichever approach is adopted, a row for the interest rate must be created and given a suitable range name, such as *Rate*, as shown in row 11 of Chart 14.1.

Modelling interest income and circular references

In practice, interest income is calculated on a daily basis, so the closing balance at the end of a day includes the interest generated during that day. This daily interest calculation implies that, over an entire accounting period, a proportion of the interest earned is based on a cash balance that includes interest earned during that period. Reality is easily replicated in a spreadsheet model by calculating the average of the opening and closing balances and applying the appropriate interest rate to the average to generate the interest income for the period. The interest income generated is included in the calculation of the closing balance. This approach, however, creates a circular reference because interest is based, in part, on the closing balance, but the closing balance includes interest that is based on the closing balance, and so on. In simple models the introduction of such a circular reference may not be too detrimental to the operation of the model, and the computation described above can be used for the interest calculation. If the modeller wishes to avoid circular references, one of the two approaches below can be adopted.

Alternative approaches to modelling interest income

A straightforward modification to the approach described above involves calculating interest based on the average balance of the previous period. This removes the circularity but introduces the implied assumption that interest is paid in arrears, with a delay of one period.

Chart 14.1 **Interest income model**

	A	B	C	D	E	F	G	H
1	Interest				2000	2001	2002	2003
2								
3	Cash account							
4	Opening balance	*Opening_balance*			100.0	136.3	177.2	223.2
5	Cash movement	*Cash_movement*			25.0	26.0	27.0	28.0
6	Interim balance	*Interim*			125.0	162.3	204.2	251.2
7	Interest income				11.3	14.9	19.1	23.7
8	Closing balance				136.3	177.2	223.2	275.0
9								
10	Interest calculation							
11	Interest rate	*Rate*			10.0%	10.0%	10.0%	10.0%
12	Average balance	*Average_balance*			112.5	149.3	190.7	237.2
13	Interest income	*Interest_income*			11.3	14.9	19.1	23.7

The example in Chart 14.1 avoids a circular reference and assumes that interest is paid at the end of the period. This is achieved by calculating an interim cash balance in row 6 before applying the interest rate to the average of the opening and interim balance to derive the interest income for the interim period. The interest income is then added to the interim balance to derive the final closing balance. Although this approach improves the modelling of the timing of interest income payments, it understates the interest income as interest income is not incorporated in the average balance.

The column and row headings and range names should be established before defining the ranges. User inputs should be made before performing the calculations. Range names are indicated in column B, and relative references have been created for the previous year with the range name *Last_year* and also for the previous period's closing balance with the name *Previous_closing_balance*. In the case of *Previous_closing_balance*, the relative reference could be created in G4 and should refer to F8, the previous period's closing balance. For the purposes of the example, inputs such as the first year, the opening cash balance, the cash movement for the period and the interest rate are included on the same sheet as the workings. In a full model these inputs would be drawn from the workings and input sheets created elsewhere in the model. The opening cash balance may be drawn from the opening balance sheet and the cash movement may be picked up from the cashflow statement.

A detailed explanation of the spreadsheet is presented in Chart 14.2. The calculations are based on column G, which corresponds to the year 2002.

Chart 14.2 **Interest income workings**

Row	Calculation	Actual calculation	Answer
1	=Last_year+1	=2001+1	2002
Opening balance	=Previous_closing_balance	=177.2	177.2
Cash movement	User input	27	27
Interim balance	=Opening_balance+Cash_movement	=177.2+27	204.2
Interest income	=Interest_income	=Interest_income	19.1
Closing balance	=Interim+Interest_income	=204.2+19.1	223.2
Interest rate	User input	10%	10%
Average balance	=AVERAGE(G4,G6)	=(177.2+204.2)/2	190.7
Interest income	=Average_balance*Rate	=190.7*10%	19.1

To convert the above model to the simple interest model described at the start of this section the interim balance row should be removed. The average balance should now be calculated on the basis of the opening and closing balances rather than the opening and interim balances. The closing balance should be equal to the opening (rather than the interim) balance plus the cash movement for the period plus the interest income. To solve the circular reference, from the TOOLS menu select OPTIONS→CALCULATION and check the iteration box. The model will now calculate the interest.

The results of the workings can then be taken to the appropriate results pages of the model. The interest income line would be included in the profit and loss account after operating profits and also in the cashflow statement. This implies there are no timing delays between the interest income or expense being recognised in the profit and loss account and being received as cash in the cashflow statement. The closing cash balances should be included in the balance sheet under short-term cash deposits.

BAD DEBT

Accounting for bad debts

The relationship between sales, sales receipts and the trade debtors figure in the balance sheet was discussed in Chapter 13. This section examines the proportion of sales revenue that the modeller believes may not be recoverable from the customer. A customer may not pay a particular debt for a number of reasons: bankruptcy, dishonesty, fraud, or perhaps a dispute with the vendor over the goods or services supplied. A bad debt is a debt that is considered to be uncollectable.

Provisions for doubtful debts

During day-to-day operations, a business normally makes provision for doubtful debts using the following accounting entries:

- ◪ Dr: Bad debt expense account
- ◪ Cr: Provision for doubtful debts

The provision will contain a general amount based on experience as well as specific amounts for debts where the recoverability is known to be in doubt. The provision is then set against the actual debtors' figure to give a net debtors figure in the balance sheet. Any movements in the provision for doubtful debts are taken to the profit and loss account, but the cash movement for the period is unaffected.

When modelling it must be assumed that a certain proportion of debts will not be recoverable. The model must reflect the impact not only on the balance sheet and profit and loss account but also on the cashflow statement. Bad debt workings eliminate or write-off a proportion of sales revenue as bad debts rather than making a suitable provision, as is it necessary to recognise the impact on the cashflow. The accounting entries are as follows:

- ◪ Dr: Bad debt expense account in the profit and loss account
- ◪ Cr: Debtors' account

Modelling bad debt expenses

The user must enter a bad debt rate for each period of the forecast. This should be entered as a percentage of sales. Assumptions for sales are also required, or sales may be drawn from the revenue forecasting section of the model.

A simple approach to forecasting bad debt is simply to leave the debtors' working untouched and deduct bad debt as a separate line in the profit and loss account. The calculation involves multiplying the sales line by the bad debt rate. The impact at the cashflow level is the same as the more rigorous approach below, but the impact on debtors is ignored, resulting in debtors being overstated.

The more rigorous approach used in Chart 14.3 captures the effect on the debtors' balance. The bad debt expense figures would be included in the profit and loss account under operating costs.

Chart 14.3 **Bad debt modelling**

	A	B	C	D	E	F	G	H	I	J
1	Bad debt				2000	2001	2002	2003	2004	2005
2										
3	Sales	Sales			1,000.0	2,000.0	2,500.0	2,500.0	3,000.0	3,200.0
4	Debtor days	Debtor_days			30.0	30.0	30.0	30.0	30.0	30.0
5	Bad debt rate	Bad_debt_rate			5.0%	5.0%	5.0%	5.0%	5.0%	5.0%
6										
7	Debtors account									
8	Opening balance	Opening_balance			100.0	78.1	156.2	195.2	195.2	234.2
9	Sales				1,000.0	2,000.0	2,500.0	2,500.0	3,000.0	3,200.0
10	Bad debt expense	Bad_debt			(50.0)	(100.0)	(125.0)	(125.0)	(150.0)	(160.0)
11	Cash received	Cash_received			(971.9)	(1,821.9)	(2,336.0)	(2,375.0)	(2,811.0)	(3,024.4)
12	Closing balance				78.1	156.2	195.2	195.2	234.2	249.9
13										
14	Operating profit									
15	Sales				1,000.0	2,000.0	2,500.0	2,500.0	3,000.0	3,200.0
16	Bad debt				(50.0)	(100.0)	(125.0)	(125.0)	(150.0)	(160.0)
17	Operating profit				950.0	1,900.0	2,375.0	2,375.0	2,850.0	3,040.0
18	Change in working capital				21.9	(78.1)	(39.0)	(0.0)	(39.0)	(15.6)
19	Cash flow				971.9	1,821.9	2,336.0	2,375.0	2,811.0	3,024.4

The workings relate to column G. Relative range names for the closing balance (*Closing_balance*) – for example, cell F8 should have a relative reference to cell E12 – and the last year (*Last_year*) should also be set up in row 1. Cell E8 is an input.

Chart 14.4 **Bad debt expense workings**

Row	Calculation	Actual calculation	Answer
1	=*Last_year*+1	=2001+1	2002
Sales	User input	2500	2,500.0
Debtor days	User input	30	30.0
Bad debt rate	User input	5%	5%
Debtors account			
Opening balance	=*Closing_balance*	=156.2	156.2
Sales	=*Sales*	=2500	2,500.0
Bad debt expense	=−*Sales**Bad_debt_rate	=−2500*5%	(125.0)
Cash received	=−*Opening_balance*−(*Sales*+ *Bad_debt*)*((365−*Debtor_ days*)/365)	=−156.2−(2,500−125)* ((365−30)/365)	(2,336.0)
Closing balance	=*Opening_balance*+*Sales*+ *Cash_received*+*Bad_debt*	=156.2+2500−2336−125	195.2
Sales	=*Sales*	=2500	2,500.0
Bad debt	=*Bad_debt*	=(125)	(125.0)
Operating profit	=G15+G16	=2500+(125)	2,375.0
Change in working capital	=−(G12−G8)	=−(195.2−156.2)	(39.0)
Cash flow	=G17+G18	=2375+(39)	2,336.0

The cash received calculation models the fact that at any time there will be an amount of sales revenue that has been recorded in the profit and loss account but the associated cash has not yet been received by the business. The amount of cash outstanding at the end of a period is calculated using the debtor days assumption. The debtor days figure is calculated by dividing the value of the debtors in the balance sheet at the end of the period by the total value of sales during that period, multiplied by 365 to give a debtor days figure. A debtor days figure of 30 implies that cash equivalent to 30 days' worth of sales remains outstanding at the end of the period.

The cash received calculation assumes that, during a period, the cash received is equal to the opening balance plus the value of sales, minus bad debt adjusted for the cash that remains outstanding.

The bad debt expense figures would be included in the profit and loss account under operating costs.

TAXATION WORKINGS

The challenges of modelling taxation

Companies can develop highly complex organisational structures to minimise their tax liabilities. The structures may, for example, involve offshore entities and mixer companies, and may try to offset losses from one part of the business against profits from another in the country with the most benign tax regime.

At the single company level the modeller can be faced with a range of modelling issues that depend on the country in which the business is based and the tax regime in operation there. The example in this chapter is based on UK corporation tax, but a generic approach that can be adopted for all taxation workings is also described.

Forms of taxation

Chart 14.5 provides a description of the typical taxes that the modeller may have to contend with. A crucial question to answer is whether a particular tax is itself tax deductible for the purposes of another tax, such as corporation tax. In some countries there can be a tax on total revenue. The revenue tax, however, can be charged in the profit and loss account above the profit before corporation tax. The revenue tax is said to be chargeable against corporation tax as it reduces the profits on which corporation tax is based. Any item, such as a tax or a cost, is said to be tax deductible if it can be charged against corporation tax.

Chart 14.5 **Forms of taxation**

Tax type	Comments
Revenue tax	A tax typically based on gross or net revenue that may be chargeable against other taxes such as corporation tax.
Corporation tax	A charge on the business's profits. The definition of profits liable to corporation tax may alter depending on the tax regime in operation.
Sales tax	A tax collected by the business on behalf of the authorities that arises whenever the customer makes a purchase, such as value added tax (VAT) in the UK.
Withholding tax	A tax typically placed on interest and dividend payments that are remitted to foreign lenders or investors.
Tax on assets	A charge on the market or historic value of the assets of the business that may be chargeable against other taxes such as corporation tax.

Tax affects the level of free cashflow generated by the business and consequently can have a significant impact on the business's valuation. In the case of sales tax the only effect is one of timing of cashflow, as the sales tax does not alter the level of cash but only the timing of cashflow. Where there is a reasonable balance between purchases and sales that attract a sales tax, many modellers will choose to ignore the modelling of the tax, as the effect is largely valuation and cashflow neutral. However, in businesses where there are significant mismatches between sales and purchases that attract a sales tax and these mismatches may reverse over time, it may be appropriate to model potentially material cashflow timing affects.

Generic approach to corporation taxation workings

The first stage in modelling any form of taxation is to create row headings for the profits and any adjustments to profit that will be liable to corporation tax. These will include the corporation tax creditor (the amount owed at the end of a period to the tax authorities) and also an account for any losses that have been incurred and that can be used to reduce profits in the future. The corporation tax liability will be taken to the profit and loss account, the corporation tax paid will be transferred to the cashflow statement and the closing tax creditor will be placed in the balance sheet. The basis of the calculation should be described in the taxation authorities' literature and the workings should replicate the tax regime of the country.

The tax creditor working will consist of an opening balance, which will either be drawn from the previous period's closing balance or be a user input if at the start of the forecast period. The opening balance should then be augmented by the taxation charge computed in the profit working. The profit working adjusts the profit before tax figure taken directly from the profit and loss and adjusts the profit to profits liable to corporation tax. These adjustments may include removing depreciation charges and replacing them with writing down allowances for capital goods. The modeller must then compute the tax paid in cash during the period. The amount of cash paid will depend on the tax regime of the country. Normally, the tax is paid in the following tax year; UK corporation tax is currently paid nine months after the end of the business year. Other taxes may be paid quarterly or even monthly. The amount of cash actually paid should be taken to the cashflow statement under the heading "tax paid". Lastly, the closing tax creditor balance can be computed as:

$$\text{Opening balance} + \text{tax charge} - \text{tax paid} = \text{closing balance}$$

The closing tax creditor balance can then be linked to the balance sheet. The application of this generic approach can be seen in the detailed example of corporation tax presented in Chart 14.6 on the next page. Row and column headings and range names should be created first. Range names have been created for all user inputs and a number of the intermediate workings' results. A relative range name has been created for the previous year (*Last_year*) in row 1. Additional relative range names have been used in the corporation tax creditor account and also in the losses account. In the case of the former, cell H17 should contain a relative reference, *Previous_closing_tax_creditor*, to cell G20. In the case of the latter, cell H24 should contain a relative reference, *Previous_closing_tax_loss*, to cell G28. Before creating the formulae the user inputs should be entered – cells E1, E23 and E24 are inputs, as are the inputs in rows 4, 5, 6, 7 and 10.

Chart 14.6 **Taxation workings**

	A	B	C	D	E	F	G	H
1	**Taxation**				2000	2001	2002	2003
2								
3	**Assumptions**							
4	Accounting profit/loss before tax	Accounting_profit			(3,000.0)	(2,000.0)	2,000.0	10,000.0
5	Rate	Taxation_rate			30%	30%	30%	30%
6	Payment delay	Payment_delay			180	180	180	180
7	Number of years of loss carry-forward	Years_forward			3			
8								
9	**Profit liable to corporation tax**							
10	Adjustments	Adjustments			(2,000.0)	(1,000.0)	(500.0)	1,500.0
11	Adjusted profit/loss before tax	Adjusted_PBT			(5,000.0)	(3,000.0)	1,500.0	11,500.0
12	Profit before the utilisation of losses	Profit_before_losses			0.0	0.0	1,500.0	11,500.0
13	Losses utilised				0.0	0.0	(1,500.0)	(9,500.0)
14	Profit before tax liable to corporation tax	Profit_liable_to_corporation_tax			0.0	0.0	0.0	2,000.0
15								
16	**Corporation tax creditors**							
17	Opening corporation tax creditor	Opening_tax_creditor				0.0	0.0	0.0
18	Corporation tax charge in the year	Tax_charge			0.0	0.0	0.0	600.0
19	Corporation tax paid				0.0	0.0	0.0	(304.1)
20	Closing corporation tax creditor				0.0	0.0	0.0	295.9
21								
22	**Losses account**							
23	Year				0	1	2	3
24	Opening losses				3,000.0	8,000.0	11,000.0	9,500.0
25	Tax losses lapsed				0.0	0.0	0.0	0.0
26	Increase in losses				5,000.0	3,000.0	0.0	0.0
27	Losses utilised	Losses_utilised			0.0	0.0	(1,500.0)	(9,500.0)
28	Closing losses				8,000.0	11,000.0	9,500.0	0.0
29								
30								
31		Year	Tax loss					
32	Profit	0	5,000.0		0.0	0.0	1,500.0	11,500.0
33	Opening losses				3,000.0	8,000.0	8,000.0	6,500.0
34	Tax losses generated				5,000.0	0.0	0.0	0.0
35	Tax losses utilised				0.0	0.0	(1,500.0)	(6,500.0)
36	Tax losss lapsed				0.0	0.0	0.0	0.0
37	Closing losses				8,000.0	8,000.0	6,500.0	0.0
38								
39	Profit	1	3,000.0		0.0	0.0	0.0	5,000.0
40	Opening losses				0.0	0.0	3,000.0	3,000.0
41	Tax losses generated				0.0	3,000.0	0.0	0.0
42	Tax losses utilised				0.0	0.0	0.0	(3,000.0)
43	Tax losss lapsed				0.0	0.0	0.0	0.0
44	Closing losses				0.0	3,000.0	3,000.0	0.0
45								
46	Profit	2	0.0		0.0	0.0	0.0	2,000.0
47	Opening losses				0.0	0.0	0.0	0.0
48	Tax losses generated				0.0	0.0	0.0	0.0
49	Tax losses utilised				0.0	0.0	0.0	0.0
50	Tax losss lapsed				0.0	0.0	0.0	0.0
51	Closing losses				0.0	0.0	0.0	0.0
52								
53	Profit	3	0.0		0.0	0.0	0.0	2,000.0
54	Opening losses				0.0	0.0	0.0	0.0
55	Tax losses generated				0.0	0.0	0.0	0.0
56	Tax losses utilised				0.0	0.0	0.0	0.0
57	Tax losss lapsed				0.0	0.0	0.0	0.0
58	Closing losses				0.0	0.0	0.0	0.0

The losses workings are the most involved. In some countries the tax regime allows the losses from earlier periods to be used to reduce the profits of later periods, which is referred to as utilising the losses. In this example, it is assumed that losses can be carried forward three years, but if they are not used in this period they are no longer available to reduce future profits and are said to have lapsed. Individual loss accounts have been set up for the losses of each year so that their utilisation and when they are no longer available to reduce profits can be modelled. Accounts for all the subsequent years are all identical to the second account for year 1 or 2001. Rows 39 to 44 can be copied and pasted to rows 46 to 51 and also to rows 53 to 58. The year counter that begins at 0 and increases for each year is used to track the age of the losses. The detailed explanation of the example is shown in Chart 14.7 and refers to column H unless stated otherwise.

Chart 14.7 **Detailed taxation workings**

Row	Calculation	Actual calculation	Answer
Assumptions	=Last_year+1	=2002+1	2003
Accounting profit/loss before tax	User input	10000	10,000.0
Rate	User input	30%	30.0%
Payment Delay	User input	180	180
Number of years for loss carry-forward (column E)	User input	3	3
Adjustments	User input	1500	1,500.0
Adjusted profit/loss before tax	=Accounting_profit +Adjustments	=10000+1500	11,500.0
Profit before the utilisation of losses	=MAX(0,H11)	=MAX(0,11500)	11,500.0
Losses utilised	=Losses_utilised	=(9500)	(9,500.0)
Profit before tax liable to corporation tax	=Profit_before_ losses+Losses_ utilised	=11500−9500	2,000.0
Opening corporation tax creditor	=Previous_closing_ tax_creditor	=0	0.0
Corporation tax charge in the year	=Profit_liable_to_ corporation_tax* Taxation_rate	=2000*30%	600.0
CT Paid	=−Opening_tax_ creditor−(Tax_ charge*(365− Payment_delay) /365)	=−0.0−(600*(365− 180)/365)	(304.1)
Closing corporation tax creditor	=SUM(H17:H19)	=0.0+600−(304.1)	295.9
Year	=G23+1	=2+1	3
Opening losses	=Previous_closing_ tax_loss	=9500	9,500.0
Tax losses lapsed during the period	=H36+H43+H50 +H57	=0+0+...+0	0.0
Increase in tax losses in the period	=H34+H41+H48 +H55	=0+0+...+0	0.0
Tax losses utilised	=H35+H42+H49 +H56	=−6500−3000 +0+...+0	(9,500.0)
Closing losses	=SUM(H24:H27)	=9500−9500	0.0
Row 32 Profit	=MAX(0,H11)	=MAX(0,11500)	11,500.0
Row 33 Opening losses	=IF(H23=0, H24,G37)	=IF(3=0,9500, 6500)	6,500.0
Row 34 Tax losses generated	=IF($B32−H$23, $C32,0)	=IF(0=3,5000,0)	0.0

Row	Calculation	Actual calculation	Answer
Row 35 Tax losses utilised	=−IF($B32+*Years_ forward*>=H$23, MIN(H33,H32),0)	=−IF(0+3>=3, MIN(6500, 11500),0)	(6,500.0)
Row 36 Tax losses lapsed	=−IF($B32+*Years_ forward*+1=H$23, MAX(0,H33),0)	=−IF(0+3+ 1=3,MAX(0, 6500),0)	0.0
Row 37 Closing losses	=SUM(H33:H36)	=6500+0− 6500+0	0.0
Row 39 Profit	=H32+H35	=11,500−6,500	5,000.0
Row 40 Opening losses	=G44	=3000	3,000.0
Row 41 Tax losses generated	=IF($B39=H$23, $C39,0)	=IF(1=3,0,0)	0.0
Row 42 Tax losses utilised	=−IF($B39+*Years_ forward*>=H$23, MIN(H40,H39),0)	=−IF(1+3>=3, MIN(3000, 5000),0)	(3,000.0)
Row 43 Tax losses lapsed	=−IF($B39+*Years_ forward*+1=H$23, MAX(0,H40),0)	=−IF(1+3=3, MAX(0,3000),0)	0.0
Row 44 Closing losses	=SUM(H40:H43)	=3000+0− 3000+0	0.0

Profit and loss account and valuation considerations

The modeller must consider the issue of valuation when computing corporation tax charges. Chapter 15 discusses how the free cashflow for valuation purposes should be adjusted to remove the impact of interest charges in order to avoid double counting the tax shield from financing when using a post-tax weighted average cost of capital (WACC). One approach is to perform a single corporation tax computation and then calculate the tax shield from financing by multiplying the interest charges by the tax rate and then adding this back to the free cashflow. An alternative is simply to perform two corporation tax computations. One includes interest charges and is used in the profit and loss account; the other excludes interest from the profits chargeable to corporation tax and can be used for discounted cashflow valuation purposes.

FOREIGN EXCHANGE CALCULATIONS

Principles of foreign exchange accounting

This book discusses foreign exchange gains and losses at the individual company level. Potential foreign exchange implications also arise from the consolidation of overseas subsidiaries, and a number of alternative approaches are possible. The modelling of foreign exchange gains and losses on consolidation, however, is beyond the scope of this book. The reader is advised to consult any standard accounting text, which should provide an exposition of the possible accounting treatments.

When a business transacts with a third party in another country the potential for foreign exchange gains and losses arises as a result of possible differences between the exchange rate on the date the transaction was recorded and the exchange rate on the date the cash is received. Consider the following example:

- A UK-based firm sells $1,500 worth of goods to an American customer when the exchange rate is $1.5 to £1.
- The sale is recorded as $1,500/1.5=£1,000 in the UK company's profit and loss account.
- There is a period of 30 days before the customer has to settle the account during which the pound weakens to $1.4 to £1.
- The amount actually received is therefore $1,500/1.4=£1,071.
- The difference between the £1,000 originally recorded and the amount actually received represents a foreign exchange gain and is taken to the profit and loss as part of the operating profit for the year.

Foreign exchange gains and losses can arise on a number of transactions, such as importing raw materials, exporting goods and raising overseas finance.

Standard accounting policies require that transactions during an accounting period should be translated at the rate of exchange in effect at the date of transaction. However, in the model it is assumed that all transactions take place in the middle of the period, allowing the mid-period exchange rate to be used for all transactions in that particular currency. The mid-period rate is calculated as the average of the opening and closing exchange rates for the period and assumes a linear movement between the opening and closing positions.

Foreign exchange gains and losses can also arise when a transaction takes place at the average rate for the period, such as a purchase of fixed assets, but the resulting creditor in the balance sheet is recorded at a different rate at the end of the period.

Monetary items, such as debtor, creditor or loan balances outstanding in the balance sheet at the end of the period, should be translated at the closing rate for the period or the rate at which the transaction is contracted to settle. For simplicity, the closing rate for all similarly denominated balances is used. Once again, the difference between the transaction rate and the rate used to convert the closing balance generates a foreign exchange gain or loss, after adjustments have been made for any cash received or paid in the period.

Gains or losses from transactions are normally included under "other operating income or charges" in the profit and loss account. Gains or losses arising from financing arrangements are disclosed separately and usually as part of "other interest receivable (payable) and similar income (charges)".

Generic approach to modelling foreign exchange gains and losses

Before embarking on a potentially complex foreign exchange working the modeller should examine whether the inclusion of the workings will have a significant impact on the business decision. The likely importance of foreign exchange gains and losses depends on the levels of exports and imports and the volatility of the currencies involved. Where trade takes place between businesses in stable western economies, foreign exchange implications can usually be ignored. However, if a business in a developing country is being modelled and exchange rates are known to be unstable, and if imports of raw materials are high and the business makes a considerable proportion of sales overseas, detailed modelling of foreign exchange gains and losses may well be essential.

Modelling foreign exchange gains and losses on overseas revenue and costs

To model foreign exchange gains and losses, a forecast of the closing exchange rate for each currency in which the business conducts a material number of transactions will be required. Modelling the closing exchange rate for a number of years was discussed in Chapter 9. The calculated closing exchange rates of adjacent periods can be used to calculate a mid-period rate, by using a simple average of the two adjacent closing rates. This mid-period rate represents the rate at which transactions will be recorded. The revenue and costs within the profit and loss should then be calculated based on translating any local currency figures at the mid-period rate. Any outstanding monetary balances at the end of the period should be recorded at the closing balance sheet rates. Lastly, the differences between the value of the transaction and the value of the monetary balances, allowing for cash remitted or paid during the period (at the average rate), can be recorded as foreign exchange gains and losses in the appropriate line of the profit and loss account.

Modelling foreign exchange gains and losses on overseas financing

The example in Chart 14.8 demonstrates many of the general principles. It is concerned with financing using overseas borrowings, but the structure of the code is applicable to overseas debtor and creditor transactions.

To calculate all the required exchange rates a forecast is required for the closing rate for an additional period beyond the last transactions.

Foreign exchange calculations

Chart 14.8 Foreign exchange workings

	A	B	C	D 1999	E 2000	F 2001	G 2002	H 2003	I 2004
1	Foreign exchange			1999	2000	2001	2002	2003	2004
2									
3	Exchange rate (mid-point) local / US$	Mid_rate		2.50	3.00	4.00	4.00	4.00	2.00
4	Closing balance sheet rate	Closing_rate		2.75	3.50	4.00	4.00	3.00	2.00
5	Interest rate	Interest_rate			10%	10%	10%	10%	10%
6									
7	Balance sheet - local								
8	Cash			100.0	103.4	96.6	104.8	101.0	
9									
10	Debt			120.0	234.4	367.9	467.9	305.9	
11	Profit and loss reserves			(20.0)	(131.0)	(271.3)	(363.0)	(204.9)	
12									
13	Shareholder's funds			100.0	103.4	96.6	104.8	101.0	
14									
15	Profit and loss account - local								
16	Operating profit	Op_profit			(50.0)	(75.0)	(50.0)	100.0	
17	Interest charges	Interest			(16.6)	(31.8)	(41.8)	(43.8)	
18	Unrealised forex gains / (losses)				(44.4)	(33.5)	0.0	102.0	
19									
20	Profit or loss for the period	Period_profit_loss			(111.0)	(140.3)	(91.8)	158.2	
21									
22	Cashflow statement - local								
23	Operating cash flow				(50.0)	(75.0)	(50.0)	100.0	
24	Debt raised / (repaid)	Debt_raised_repaid			70.0	100.0	100.0	(60.0)	
25	Interest paid				(10.0)	(31.8)	(41.8)	(43.8)	
26									
27	Cash movement in the period	Cash_movement			3.4	(6.8)	8.2	(3.8)	
28									
29	Debt account - US$								
30	Opening balance				43.6	67.0	92.0	117.0	
31	Net movement				23.3	25.0	25.0	(15.0)	
32	Closing balance	Closing_debt		43.6	67.0	92.0	117.0	102.0	
33									
34	Average debt	Average_debt			55.3	79.5	104.5	109.5	
35									
36	Foreign exchange workings - local								
37	Opening balance at opening rate				120.0	234.4	367.9	467.9	
38	Opening balance at closing rate				152.7	267.9	367.9	350.9	
39	Opening gain / (loss)				(32.7)	(33.5)	0.0	117.0	
40									
41	Movement at mid-rate				70.0	100.0	100.0	(60.0)	
42	Movement at closing rate				81.7	100.0	100.0	(45.0)	
43	Movement gain / (loss)				(11.7)	0.0	0.0	(15.0)	
44									
45	Total gain / (loss)	Forex_gain_loss			(44.4)	(33.5)	0.0	102.0	
46									
47	Balance				0.0	0.0	0.0	0.0	

This example includes a simplified profit and loss account, balance sheet and cashflow statement. For simplicity, it has been assumed that there are no working capital movements so that operating profits and the cashflow from operating activities are identical. The debt account and interest charges have been maintained in the currency in which the debt has been denominated. Interest charges are translated into the profit and loss account at the mid-period rate for the period and the closing debt balance is included in the balance sheet based on the closing period rate.

The foreign exchange workings have been broken down into two stages for clarity. The difference between the value of the opening balance at the opening exchange rate for the period and the value of the opening balance using the closing exchange rate is the first stage in computing the foreign exchange gain or loss. The results of this calculation are combined with the difference between the value of an increase or decrease in the debt balance during the period, recorded at both the mid-period rate and the closing period rate. The combination of these two calculations gives the overall foreign exchange gain or loss. The gain or loss has been recorded in the profit and loss account. Lastly, a check has been performed on the balance sheet to ensure that it balances after conducting these foreign exchange operations.

The detailed workings are explained in Chart 14.9. The example refers to row F or year 2001 unless stated otherwise. Headings and range names should be created first. A relative range name for the last year (*Last_year*) is required in row 1. Cells D1, D8, D10 and D11 are inputs, as are rows 3, 5, 16 and 24. Ensure that the formula in cell D32 is entered correctly, as this entry is different from the other formulae in this row.

Chart 14.9 **Detailed foreign exchange workings**

Row	Calculation	Actual calculation	Answer
1	=Last_year+1	=2000+1	2001
Exchange rate (mid-point) local/US$	User input	4	4
Closing balance sheet rate	=AVERAGE(F3,G3)	=(4+4)/2	4
Interest rate	User input	10%	10%
Balance sheet – local			
Cash	=Last_year+ Cash_movement	=103.4−6.8	96.6
Debt	=Closing_debt* Closing_rate	=92.0*4	367.9
Profit and loss reserves	=Last_year+ Period_profit_loss	=(131.0)−140.3	(271.3)
Shareholder funds	=F10+F11	=367.9+(271.3)	96.6
Profit and loss account – local			
Operating profit	User input	(75)	(75.0)
Interest charges	=−Average_debt* Interest_rate*Mid_rate	=−79.5*10%*4	(31.8)
Unrealised foreign exchange gain/(loss)	=Forex_gain_loss	=Forex_gain_loss	(33.5)
Profit and loss for the period	=SUM(F16:F18)	=(75)+(31.8)+(33.5)	(140.3)
Cashflow statement – local			
Operating cashflow	=Op_profit	=Op_profit	(75)
Debt raised/(repaid)	User input	User input	100
Interest paid	=Interest	=Interest	(31.8)
Cash movement in the period	=SUM(F23:F25)	=(75)+100+(31.8)	(6.8)
Debt account − US$			
Cell D32	=D10/D4	=120/2.75	43.6
Opening balance	=E32	=67	67.0
Net movement	=Debt_raised_repaid/ Mid_rate	=100/4	25.0
Closing balance	=SUM(F30:F31)	=67+25	92.0
Average debt	=AVERAGE(F30,F32)	=(67+92)/2	79.5
Foreign exchange workings – local			
Opening balance at opening rate	=F30*E4	=67*3.50	234.4
Opening balance at closing rate	=F30*Closing_rate	=67*4	267.9
Opening gain/(loss)	=F37−F38	=234.4−267.9	(33.5)
Movement at mid-rate	=F31*Mid_rate	=25*4	100.0
Movement at closing rate	=F31*Closing_rate	=25*4	100.0

Row	Calculation	Actual calculation	Answer
Movement gain/(loss)	=F41−F42	=100−100	0
Total gain/(loss)	=F39+F43	=(33.5)+0	(33.5)
Balance	=F8−(F10+F11)	=96.6−(367.9−271.3)	0

15 Valuation approaches

Previous chapters have examined various modelling techniques for developing a forecast of a project's or a company's future financial statements. Although the financial statements provide valuable information about revenue, profitability and growth they do not provide an indication of the value of a project or business. This chapter introduces a number of approaches and modelling techniques for performing valuations. It starts with some basic definitions and valuation theory. This is then applied to the problem of valuing an entire company. The second half of the chapter covers the valuation of specific company projects. For a more detailed exposition of the techniques used see *Principles of Corporate Finance* by Richard Brealey and Stewart Myers.[1]

VALUATION DEFINITIONS

Enterprise or firm value

The value of a company is based on an expectation of its ability to generate future cashflow. The enterprise value or firm value of a company is the value of the future cashflow that is attributable to both the debt and the equity holders within the business. This cashflow is called free cashflow (FCF) and can be defined as follows:

Operating profits, adjusted for movements in working capital, less the tax that would be paid if the business was entirely financed by equity, less capital expenditure

It is possible to demonstrate, through financial theory, that the decision to undertake an investment can be separated from the decision about how that investment is financed. A valuation based on an analysis of FCF allows us to examine the viability of an investment in its own right and then to examine how to finance the investment as a secondary decision.

Equity value

The equity value of a company is the value of the future cashflow that flows only to the equity holders. This cashflow can be defined as follows:

Operating profits, adjusted for movements in working capital, less interest and debt principal repayments, less the tax paid based on the actual capital structure of the company, less capital expenditure

The equity value of a company is often referred to as the market capitalisation of the company. In the case of a listed company, the equity value divided by the closing number of shares in issue at the end of the year should give the share price for the company.

---

1 6th edition, McGraw-Hill, 2000.

The relationship between equity value and enterprise value can be written as follows:

Enterprise value–today's value of future interest and principal payments=
equity value

Normally, the value of the interest and principal payments is assumed to be approximated by the carrying value of debt in the balance sheet. As a result the equation can be rewritten:

Enterprise value–net debt=equity value

VALUING A COMPANY

P/E ratios

The easiest way to value a company is to look at the values of similar companies. To make this comparison, markets have often used price/earnings (P/E) ratios. The P/E ratio is the ratio of the equity value of a company to the total earnings of the company, where earnings are defined as:

Profits after tax, less preference dividends, less minority interests

The P/E ratio can also be calculated by dividing the price of one of the company's shares by the earnings per share.

To see how P/E ratios might be used for valuation purposes, consider two companies: a company that is traded on a stockmarket and a similar company that is not traded. A P/E ratio will be useful as it provides a relative measure of value that can be used across similar companies.

For the traded company, its earnings per share can be obtained from the company's accounts. It is also possible to observe its share price on the stockmarket. Combining the two generates a measure of relative value per unit of earnings. The P/E ratio is a measure of value per unit of earnings.

To value the untraded company, the techniques developed earlier in this book can be used to create a forecast for the future earnings of the company. The forecast earnings can then be multiplied by the P/E ratio to give an indicative valuation of the company. For example:

- The P/E ratio for the traded company is 28.
- The earnings per share from the forecast for the company to be valued is $0.52.
- The implied price per share is therefore the P/E ratio multiplied by the earnings per share.
- 28 multiplied by $0.52 indicates a price per share of $14.56.

If it is assumed that there are 10m shares in issue, then the total value of the company would be:

- The price per share multiplied by the number of shares.
- $14.56 multiplied by 10,000,000.
- The value of the company would be $145.6m.

Limitations of P/E ratios

Despite the widespread use of P/E ratios for valuation purposes, there are a number of limitations. The first is finding a suitable similar company. Should such a company be found, the differences in accounting treatments, for example for fixed assets and intangibles, can make earnings comparisons difficult. Even if these problems can be overcome there can be a more fundamental problem. Some companies are loss making so they do not have a positive earnings per share figure to which a P/E ratio can be applied.

EBITDA multiples

One solution is to use a measure of profitability such as earnings before interest, tax, depreciation and amortisation (often written as EBITDA), which for new ventures generally turns positive earlier than profit after tax on which earnings per share calculations are based. Many analysts prefer to use EBITDA as a matter of course, because it is calculated before depreciation and amortisation have been deducted and is therefore less susceptible to differences in accounting policies.

An important difference to note in using EBITDA for valuation purposes is that as EBITDA is before interest charges, it must be compared with the enterprise value (EV) rather than the equity value of the business. Consequently, analysts often refer to "enterprise value to EBITDA multiples" as a basis for valuation, but they can be used in exactly the same way as P/E ratios (although the ratio must be applied to EBITDA, not earnings).

Revenue multiples

Even when EBITDA is negative, company comparisons can still be made using sales revenue that is always positive. Many of the new Internet businesses were valued on the basis of enterprise value to revenue ratios. The basis of the approach is identical to the use of P/E and EV to EBITDA ratios. Of course, some Internet companies did not even have revenue so some analysts resorted to ratios of value per customer.

DISCOUNTED CASHFLOW THEORY

One way to value a business or project could be to add all the amounts of cash across all the years of the forecast. However, this assumes that all income is equally valuable, regardless of when it is earned. For example, if you had the choice of being given $100 now or $100 in ten years' time, you would probably take the money now. There are two reasons for this:

- Risk, in terms of actually being able to turn a future expectation into cash.
- The time value of money (or the effect of interest). By putting $100 on deposit now it will earn interest making it worth much more in ten years' time.

The concept of value is to calculate a project total that reflects both the time value of money and the risk associated with the investment. This is the role of discounted cashflow (DCF) techniques, which can be applied to both companies and individual projects irrespective of their stage of maturity. Ultimately, this technique will be a key element in the decision to accept or reject an investment.

DISCOUNTED CASHFLOWS

If $100 is deposited in an account that pays interest annually at 10% gross, the balance on that account would grow as follows:

Now		1 year		2 years		3 years
$100	→	$110	→	$121	→	$133.1

This is the principle of compound interest. The principle can be used to calculate the value of an amount at a future point in time. The formula is:

$$X*(1+r)^n$$
where:
X is the amount
r is the interest rate expressed as a fraction (eg 10% = 0.1)
n is the number of years

The principle of discounting is the opposite of compounding. Discounting is used to calculate how much a future amount is worth now. Using the above example in reverse, if a project had a positive cashflow of $121 in year 2 this is the equivalent of a positive cashflow of $100 now. The value now is known as the present value. The formula to calculate a present value is:

$$X*(1/(1+r)^n)$$
where: X and n are the same as above, but r is often referred to as the discount rate

An overall project value can be calculated as the total of the present values for each future year of a project. Although the principle of compounding may be easier to understand, discounting is the basis for many business valuation techniques. Chart 15.1 shows an example with a discount rate at 10%.

Chart 15.1 **A project with a discount rate of 10%**

	Cashflow	Discount calculation	Present value of each cashflow
Invest now	(1000)	(1000)*1	1000
Receive in one year	500	500*1/1.1	454
Receive in two years	700	700*1/1.21	579
Total	200		33

The present value of the future cashflow is $1,033. The overall value, being the combination of the initial investment and the present value of the future cashflows, is called the net present value (NPV) of the project. The NPV of this example is $33. Finance theory indicates that, in the absence of any constraints on the availability of investment funds, the business will undertake projects that generate a positive NPV when calculated at the appropriate discount rate.

Most spreadsheets contain an NPV function to calculate these values. However, they may have some in-built conventions that need to be remembered. In Excel the syntax is:

=NPV (rate, values) where the values can be a range, but must start with year 1

Therefore to calculate the NPV of the example above the formula would have to contain:

$$=NPV(10\%,500,700)-1000$$

The value at time 0 is outside the NPV calculation.

PRACTICAL APPROACHES TO DCF ANALYSIS

Having examined the theoretical approach to DCF analysis, here are some of the practical considerations. The value of a firm can be calculated in a number of different ways, using different cashflows and their appropriate discount rates. Underlying all these approaches it is important to have consistency between the cashflows and the discount rate that is used.

For example, assume that a forecast has been generated for the profit and loss and cashflow statement for a company in nominal terms (including inflation). From the financial statements a series has been derived for the nominal free cashflow to both debt and equity holders. To ensure consistency, we must use a discount rate that reflects the cost of capital to both the debt and the equity holders. This is the discount rate that represents the average cost of capital for all the providers of finance to a company, and it is called the weighted average cost of capital (WACC). In this example, the WACC reflects the weighted average of the discount rates for both the debt and the equity holders. Once the free cashflow has been discounted, we will have a figure for the enterprise value of the business.

Calculating the WACC

Assume that:

- ◪ A is the proportion of the business financed by equity
- ◪ E is the cost of equity in nominal terms
- ◪ B is the proportion of the business financed by debt
- ◪ R is the cost of debt in nominal terms
- ◪ T is the tax rate

If the cost of equity is the discount rate that would be used to discount the cashflows only to equity holders and the cost of debt is the discount rate used to discount cashflows only to debt holders, then the WACC would be written as:

$$WACC=(A*E)+(B*R*(1-T))$$

The important element of the equation to examine is the cost of debt. The cost of debt is multiplied by 1 minus the tax rate. Interest costs are chargeable against profits for taxation and thus reduce the tax paid by the business. Multiplying the cost of debt by 1 minus the tax rate captures the tax benefit of debt financing on cashflows through the saving of tax paid. This effect is called the tax shield on financing.

However, care must be taken when calculating the amount of tax paid in the free cashflow as there is a risk of double counting the tax shield on debt financing. Normal tax charges included in the profit and loss statement are calculated on profit before tax (PBT), which is after deducting interest and therefore the interest cost lowers the actual tax paid. To avoid double counting the tax benefit of interest, the cashflows must be computed as if the business was 100% equity financed. To achieve this one of two options can be adopted:

1. Add back the tax shield on financing to the discounted cashflows; this is calculated as interest cost * tax rate.
2. Calculate the tax paid twice, once including interest charges and once without, the first for the profit and loss statement, the other for valuation purposes.

The second option was discussed in more detail in Chapter 14 (see page 160).

In calculating the WACC, the costs of debt and equity are weighted according to the market value of the debt and equity. Normally, the value of debt can be approximated by taking the carrying value in the balance sheet. The value of equity should be the market value of the equity. Unfortunately, there is a problem here.

To calculate the market value of equity a DCF analysis may need to be carried out. To carry out a DCF analysis a discount rate is needed. To calculate the discount rate a WACC calculation must be done, but a WACC calculation needs the market value of equity. There is a circular argument. The solution is to assume that the business will tend towards an optimal financing structure. This structure can be indicated by looking at the capital structure of other similar businesses in the industry.

From enterprise value to equity value
The discussion above focused on the discounted cashflows to debt and equity holders by the WACC to generate the enterprise value of the business. To obtain the equity value, apply the formula introduced earlier.

$$Enterprise\ value-net\ debt=equity\ value$$

However, the equity value could have been calculated directly. First, forecast the free cashflow to equity holders by deducting interest and principal repayments and also the tax paid (this time including the effects of interest). This free cashflow reflects the cash that would be attributable only to the equity holders. Then discount not by a WACC but by the cost of equity alone. The value of the discounted free cashflow to equity holders would be the equity value of the business. This approach could be followed on a nominal (including inflation) or real (excluding inflation) basis. It could also have been calculated on a pre-tax or post-tax basis. Consistency is the key, as shown below.

Cashflow	DCF rate
◪ Nominal free cashflow to equity holders	◪ Nominal cost of equity
◪ Real free cashflow to equity holders	◪ Real cost of equity
◪ Nominal free cashflow to equity holders before tax	◪ Nominal cost of equity excluding tax

To calculate the enterprise value from the equity value, simply rearrange the formula above.

$$\text{Equity value} + \text{net debt} = \text{enterprise value}$$

Terminal values

So far the discussion has covered the discounting of the future cashflow stream of a business that is captured within the detailed forecast period. Businesses, of course, do not stop generating cashflows at the end of an arbitrary forecast period. They continue, with luck, to perpetuity. These cashflows, generated beyond the detailed forecast period, should also be included in the NPV in order to understand the true value of the business. In the case of many business plans for telecommunications companies, because of the heavy initial investments, the discounted value of the free cashflows over a ten-year period are often negative. It is only the magnitude of the terminal value that yields a positive overall NPV for the project.

There are many approaches to calculating the terminal value for a business. However, two of the most common approaches are the use of perpetuity growth models and company comparable exit multiples, such as the enterprise value/EBITDA multiples discussed earlier.

Growth rate models

There are a variety of different perpetuity growth models that can be used. In its simplest form the present value of a perpetuity, an amount paid at the same point each period to infinity, can be calculated using the following formula:

$$\frac{\underline{\text{Year ten cashflow}}}{\text{Discount rate}}$$

This formula will give the present value at the mid-point of year ten of the year ten cashflow received to infinity. To be able to add the terminal value to the present value of the discounted detailed cashflows, the terminal value itself must be discounted back to the start of the forecast period by the year ten discount factor.

Many companies would hope that their business continues to grow after the end of the detailed forecast period. The expectations of growth may be quite low, for example in line with the growth in the country's GDP, but the cashflows will at least continue to grow to perpetuity.

A common model for calculating the terminal value with growth is the Gordon Growth Model:

$$\frac{\text{Year ten cashflow}*(1+\text{growth rate})}{(\text{Discount rate}-\text{growth rate})}$$

Once again, the result of this calculation must be discounted back to the start of the forecast period by the year ten discount factor to be included with the net present value of the detailed cashflows.

Beware of this method as it depends on the assumption that it grows in perpetuity. The product life cycle theory would suggest otherwise. It is advisable to generate a range of valuations using different terminal value growth rate assumptions. The modeller should also look closely at the last year of the forecast to ensure that the final year cashflow is representative of the cashflows that will be generated to perpetuity. All the perpetuity calculations assume that the business has achieved a steady state. The forecast period must be sufficiently long to ensure that this state as has been achieved before the calculation is performed.

All these methods can significantly enhance the value of the project and should be used with caution. It is best practice to work out the value of the opportunity including and excluding the terminal value to understand the degree of dependence that is based on realising the terminal value.

EBITDA exit multiples

An alternative to using a growth model calculation is to return to the use of company-comparable multiples. In this method the final year EBITDA figure is multiplied by a suitable enterprise value to EBITDA multiple to give the enterprise value of the business at year ten. This figure must be then discounted back to the start of the detailed forecast period to be combined with the present value of the detailed cashflows. Once again, because of the importance of the terminal value it is advisable to calculate a range of values based on different EBITDA exit multiples.

Valuation range

Valuing a company is not an exact science, and modellers are advised to adopt a number of different valuation methods to create a range of possible valuations. It is best not to rely on just one valuation approach. However, if there are significant variations in values based on a number of different methods, the reasons behind the variations should be explored. If, after extensive review, no explanation can be found for the difference between a DCF valuation and the current share price of a company, then this may represent a buying or selling opportunity!

Company valuation example

This example examines the code required to develop a simple company valuation using DCF analysis. It first calculates the NPV of the ten years of cashflows that have been forecast in detail before calculating terminal values based on the Gordon Growth Model and also using EBITDA exit multiples. The combination of the NPV of the detailed cashflows and the terminal values gives a range of enterprise values for the company. Lastly, the net book value of the debt is deducted to derive the equity value. The free cashflow figure calculated in the example is post-tax and in nominal terms, so a nominal post-tax discount rate and a nominal terminal value growth rate are used to ensure consistency. The discount rate represents the WACC for the company based on an assumption for the optimal gearing, or debt/equity ratio, for the business.

Chart 15.2 **Valuation input assumptions**

	A	B	C	D	E	F	G	H	I	J	K	L	M	N	O
1	Valuation assumptions														
2															
3	Description	Range name			Input										
4															
5	Nominal post tax discount rate	Discount_rate			10.0%										
6	Nominal terminal value growth rate	Terminal_value_growth_rate			2.5%										
7	EBITDA exit multiple	EBITDA_exit_multiple			10										
8	Net book value of debt	Net_book_value_of_debt			16000										
9															
10		Year			2000	2001	2002	2003	2004	2005	2006	2007	2008	2009	2010
11	Operating profit (EBITDA)	Operating_profit			-3000	-2660	-1520	170	1940	3180	4400	5470	6230	6860	7050
12	Movements in working capital	Movements_in_working_capital			15	25	28.7	25	13.5	2	-6	-11.7	-16.3	-18.7	-20.9
13	Tax paid (100% equity)	Tax_paid									440	820	1558	2058	2115
14	Capital expenditure	Capital_expenditure			3000	1000	250	260	100	100	100	400	125	125	125

Chart 15.2 shows the input assumptions required to carry out the valuation. The inputs for operating profit, movements in working capital, the tax paid (calculated as if the business were 100% equity financed) and capital expenditure would normally be drawn from other sections within the model. To simplify the example, these are provided as inputs. All figures are nominal. The valuation workings are shown in Chart 15.3.

Chart 15.3 **Valuation workings**

	A	B	C	D	E	F	G	H	I	J	K	L	M	N	O
1	Valuation workings														
2															
3	Net present value of free cash flows				2000	2001	2002	2003	2004	2005	2006	2007	2008	2009	2010
4															
5	Free cash flow	Free_cash_flow			(5,985.0)	(3,635.0)	(1,741.3)	(55.0)	1,853.5	3,062.0	3,854.0	4,238.3	4,530.7	4,658.3	4,789.1
6															
7	Reference year	Reference_year			1	2	3	4	5	6	7	8	9	10	11
8															
9	Discount factor	Discount_factor			1.05	1.15	1.27	1.40	1.54	1.69	1.86	2.04	2.25	2.47	2.72
10															
11	Discounted free cash flow	Discounted_free_cash_flow			(5,706.5)	(3,150.8)	(1,372.1)	(39.4)	1,207.1	1,012.8	2,074.2	2,073.7	2,015.2	1,883.6	1,760.5
12															
13	Total NPV of free cash flows				2,558.4										
14															
16	Terminal value based on the Gordon Growth Model														
17															
18	Terminal value at year 11				65,451.0										
19															
20	Terminal value at year 0	Terminal_value_growth_model			24,059.9										
21															
22															
23	Terminal value based on EBITDA exit multiple														
24															
25	Terminal value at year 11				70,500.0										
26															
27	Terminal value at year 0	Terminal_value_EBITDA			25,915.9										
28															
29															
30	Enterprise value				Gordon Growth	EBITDA Exit									
31					Model	Multiple									
32	NPV of free cash flows				2,558.4	2,558.4									
33	Terminal value				24,059.9	25,915.9									
34															
35	Enterprise value				26,618.3	28,474.3									
36															
37	Equity value				10,618.3	12,474.3									

The workings begin by calculating the free cashflow to both debt and equity holders, based on the formula shown on page 171. A reference year is created to ensure that the same formulae can be used in each year. The calculation of the discount factor is one of the most important calculations.

Before performing a valuation it is important to decide the date at which the company is to be valued. This is the date to which all future cashflows are discounted. In this example, the company is valued at the start of 2000, which is referred to as year 0. During 2000 the company has negative free cashflow of $5,985. As in previous examples, it is assumed that all cashflows occur mid-way through the year. The negative free cashflow of $5,985 is therefore assumed to take place on June 30th 2000, six months from the date of valuation (January 1st 2000). This initial cashflow must therefore be discounted by only six months. In the detailed analysis in Chart 15.4, the discount rate is adjusted accordingly. Subsequent cashflows occur 12 months later, and the discount factor can be calculated without any further adjustments to the discount rate.

Chart 15.4 provides a detailed analysis of the example. Workings relate to 2000 unless stated otherwise. Range names in addition to those shown in column B have been created as follows:

- Final_year_cash_flow for cell O5 on the valuation workings sheet
- Final_year_EBITDA for cell O11 on the inputs assumptions sheet

Chart 15.4 **Valuation workings code**

Row	Calculation	Actual calculation	Answer
Free cashflow	=Operating_profit+Movements_ in_working_capital–Capital_ expenditure–Tax_paid	=−3000+15−3000−0	(5,985.0)
			(5,985.0)
Reference year	Input	1	1
Discount factor	=IF(Reference_year=1,(1+ Discount_rate)^0.5,D9* (1+Discount_rate))	TRUE(1+10%)^0.5	1.05
Discounted free cashflow	=Free_cash_flow/Discount_factor	=(5985)/1.05	(5,706.5)
Total NPV of free cashflow	=SUM(Discounted_free_ cash_flow)	=(5706.5)+(3150.8)+... +1760.5	2,558.4
Terminal value at year 11 (row 18)	=Final_year_cash_flow *(1+Terminal_value_growth_ rate)/(Discount_rate–Terminal_ value_growth_rate)	=(4789.1*(1+2.5%))/ (10%−2.5%)	65,451.0
Terminal value at year 0 (row 20)	=E18/O9	=65451.0/2.72	24,059.9
Terminal value at year 11 (row 25)	=Final_year_EBITDA*EBITDA _exit_multiple	=7050*10	70,500.0
Terminal value at year 0 (row 27)	=E25/O9	=70500/2.72	25,915.9
Gordon Growth Model (column E)			
NPV of free cashflows	=E13	=2558.4	2,558.4
Terminal value	=Terminal_value_growth_model	=24059.9	24,059.9
Enterprise value	=E32+E33	=2558.4+24059.9	26,618.3
Equity value	=E35–Net_book_value_of_debt	=26618.2−16000	10,618.3
EBITDA exit multiple (column G)			
NPV of free cashflows	=E13	=2558.4	2,558.4
Terminal value	=Terminal_value_EBITDA	=25915.9	25,915.9
Enterprise value	=G32+G33	=2558.4+25915.9	28,474.3
Equity value	=G35–Net_book_value_of_debt	=28474.2−16000	12,474.3

PROJECT VALUATIONS

So far this chapter has concentrated on the valuation of complete businesses. However, the use of discounted cashflow techniques is equally valuable to the examination of individual projects within a company.

Identifying the cashflows

As discussed above, DCF techniques focus on cashflows. This may seem obvious, but in practice it can be quite difficult to separate profit flows from cashflows. A spreadsheet model can often double in size to calculate both sets of data. Some of the principal areas of difference are summarised in Chart 15.5.

Chart 15.5 **Differences between profit flow and cashflow**

Type of data	Profit flow	Cashflow
Sales	Recognised when the invoice is raised	Recognised when a debtor pays
Cost of sales	Recognised when the sales invoice is raised (held in stock until this point)	Recognised when cash is paid out for the items bought into stock
Overheads	Spread evenly using the concepts of accruals and prepayments	Recognised when the cash is paid for each overhead
Tax	Based on profits	Paid by instalments or in the year after earned
Fixed assets	Cost is spread over the period of use by way of depreciation	Recognised in total at time of purchase (unless by paid by instalments)

Chapter 12 explores the way in which some of these types of flows can be modelled.

Relevant cashflows

To understand the quality of a project, the discounting techniques should only be applied to the cashflows that result from the operation of the project. These cashflows are distinct from the cashflows required to finance the project. The reason for this separation is to understand whether the project is worthwhile as a venture in its own right. If the venture is viable then the issue of how to fund the project involves a separate set of decisions, perhaps requiring its own model (see Chapter 13).

It is also true that the funding is usually an organisational issue that involves factors beyond the scope of a single project. A principle espoused by many corporate treasurers is that "all cash belongs to mother". This means that all cash generated by projects becomes the cash of the organisation. Although a model may show cash surpluses and deficits evening out during a project, they are likely to be substantially different for an organisation. The project surpluses are taken by the organisation as they are earned and are applied elsewhere in the organisation. Each cash deficit will need to be specifically sourced.

Take, for example, a proposal to justify buying a new machine. The proposal should focus on the cashflow benefits that the new machine would bring to the company. If the project is to go ahead, it is a separate decision to decide how the purchase will be funded. The purchase could be by cash, loan or lease.

The main types of cashflow to include and exclude are shown in Chart 15.6.

Chart 15.6 **Types of cashflow to include and exclude**

Cashflows to include	Cashflows to exclude
Cash generated from sales	Equity or loan finance (received or repaid)
Cash paid for purchases	Dividend or interest on the finance
Cash paid for running costs	Lease payments
Cash paid and received on the purchase or sale of assets	Interest received on surplus deposits
The equivalent cash purchase cost for assets that would otherwise have been leased	
Tax payments or receipts	

There are some exceptions to the principles set out above for corporate acquisitions or corporate-level planning models. In these cases, an objective is to calculate shareholder value. This requires the model to include loan finance cashflows to leave the net cashflows attributable to the equity investors.

The cash effect of change

It can be difficult to know where to start when building the cashflows for a project. For example, a modeller is asked to assess the impact of new packaging on the manufacturing costs of a product. The modeller could build a model of the current costs and a model of the new costs and compare the results of each. This would be an accurate and perhaps time-consuming process. The more efficient way to assess the problem is to build one model that focuses on the effect of changing from the current situation to the new situation.

To build such a model, start by assuming that production of the old packaging will continue and then identify any receipts and payments that will be different when switching to the new packaging. The benefits of this approach are that there is only one model and that it focuses exclusively on those aspects of manufacturing that will be affected by the change. Anything that is unaffected by the change is ignored.

This approach can be applied to any project – an acquisition, a product launch, a closure or capital expenditure. The important point is to focus on the cash effect of the changes that will take place as a consequence of the project.

Dealing with allocated overheads

In compiling the project cashflows, there can often be a conflict between assessing the project on its own and assessing it as part of the business. In Chart 15.6 one of the items is "cash paid for running costs". This category can comprise central overheads that are allocated to a product or department.

Take, for example, a new product launch in a factory that already makes several other products. The cost of the factory (rent, heat, light and canteen) is allocated to products on a $ per tonne basis. On the launch of this new product the organisation is unlikely to be spending much more on the factory, yet part of the cost is now being attributed to the new product.

If the factory cost were ignored in the model of the new product, the financial evaluation would show unrealistically low manufacturing costs. The implication could be that the new product would only be viable providing the other products in the factory were able to cover the factory costs. This is the principle (and danger) of marginal costing.

To deal with this problem, some companies have developed a principle that they apply to all projects. Treat the project as part of the company and not stand-alone, and develop the cashflows for overheads as follows:

- If the project is to add incremental business to the company, then assume its share of allocated overheads is a real cashflow cost.
- If the project is to remove business from the company, then assume there will be no cashflow saving in the allocated overheads.

This principle is perhaps prudent in the impact it can have on projects and may be seen as negating the economy of scale effect. In any proposal it is worth stating clearly the way overheads have been treated.

Group versus project

In assessing a project it is difficult to know whether to bring in synergies that may be realised by combining a project with an organisation. At all times it is worth knowing whether a project stands on its own feet or whether its value is only realisable by combination with others. In bid situations for companies it is likely that the highest bid will come from the party that relies on one or more of the following:

- Higher expectations of value.
- Greater synergies identifiable.
- Lower acceptable returns.

Therefore the bid price is partly dependent on synergy gains.

Synergy gains are derived from several sources:

- Economies of scale, where corporate functions provide services to the whole organisation, such as treasury, investor relations, human resources and IT, and can be used without necessarily incurring incremental cost.
- Supply chain efficiencies, where the output of one part of the group is the input to the next; for example, tour operators owning their own airlines.
- The buying power of the company as a whole, which enables input costs to be reduced for all parts of the company.

In a model it is important to state what assumptions on synergy have been assumed in deriving the valuation. Many organisations will admit that synergies are often valued but rarely achieved, particularly when head-count savings are incorporated.

Treatment of surplus cash

Most projects are concerned with part of an organisation. If the project generates a cash surplus, this is applied to fund other projects. If there are no other projects in the organisation, then the surplus is used to repay borrowings. It is rare for the surplus cash to be put on deposit and left there until the end of a project. Therefore the discount rate used in a project will stay constant throughout the life of the project, regardless of when it moves into a net positive cash position.

Conventions for setting out the cashflows

Sign convention

In the model it is important to be disciplined about the sign convention given to the cashflows. The most common convention is that a receipt is positive and a payment is negative. Although the cell formulae can be coded to add receipts and deduct payments, it is much better to see the minus sign by each of the payments. Consequently, the cell formulae are easier with only additions being required.

Timing

Most models are designed with annual time intervals between each cashflow. The standard layout is shown in Chart 15.7 (this is for illustration only and does not form part of a detailed worked example).

Chart 15.7 **A standard timing layout**

	A	B	C	D	E	F	G	H	I	J
1	**Model title**									
2										
3	Year number	Year_number			0	1	2	3	4	5
4	Years	Actual_years			2000	2001	2002	2003	2004	2005
5										
6	**Summary cashflow**									
7	Capital				(1,000)					
8	Sales					100	300	700	1,200	1,500
9	Costs					(210)	(240)	(300)	(390)	(430)
10	Net cashflow				(1,000)	(110)	60	400	810	1,070
11										

Time 0 is the moment the first cashflow takes place. Time 1 is one year after the first cashflow takes place, time 2 is two years after the first cashflow takes place, and so on.

With these annual intervals it can be difficult to identify the appropriate period in which to place a cashflow. A general rule is to be prudent and if necessary accelerate payments and defer receipts. In the example in Chart 15.7, the capital cost has been put at time 0, although with a large capital spend it may be spread over the first few months of the project. The receipts are all placed at the end of the years in which they are earned.

The effect of these prudent timings is to reduce the NPV of a project. It is impossible to generalise on their actual impact owing to the scale of the compromises made and the interest rate used for discounting.

Short time intervals

For projects that conclude in less than five years, it may be preferable to lay out the cashflows using more frequent time intervals than the typical annual layout. Monthly, quarterly and semi-annual are all used. Other intervals are rare.

The danger is that the discount rate applied is not a simple fraction of an annual rate. For example, an annual model using a 12% discount rate is not the same as quarterly model using a 3% rate. The required rate is one that, when compounded for a year, equals the annual rate.

To convert an annual rate into a shorter period use:

$$\text{Short period rate} = (\sqrt[n]{(1+\text{annual rate})}) - 1$$

where n equals the number of short periods in a year and is applied as the nth root of the amount in brackets. The annual rate must be in percentage format eg 12% or 0.12

For example, 12% on a quarterly basis is:

$$(\sqrt[4]{(1.12)}) - 1 = 0.02874 = 2.874\%$$

In Excel this is written as:

$$=(1.12{\wedge}(1/4)) - 1$$

To convert a short period rate into an annual rate use:

$$\text{annual rate} = ((1+\text{short period rate}){\wedge}(\text{the number of short periods in a year})) - 1$$

For example, a quarterly rate of 3% is an annual rate of

$$=((1.03){\wedge}4) - 1 = 12.55\%$$

MEASURING RISK

In investment appraisal terms, risk is seen as the length of time taken to recover investment. This is based on the principle that it is easier to forecast next year than it would be to forecast, say, year ten.

Payback

The simplest method of appraising risk is to take the payback period. This is the length of time for the project to reach the cash breakeven point where the cash inflows match the cash outflows. The longer the payback the more risk there is in the project.

Take, for example, the project shown in Chart 15.8.

Chart 15.8 **The payback period**

	A	B	C	D	E	F	G	H	I	J	K
1	**Model title**										
2											
3	Year number	Year_number			0	1	2	3	4	5	Total
4	Years	Actual_years			2000	2001	2002	2003	2004	2005	
5											
6	**Net cashflows**										
7	Actual cashflow in year				(10,000)	5,000	4,000	3,000	2,000	1,000	5,000
8	Cumulative cashflow				(10,000)	(5,000)	(1,000)	2,000	4,000	5,000	

The payback is two years and four months (assuming cash is earned evenly through each year).

To work out this number:

- ☑ Find when the net investment changes from being negative to positive.
- ☑ The payback period is the year of the last negative net investment – (last negative net investment/cash movement in the year of the first positive net investment) $=2+(1000/3000)=2.333$.

Spreadsheets have no specific formula for calculating payback, so one method of working it out is shown in Chart 15.9.

Chart 15.9 **Payback period workings**

	A	B	C	D	E	F	G	H	I	J	K	L
1	**Model title**											
2												
3	Year number	Year_number			0	1	2	3	4	5	Total	
4	Years	Actual_years			2000	2001	2002	2003	2004	2005		
5												
6	**Net cashflows**											
7	Actual cashflow in year				(10,000)	5,000	4,000	3,000	2,000	1,000	5,000	
8	Cumulative cashflow	Current_year_net_investment			(10,000)	(5,000)	(1,000)	2,000	4,000	5,000		
9												
10	Payback	Payback			0	0	2.33333	0	0	0	2.33333	
11	No of months										28	
12	Payback in words										2 years 4 months	

The calculation for payback in year 2 is as shown in Chart 15.10. Rows 3, 4 and 7 are inputs. Relative range names are required for:

- ☑ Next_year_net_investment, for example, G10 to H8
- ☑ Next_year_cashflow, for example, G10 to H7

Chart 15.10 **Code for calculation for year 2**

Row	Calculation	Actual calculation	Answer
Payback	=IF(AND(*Current_year_net investment*<0,*Next_year_net investment*>=0),*Year_number* –(*Current_year_net_investment/ Next_year_cashflow*),0)	=IF(AND(−1000<0,2000>=0), 2−(−1000/3000),0)	2.33333

The calculations for column K are shown in Chart 15.11.

Chart 15.11 **Code for calculation for column K**

Row	Calculation	Actual calculation	Answer
Payback	−Max(Payback)	=MAX(0,0,2.333,0,0,0)	2.33333
No. of months	=ROUND(K10*12,0)	=ROUND(2.333×12,0)	28
Payback in words	=CONCATENATE(INT(K11/ 12)," years ",K11−(INT (K11/12)*12)," months")	=CONCATENATE(INT (28/12)," years ",28− (INT(28/12)*12), " months")	2 years 4 months

In row 10 MAX is used to find the highest payback, should the cashflows give rise to more than one payback point.

Rows 11 and 12 work in months to ensure than when the payback period is converted to words there are no instances of the fractional part reading 12 months; for example, 3 years 12 months, which should be converted to 4 years.

Many companies use the payback measure as a way of dismissing projects that do not pay back within a set time period. If a project has a payback of over ten years, then there will be a high dependence on the forecasting of cashflows in years five to ten. This is likely to increase the risk of the venture.

The problem with payback is that it is very short term. It fails to consider cashflows beyond the payback period (for example, the project could make $2,000,000 in year 6 and its payback would still be 2 years 4 months).

Payback makes no allowance for interest and therefore does not measure return.

Discounted payback

To avoid the potentially misleading situation of straight payback being calculated ignoring interest rates, a more realistic method is to calculate payback using the present value of each cashflow. This is known as discounted payback and is shown in Chart 15.12.

Chart 15.12 **Discounted payback workings**

	A	B	C	D	E	F	G	H	I	J	K	L
1	Model title											
2												
3	Year number	Year_number			0	1	2	3	4	5	Total	
4	Years	Actual_years			2000	2001	2002	2003	2004	2005		
5												
6	Net cashflows											
7	Actual cashflow in year				(10,000)	5,000	4,000	3,000	2,000	1,000	5,000	
8	Present value (10%)				(10,000)	4,545	3,306	2,254	1,366	621	2,092	
9	Cumulative discounted cashflow				(10,000)	(5,455)	(2,149)	105	1,471	2,092		
10												
11	Payback				0	0	2.95341	0	0	0	2.95341	
12	No of months										35	
13	Payback in words										2 years 11 months	

In row 8 the cashflows have been discounted by 10% to find their present values.

Row 9 adds the present value amounts to find the cumulative NPV.

Rows 11, 12 and 13 contain the same formulae as those used for the previous payback calculation.

Internal rate of return

There are two problems associated with using NPV as a measure:

- ☑ The discount rate has to be calculated or assumed in advance.
- ☑ The size and scale of projects are infinitely variable, so the NPV of one project cannot be easily compared with another.

To compensate for these it is possible to use a form of breakeven analysis that identifies the interest rate where the project has an NPV of zero (it can also be known as the highest interest rate the project could support before generating a negative NPV). This point is known as the internal rate of return or IRR.

Take the project used above and apply a discount rate of 20%, as shown in Chart 15.13. The following charts are for illustrative purposes only and do not form part of a detailed worked example.

Chart 15.13 **Applying a discount rate**

	A	B	C	D	E	F	G	H	I	J	K
1	Model title										
2											
3	Year number	Year_number			0	1	2	3	4	5	Total
4	Years	Actual_years			2000	2001	2002	2003	2004	2005	
5											
6	Net cashflows										
7	Actual cashflow in year				(10,000)	5,000	4,000	3,000	2,000	1,000	5,000
8	Present value (10%)				(10,000)	4,545	3,306	2,254	1,366	621	2,092
9	Present value (20%)				(10,000)	4,167	2,778	1,736	965	402	48

As the discount rate increases so the NPV of the project will fall. The graph in Chart 15.14 shows the NPV for a range of discount rates.

Chart 15.14 **The NPV of a project with a range of interest rates**

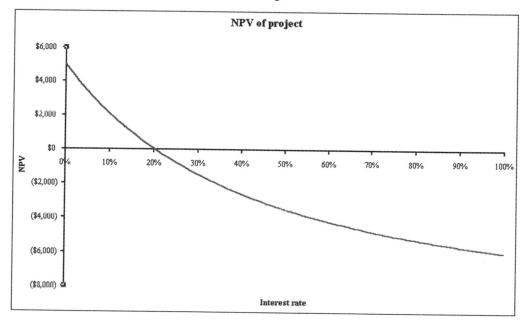

The graph is a curved shape so the IRR has to be found by trial and error or interpolation between two known points. Even spreadsheets use a trial and error iterative process to find the breakeven point. In the example it was possible to find the point almost exactly.

In spreadsheets the IRR function can be used to find the breakeven interest rate. The syntax is:

$$=IRR(range,guess)$$

The range is the cashflows in the model and the guess is the point near where the IRR is expected to be found. If no guess is used the formula assumes 10%.

Note that the range for IRR is time 0 to time N, whereas with NPV above the range is time 1 to time N.

Applying the function to the data in Chart 15.13, the IRR works out at 20.3%. The code is:

$$=IRR(E7:J7)=20.3\%$$

The IRR gives no indication of the scale of a project. It could be worth $5 or $5m.

This is probably the best method of identifying "room for error", as a high IRR means the project could underperform and still cover the WACC. Most organisations consider IRR and NPV to ensure that a large, profitable project is not rejected in favour of a smaller project with a higher rate of return.

More than one IRR

For projects that swing back and forth with years of surplus cash and years of investment, it is possible to have more than one IRR for the project. Take the example in Chart 15.15.

Chart 15.15 **A project with more than one IRR**

	D	E	F	G	H	I	J	K	L	M
1										
2										
3	Year	0	1	2	3	4	5	6	7	8
4										
5	Cashflow	(100)	(500)	(50)	500	1,000	500	0	(500)	(1,000)

The graph of NPV values for different interest rates is shown in Chart 15.16.

Chart 15.16 **NPV of a project with different interest rates**

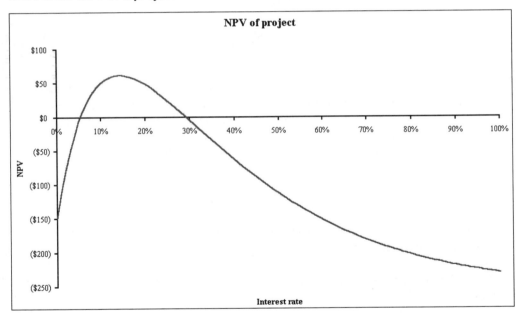

There are two IRR points. One is at about 5% and the other at around 29%. Which is correct? Mathematically, both are correct. For investment purposes, the shape of the graph shows that this project will be successful if interest rates are more than 5% but less than 29%.

Using the IRR function in a spreadsheet can give unpredictable results, and for this set of data:

IRR(E5:M5,10%)=5.4%
IRR(E5:M5,30%)=29.3%

This problem arises only if there is more than one change of sign in the series of cashflow data. If the project profile follows the typical investment in early years followed by a surplus in later years, there will be only one IRR point.

SUMMARY

Because of the problems of taking any one of the value measures it is normal for a project to be assessed using all four measures:

- The payback
- The NPV at the company WACC
- The discounted payback at the company WACC
- The project IRR

Only by using this set of measures is it possible both to compare options within projects and to make comparisons with other projects.

All the discounting techniques explained above are only as accurate as the underlying cashflows from which they are calculated. Therefore in any business proposal it is vital that the time is spent making the model assumptions as accurate as possible.

With discounting techniques "garbage in = garbage out".

16 Analytical ratios and reviewing the financial statements

In building a model to explore the potential of a project the output area typically presents results in the form of a profit and loss account, cashflow statement and balance sheet. These results portray the potential consequence of one set of assumptions. By creating a model to project results for a number of years, different assumptions can be used to obtain different sets of results. This will enable the best way forward to be identified. This chapter looks at ways of evaluating the quality of a project to help modellers make choices between different scenarios.

To evaluate any project it is necessary to identify quantitative criteria that define its success. For example, a model built to evaluate the acquisition or disposal of a business focuses on one crucial factor – the price. Therefore as different scenarios are entered into the input area they can be evaluated in terms of the changes in price that result.

In many companies an overall success factor is applied to all projects, whether they are for business reorganisation, asset purchase, budgeting or strategic planning – the enhancement of shareholder value. A model can then be used to quantify the change in shareholder value that is created by alternative scenarios.

SHAREHOLDER VALUE

The objective for most organisations is to deliver a growing return to shareholders (the owners in the case of an unincorporated business or partnership). This is achieved by generating growing profits and realising them in cash. The cash can then be used for reinvestment in the business, repayment of funding or distribution to shareholders.

Chart 16.1 **Shareholder value framework**

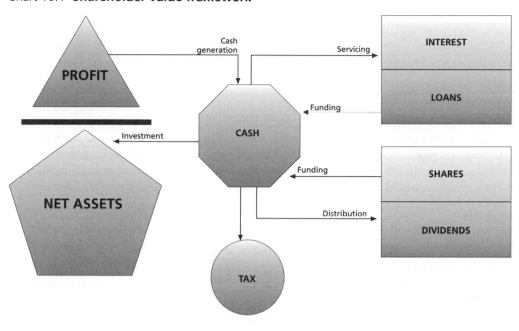

One common method of quantifying shareholder value is to calculate the net present value (NPV) of the future cashflows generated by a project (see Chapter 15 for the principles of discounted cashflow). The result gives a single number that represents the worth of the whole project today.

This shareholder value number may be helpful in overall terms, but it can be difficult to use when analysing the detailed elements of a project. What is needed is a set of indicators that, while being congruent with the principle of shareholder value, provides information about a range of project attributes. These indicators are known as ratios.

Ratio analysis

Ratios provide indicators that through comparison enable the identification of the strengths and weaknesses of the project. The benefit of ratios is that in comparison they remove the effects of scale, inflation and foreign currency. Thus they can be easily generated and applied.

Ratios fall into two categories:

- ▧ External analysis – measures of business performance for investors, bankers or suppliers to monitor the performance and risk of their money.
- ▧ Internal analysis – measures of operational performance to provide early-warning systems to management for project control.

This chapter concentrates on the second category, which will help in the evolution of a model and the assumptions used to determine results. The first category is covered in *The Economist Guide to Analysing Companies*.

INTERNAL RATIO ANALYSIS

These ratios quantify the relationship between different outputs of a project, such as profit as a percentage of sales (usually known as the profit margin). This ratio indicates the proportion of sales income that is turned into profit after costs have been deducted.

On its own a profit margin number could be fairly meaningless. The benefit of the ratio is realised when one year of data is compared with similar calculations for other years and indeed similar projects or competitors (the process of benchmarking). The profit margin may be rising or falling over time indicting potential strength or weakness in a project. If a project has a rising profit margin that makes it more profitable over time, this could be because of cost efficiencies or price increases. To identify why the profit margin is rising other ratios are needed. Therefore from a complete set of ratios a qualitative judgment can be made about the implementation of a project.

The benefit of using a model is that in the output area, spreadsheet formulae can be used to calculate a wide range of ratios over a number of years. From these ratios the data trends can be identified. These trends enable the performance of a project to be challenged as well as the identification of attributes that are improving or deteriorating over time.

There are three potential causes for declines or unusual blips in the performance:

- ◪ They are genuine attributes of the project.
- ◪ Invalid assumptions have been entered in the input area.
- ◪ Formulae errors have made inappropriate calculations with the inputs.

The first response should be to investigate and correct any formulae errors before adjusting a valid assumption. Methods to do this are described in Chapter 17.

In evaluating a model's results it is important to remember that the results are only as good as the input assumptions. Only if the model is realistic will it generate results that can support decisions. Too often managers are convinced that their project will be successful. They will adjust the project assumptions unrealistically until the outputs become presentable. Using a model to dismiss a project is just as valid as using it to approve a project.

In analysing the ratios for a model the appropriate response is to identify any weaknesses, not to tweak the assumptions until the ratios look good. The response may give rise to a genuine change of an assumption, but more realistically it could involve identifying alternative methods of operating the project and potentially recoding some of the working page to reflect this.

INTERPRETING RATIOS

Much of the interpretation of ratios is judgment, but there are some helpful functions that can be built in to aid the user.

Average

The first is to calculate the average of a set of ratios and thus identify the above and below years.

The function is:

$$=AVERAGE(range\ of\ values)$$

Rank

The final year that is modelled should be more successful than earlier years and therefore it can be helpful to know where the final year ranks in order of performance.

The function is:

$$=RANK(final\ year\ value,range\ of\ values)$$

Both of the above functions can be added in the column after the final year of the model. Other evaluation techniques require tests to be applied to the ratios and the results stored and totalled. These include the following:

High and low values

It can be helpful to know the range of ratio results and therefore to know whether there is a significant issue over the life of the project. This can be found by using the MAX and MIN function over the range of results.

Ratios moving in the right direction

It can be helpful to quantify or percentage the number of ratios that are moving in the right way (depending on the ratio this can be up, down or static).

Ways to apply this are shown in Chart 16.2.

Chart 16.2 **Evaluating how often the margin rises**

	A	B	C	D	E	F	G	H	I	J
1	Model title									
2										
3	Year number	Year_number			0	1	2	3	4	5
4	Years	Actual_years			2000	2001	2002	2003	2004	2005
5										
6										
7	Profit and loss									
8	Profit margin				5.40%	6.30%	8.20%	6.50%	5.40%	6.30%
9										
10	Margin growing	Margin_growing				1	1	0	0	1
11	Total growing					3	60%			

The calculations for year 2 are shown in Chart 16.3.

Chart 16.3 **Code for evaluating how often the margin rises**

Cell	Calculation	Actual calculation	Answer
G10	=IF(G8>F8,1,0)	=IF(8.2%>6.3%,1,0)	1
F11	=SUM(*Margin_growing*)	=SUM(F10:J10)	3
G11	=F11/(Number of years−1)	=3/(6−1)	60%

Note that as the function is looking at changes between years, there should be no calculation in the first year (column E in this example). The total number of years for the calculation is number of columns displayed −1.

USEFUL RATIOS TO CALCULATE

Below are listed some of the most common performance measures that can be used to evaluate a model. Their appropriateness will depend on the industry and situation being modelled.

Return on net assets (RONA)

The left-hand side of the shareholder value framework model shown in Chart 16.1 is driven from the basis of making a return on the cash invested in net assets. This return can be measured as a percentage. The percentage should be greater than the possible return from investing the cash in alternative options that have lower risk. Therefore the return must be greater than the bank deposit rate to be viable. Most top 100 companies have a return on net assets (RONA) in the region of 15–25%.

The calculation is:

$$\frac{\text{Operating profit (before interest, tax and non-operating activities)}}{\text{Net assets (operating fixed assets+stock+debtors−creditors)}}$$

Many textbooks will describe this as a return on investment or a return on capital employed. When dealing with these ratios it is worth knowing that there are many different methods of calculation that are used and there is no simple method of calculating a definitive rate of return. For example, sometimes the denominator is defined as "loans + shareholder funds", and from a shareholder perspective an after-tax profit may be more appropriate than one before. All these measures are ways of analysing the same profit and loss account and balance sheet. RONA is perhaps the most practical measure for operational use. This is because it defines the return in terms of the operational items created by the project. It ignores the funding items that are usually the prerogative of the treasury or finance department. The most important consideration is consistency; state the method used and thus the implication or interpretation.

Cash is deliberately omitted from this calculation for two reasons. First, operating profit excludes the interest earned from deposits. Second, cash can be considered as having drawn down too much in loans rather than being an operating asset.

Debtors and creditors will normally be limited to trading components. Items such as tax accruals should be excluded as they are not part of operating profit, nor can managers directly influence them.

When analysing RONA over time a business is looking for a sustainable return that reflects the risk of the project being undertaken.

The advantages and disadvantages of RONA are listed in Chart 16.4.

Chart 16.4 **Advantages and disadvantages of RONA**

Advantages	*Disadvantages*
• Does not reflect the growth in the business, as the return is independent of the size of business.	• Start-ups will take a while to deliver returns and the measure does not take into account the long-term potential.
• The measure is an average from all assets regardless of their individual risks.	• The measure can dissuade investors as early project years can cause a decline in return.
• Ultimately a business or project must generate a good return to justify its existence.	• A scenario with more costs and less capital can give better short-term returns.
• Easily understood by managers, as the measure is similar to an interest rate on a savings account.	• Over time depreciation will reduce the value of fixed assets and enhance the return. Fixed assets should be revalued to a market value for a fair measure.

Return on average capital employed (ROACE)

Where a business is growing rapidly its net assets can rise significantly, so it may be more appropriate to calculate a return based on the average net assets employed during the period. This measure is known as return on average capital employed (ROACE). It is calculated by taking the operating profit for the year and dividing it by the average of the opening and closing net assets.

Return on equity (ROE)

This section would not be complete without return on equity (ROE), a measure that has perhaps the strongest link to shareholder value. It is calculated as a percentage of the profit attributable to shareholders (usually after interest, tax and removal of minority interest) divided by shareholder equity (share capital + share premium + undistributable reserves). The measure shows how well the board is making the shareholders' money work.

THE DU PONT PYRAMID OF RATIOS

From RONA stem a number of supporting measures that can be combined into one framework known as the Du Pont pyramid of ratios.

Chart 16.5 **The Du Pont pyramid of ratios**

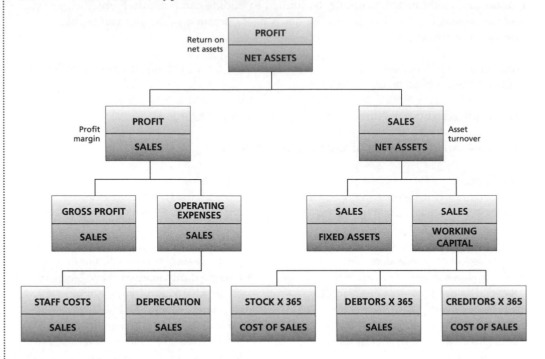

Profit margin and asset turnover

Below RONA are two measures known as the profit margin and asset turnover. The first of these, profit margin, helps evaluate the quality of profit management. The second, asset turnover, helps evaluate the quality of balance sheet management.

Profit margin

For every $1 of sales this ratio indicates the amount of operating profit achieved. It is calculated as a percentage as follows:

$$\frac{\text{Operating profit}}{\text{Sales}} \%$$

Operating profit is defined the same as for RONA and is the profit before interest, tax and non-operating items. Sales exclude any sales tax such as VAT.

In reviewing this measure the percentage should be maintained or growing over time. As the sales volume of a business grows there can be economies of scale that will often help increase the margin. The economies of scale are derived from fixed costs, such as accounting, IT and human resources, which typically do not rise as fast as sales. The costs of these departments are mainly payroll, and the headcount may stay constant over a range of sales volume levels. Conversely, as a business reduces in size it is difficult to remove these fixed costs and a margin can therefore decline.

RONA can be compared with any business, as it is a uniform indicator. However, the profit margin is particular to an industry. For example, a food retailer typically has low margins compared with telecoms operator, which has higher margins. This does not imply one company is better than another, only that the cost structure of each business is different. For a food retailer, most of the costs are in the purchase of groceries in the cost of sales, whereas for a telecoms operator the costs are mainly in the network, which is capitalised as a fixed asset.

Asset turnover

Asset turnover measures the amount of sales achieved for every $1 of money invested in the company's net assets. It is a factor and is calculated as follows:

$$\frac{\text{Sales}}{\text{Net assets}}$$

The value of sales is the same as that used for the profit margin. The net assets are the same as those used for the RONA.

The objective with the asset turnover is to achieve high asset utilisation. So if a business has invested in assets, they should be used to generate sales income. For an airline this is a key factor: the higher the seat occupancy in an aircraft, the greater is the asset turnover. However, in pursuing strategies to enhance asset turnover it is important to allow for downtime and maintenance.

Like the profit margin, the asset turnover is particular to an industry.

It is clear from the calculations for profit margin and asset turnover that sales is a common factor. RONA can be expressed as profit margin multiplied by asset turnover. For example, the RONA of a food retailer might be 5% margin × 3 asset turnover = 15%. Compare this with the RONA of a telecoms company, which might be 15% margin × 1 asset turnover = 15%. These two industries achieve a similar RONA but earn it in very different ways.

In reviewing the results of a model it is important to look at how these two measures interact. For example, a project may be to consider outsourcing manufacturing. The effect might be that net assets would fall with the sale of equipment and production costs would rise, with the payments to the outsource company exceeding the previous operating and staff costs. This would cause an increase in asset turnover and a decrease in profit margin. Ignoring non-financial factors, the decision would be worthwhile only if the overall RONA increased.

Thus if either the asset turnover or the margin falls during a project, then the other must rise to compensate and maintain the RONA.

Percentage of sales measures

On the left-hand side of the pyramid in Chart 16.5 is a set of measures that express each part of the profit and loss account as a percentage of sales. These include gross profit and operating expenses as subtotals, which are then broken down further into individual lines of staff costs, depreciation, administration, marketing, and so on.

These measures are effective in monitoring trends in component costs. For example, the staff cost percentage should stay reasonably constant year on year. If the ratio starts to rise, then the business may be paying too high salaries or becoming less productive. Both are indicators of unsustainable performance that will lead to profit decline.

This set of measures expressing everything on the profit and loss account as a percentage of sales is also known as vertical analysis. It provides a quick way to evaluate the cost structure of the business as it develops over the years of the model.

Balance sheet management

On the right-hand side of the pyramid in Chart 16.5 is a series of balance sheet measures. The first two are known as fixed asset turnover and working capital turnover (working capital is defined as stock + debtors − creditors).

Fixed asset turnover

This monitors what is sometimes known as the "sweat" of assets. The purpose of assets is to work for the company. This ratio comparing fixed assets with sales indicates how well this happens. A decline in the ratio may indicate that the company is over-provided with assets and could free up capital with some disposals. Rapid growth in the ratio may indicate that capacity constraints have been reached and more time for maintenance and repairs should be considered.

The ratio is normally confined to just tangible fixed assets – the ones used operationally. Intangible assets included in the ratio (or evaluated individually) can give rise to some strange results over the life of a model which do not help in interpreting performance. For example, goodwill may be amortised and hence the ratio is likely to rise year on year for this reason alone.

Working capital turnover

This measure indicates how well the cash cycle of stock, debtors and creditors is managed.

Chart 16.6 **Cashflow cycle**

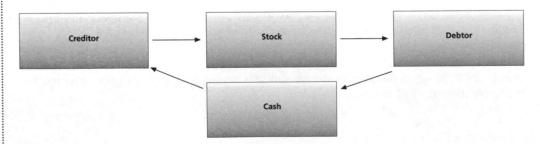

Cash is paid to a supplier who provides stock. The stock is converted to finished goods or held in a warehouse until purchased by a customer. The customer pays an invoice to bring cash back into the business. With both suppliers and customers having credit terms, the issue to manage is how long it takes cash to complete the cycle. Money tied up in this cycle has to be funded and can significantly drain the resources required for investment and to grow the company.

The overall working capital ratio can be broken down into the individual elements. These are usually referred to as day measures.

Stock days – the amount of time stock is held on site from the moment it arrives to the moment it is dispatched. It is calculated as:

$$\frac{Stock * 365}{Cost\ of\ sales}$$

Debtor days – the time taken for customers to pay their invoices. It is calculated as:

$$\frac{Debtors * 365}{Sales}$$

Creditor days – the time taken to pay suppliers' invoices. It is calculated as:

$$\frac{Creditors * 365}{Cost\ of\ sales}$$

In each of these three measures the denominator reflects an annual level of activity in the same terms as the numerator. For example, stock excludes profit and therefore cost of sales is the best approximation to annual level of stock consumption.

These ratios should stay reasonably constant over the life of the model and may indeed be set up as assumptions used in reverse to calculate the amount of stock, debt or credit to include in the balance sheet.

Further analysis

The pyramid of ratios in Chart 16.5 is a basic framework that provides a structure for developing a set of key operational ratios. This can be further developed as necessary for the relevant attributes of the project being modelled. For example, the stock day measures can be broken down into day measures for raw materials, work in progress and finished goods. The staff costs, as a percentage of sales, can be analysed between payroll, employment taxes, pension and other benefits. The level of detail required depends on the attributes that determine the principal drivers of value in the model being created.

SPECIFIC PROFITABILITY MEASURES

Some industries have specific profitability measures that are used to indicate performance. In developing a model it is helpful to identify and build in the measures that reviewers or sanctioners will need to support their evaluation and approval.

A common measure is earnings before interest, tax, depreciation and amortisation, or EBITDA. This is used instead of operating profit where the industry is heavily capital intensive. The number shows the amount of profit made from trading before the cost of its annual share of the capital investment. In fast-growing capital industries such as telecoms, it is a good indicator of whether the core operations are being managed successfully before the depreciation cost of the long-term investment of the cable network.

EBITDA can be compared with sales to give a profit-margin type measure, as explained above. These are sometimes extended, with five-year moving averages used to smooth the annual fluctuations and give a trend result for the business's performance.

INVESTMENT MEASURES

There are several capital expenditure measures that help monitor the performance of the investment being made.

Reinvestment ratio

This explores capital expenditure each year compared with depreciation for each year. If the measure is more than 100%, then the company is investing more than it depreciates, so growth in profitability should be taking place to make the investment justifiable. If the ratio is less than 100%, the business may be milking its assets and moving towards an unsustainable state.

Investment funding

Where is the money coming from to fund new investment? By comparing the cashflow generated before capital investment and financing costs with the amount invested, it can be seen whether the company is growing through organic development or external support. In the early years of a new project there is likely to be heavy reliance on external funding, but in the longer term this should decline and move to less than 50%.

INVESTOR MEASURES

These measures are only relevant for models of whole companies rather than individual projects.

Chapter 13 covered ways to monitor the mix of debt and equity in an investment. The measures here cover the traditional per share measures as well as the newer shareholder value cashflow measures.

Earnings per share

This identifies the amount of profit available to a holder of one share after all costs have been met. It is calculated by taking the profit after tax and dividing by the number of shares in issue. Complications arise when there are subsequent share issues or scrip issues, as earlier figures have to be adjusted to reflect the impact. Although these occur in real life, most models need not be concerned with such events.

Dividend cover

This measures the ability of a company to pay and sustain its dividend. It takes the earnings and divides it by the dividend amount. In the long term the ratio should stay constant or rise. A decline in the ratio may indicate that despite falling earnings the company is maintaining the level of dividend paid out and that it is raising its dividend faster than it is able to generate the earnings needed to fund the cost.

NEW MEASURES

In the 1980s and 1990s, consultancies developed new measures that have been found to have a better correlation between financial performance and share price for investors than those mentioned above. These measures are more commonly cashflow based, removing the distortions that are sometimes created by accounting policies used in traditional profit measures. They also try to reflect risk more genuinely than can simple RONA measures.

One of the most common is economic value added (EVA), developed by Stern Stewart. This is the amount of value created over and above the amount required to keep investors satisfied. It is calculated as:

$$EVA=(R-COC)\times Capital\ invested$$

$$R=Net\ operating\ profit\ after\ tax/Average\ capital$$

$$COC=Cost\ of\ capital\ (weighted\ average\ cost\ of\ capital\ after\ tax\ cost\ of\ debt\ and\ equity)$$

$$Capital=Total\ capital\ invested$$

Detailed adjustments are made to arrive at the figures for net operating profit after tax and cost of capital, so this measure has been described as "difficult" for operational managers to apply when evaluating the impact of their actions.

Other measures have similar complexity in trying to create a balance between four core factors of success: return, growth, cost of capital and free cashflow.

17 Testing and debugging

THE IMPORTANCE OF TESTING AND DEBUGGING

A typical spreadsheet user will make a keystroke error once every 30 strokes. Fortunately, most of the errors will be spotted and dealt with immediately. However, a number will remain undetected. Ironically, for a book concerned with forecasting, the only thing that can be predicted with any degree of certainty is that a completed model will contain bugs. The wrong decision, based partly on a flawed model, can be extremely costly, especially when major investments or strategic choices rest on the model's outputs.

For a model to be relied upon with confidence it must have credibility among those who use it. To be credible it must meet three important criteria:

- ✓ It must be technically accurate.
- ✓ It must provide a realistic description of the environment, or the expected future environment, in order to produce useful forecasts.
- ✓ It must be easy and quick to use.

TYPES OF ERRORS

The key components of model credibility provide a simple framework for classifying different types of errors.

Technical errors

These are caused by the incorrect formulation of an idea, principle or concept. Typical technical errors include referencing the wrong cells, the incorrect use of brackets and pure mathematical formulation errors. Even when a model contains no technical errors, however, it may still fail to deliver intuitive results because of a conceptual flaw.

Conceptual errors

These constitute a flaw in the logic, the rationale or the mechanisms depicted in the model. As the business modelling process map in Chapter 6 (Chart 6.1, page 33) indicated, developing an understanding of the logical flows and the relationships within the environment is an iterative process. The testing phase offers the modeller another opportunity to increase and test his or her understanding of the business.

User errors

These occur in poorly structured and badly documented models with limited checks on user inputs and inadequately trained users. The problems may arise as a result of human error, but the fundamental problem often lies with the design of the model.

Allow time for testing

A testing and debugging strategy must ensure the identification and removal of as many of the three types of errors as possible. The project plan must allow enough time for this important task. How much time will depend on the complexity and size of the model. If others will be using the model, time also needs to be allocated for user testing. The time required for testing, however, will be dramatically reduced if the key principles of model design (see Chapter 8) have been used from the outset. Despite the modeller's best efforts, a number of errors are likely to remain undetected. The objective of the testing and debugging strategy is to eliminate the errors that would alter significantly the model's outputs and hence influence the decision-making process.

TESTING STRATEGY

Ideally, the individual who developed the model would not be responsible for testing the model. In large organisations the internal audit department may perform this function. In the absence of a dedicated department, a peer review by a colleague would be a valuable alternative. In smaller businesses the modeller will often also be responsible for testing. To ensure that the process is carried out effectively the modeller should follow a clear testing strategy.

The testing strategy can be used throughout the development of the model. In the case of a large and complex model, the strategy can be applied to a particular sheet or even a working, once they have been completed. During the development of the model the modeller should use only the relevant testing strategy. This usually means applying step 1 of the four-stage process described below.

The testing strategy aims to eliminate all technical errors first so that the conceptual design of the model can be tested in isolation. By following the four-stage approach in Chart 17.1, the tester will not be attempting to solve a conceptual design fault when the failure to produce the expected result was simply the result of a typing mistake, which had given rise to a technical error.

Chart 17.1 **Four-stage testing and debugging strategy**

Step 1	Eliminate technical and conceptual flaws
Step 2	Range test the model
Step 3	Stress test the model
Step 4	User testing

At the testing phase, strict version control will be required (see Chapter 6), as the model is likely to evolve swiftly and many changes, often subtle, will be made. Before starting to examine the model the modeller should ensure that all hidden columns and rows are revealed to ensure that every cell potentially containing an error is reviewed.

STEP 1: ELIMINATE TECHNICAL AND CONCEPTUAL FLAWS

Step 1 provides the main body of the testing and should quickly identify most of the technical errors. This stage may also highlight some obvious conceptual flaws.

Perform a manual code review

Technical and conceptual flaws can be identified through testing the model's ability to reproduce known results, both at the final output stage and at the individual workings level. The model should be fully populated with a set of simple data inputs. These simple inputs should be whole integers, such as 10 or 1. Provided that the modeller has adopted the principle of avoiding complex formulae, the workings can be checked manually using mental arithmetic or a calculator. Simple test data will highlight some obvious flaws within the model, but the modeller should be aware of the possibility of compensating errors, where two errors of equal magnitude but of opposite sign cancel out. The modeller may be asked to review somebody else's model, which may not reflect the important principle of using simple formulae. In such cases, the complexity of the formulae may force the modeller to deconstruct them before inspection.

Deconstruct complex formulae

If a formula is extremely complex, including multiple nested IF statements, for example, and is difficult to review in the formula window of the spreadsheet, it may be useful to break it down into smaller, more manageable components. This can be done, while protecting the integrity of the model, by highlighting the formula in the formula window and using COPY→ESCAPE and then moving to a free range of cells and using PASTE. The formula has now been replicated and the references to other cells maintained. The same PASTE command can then be used again to reproduce the same formula in as many cells as there are complex elements of the formula. The developer can then strip away parts of the formula by selectively using delete so that the results of each stage of the calculation can be examined separately. An example of deconstructing a formula for a simple, non-business problem is shown in Chart 17.2.

Chart 17.2 **Deconstructing a formula**

	A	B	C	D	E	F	G	H	I
1	Radius	*Radius*			5				
2	Output selection	*Output*			3	(1 = Circumference, 2 = Area, 3 = Volume)			
3	Result				**339.3**				
4									
5					Original	Corrected			
6	Full formulae				339.3				
7	Component 1				31.4				
8	Component 2				78.5				
9	Component 3				339.3	523.6			

Row 1 of the example requests an input for the radius of a circle. The second row asks the user to select which output is required. The user enters 1 for the circumference of a circle, 2 for the area and 3 for the volume. The original formula does not seem to calculate the volume of a sphere correctly. The formula has been deconstructed in rows 5 to 9. The detailed workings are shown in Chart 17.3. All the workings relate to column E unless stated otherwise. Cell E1 has been given the range name *Radius* and cell E2 has been given the range name *Output*.

Chart 17.3 **Detailed calculations for deconstructing a formula**

Row	Calculation	Actual calculation	Answer
Radius	Input	Input	5
Output	Input	Input	3
Result	=IF(*Output*=1,2*PI()*Radius*, IF(*Output*=2,PI()*(*Radius*^2), 4*PI()*Output*^3))	=4×3.14×(3^3)	339.3
Original	=IF(*Output*=1,2*PI()*Radius*, IF(*Output*=2,PI()*(*Radius*^2), 4*PI()*Output*^3))	=4×3.14×(3^3)	339.3
Component 1	=2*PI()*Radius*	=2*3.14*5	31.4
Component 2	=PI()*(*Radius*^2)	=3.14×(5^2)	78.5
Component 3	=4*PI()*(*Output*^3)	=4*3.14*(3^3)	339.3
Corrected component 3 (column F)	=4/3*PI()*(*Radius*^3)	=4/3×3.14×(5^3)	523.6

A quick manual review of each component highlights that component 3 is the element of the formula that contains an error. Once an erroneous component has been identified, the first thing to check is that the model is referencing the correct cells from elsewhere in the model.

Use the auditing toolbar

A useful tool for tracing the cells that feed into a formula is the auditing toolbar of Excel or its equivalent. TOOLS→AUDITING→SHOW AUDITING TOOLBAR should reveal the auditing toolbar. Clicking on the icon TRACE PRECEDENTS will provide arrows from all the cells featuring in the formula. Double clicking on the arrows will take you to that particular cell. The user can quickly check that the appropriate cells are being used in the formula. If this technique is applied to cell E9, it will soon be clear that the formula is incorrectly referenced to the output row rather than the radius row. The use of range names reduces the incidence of misreferencing cells and makes auditing the formulae much more straightforward. In this example, a simple examination of the cell would have been sufficient to identify an incorrect reference. The corrected formula can be entered in column F, adjacent to the cell containing the error.

Examine mathematical operations

Once all the references have been checked, the modeller can conclude that the error arises in the calculations within each component or in the interaction between the various components. Examining the incremental breakdown of a formula allows the combination of individual components' results to be checked manually. Errors can also be caused by the incorrect use of brackets combined with the spreadsheet's sequential approach to mathematical operations. These types of errors should be eliminated. In this example, the formula has been incorrectly entered, representing a flaw in the logic.

Rather than entering the correct formula for the volume of a sphere:

$$=4/3*PI()*(Radius^3)$$

the following formula, corrected for the misreferenced cell, was entered:

$$=4*PI()*(Radius^3)$$

The modeller should continue to deconstruct formulae and check the cell references and mathematical operations until the problem has been identified. The correct formula for the component can then be developed, and the corrected formula can be copied and pasted over the original incorrect component via the formula window.

Check column and row consistency

Once the modeller is happy with the results of an individual column, he should check that the same formula appears in each year. As the modeller has used identical test data for each period, the results should be the same in each column. However, in the case of cash balances, where the results are developed from the results of the previous period, this will not be the case. A useful tool for checking row and column inconsistencies is Excel's GO TO function.

- ◪ Highlight the block of cells to be reviewed.
- ◪ From the EDIT menu select GO TO→SPECIAL.
- ◪ In the dialog box that appears select ROW DIFFERENCES.

The model will automatically move to a cell that is different from any other cells within the row. Any differences should be examined and then corrected. If the error persists, the modeller should recognise that the error might be in a preceding working. Once again, the use of the audit toolbar to trace cells referenced by the formula and the use of simple, identical data will allow the modeller to find and correct the rogue cell quickly.

Having tested the model in detail, using simple test data, the modeller should employ a number of additional error-busting techniques before using actual data.

Use FIND to locate hidden errors

During the development process, columns, rows and even sheets containing cells that were referenced elsewhere in the model may be deleted. Normally, this action would result in a #REF! error indicating that the referenced cell no longer existed. In some instances, such as where an IF statement has been used, the #REF! error may not actually appear under a certain set of assumptions within the model. Only when the conditions affecting the IF statement change will the #REF! error make itself known.

By selecting EDIT→FIND and then typing #REF!, the spreadsheet will search the entire sheet for instances of #REF!. These can then be corrected. Exactly the same search and correct technique should be used with the other common errors #N/A! and DIV/o!.

Set all inputs to zero

In normal use, input cells will be populated with data producing results that do not interfere with the normal operation of the model. However, users may place a zero or even no input into a key cell. If, at any stage, the spreadsheet attempts to divide by zero a #DIV/o! error will be reported. These #DIV/o! cell results can then affect all the dependent cells with the same error message. Often the whole model will be awash with #DIV/o!, particularly when its financial performance is derived from a large number of endogenous variables.

The modeller should set all input cells to zero and use the FIND function described above to identify all cells containing #DIV/o!. Two of the simplest solutions for avoiding the #DIV/o! result are to use either the ISERROR function or an IF statement. These approaches were discussed in Chapter 7.

Manage circular references

Circular references can often be introduced erroneously into a model. The spreadsheet will usually provide a warning that a circular reference has been established and the modeller can use the auditing feature to trace the dependencies and make the appropriate corrections. However, if a circular reference is an integral part of the design, such as in the case of interest calculations, then the spreadsheet package must be instructed to find a set of values that satisfy the circularity. The values represent an equilibrium that is effectively the solution to a set of simultaneous equations. To allow the spreadsheet to solve the circular reference, the modeller should select TOOLS→OPTIONS→CALCULATION TAB→ITERATION. The model uses an iterative process where a range of values is used until a consistent set of results is found.

Additional error handling may be required in the presence of circular references because if, for example, a #DIV/o!, #N/A! or #REF! occurs the model will be unable to find a solution and the errors become compounded by the circularity. This is common in the case of items that influence all the financial statements such as taxation, cash and dividend calculations. Tracing the source of the circularity can be quite difficult, even with the help of the auditing feature. Often it is easier to select one column and to delete the suspect cells in turn (confident in the knowledge that the cell can be reproduced by simply copying the formula from an adjacent column) until the error is eliminated. This technique will pinpoint the offending cell generating the error within the circular reference. An error-trapping formula will be required in the cell, and the use of the ISERROR function or an IF statement will usually be required. Now, when the conditions are such that an error would have occurred, the model can continue to function. Separate warnings can be incorporated into the model to inform the user that an erroneous input has been made.

Having used simple test data and the error detection techniques described above, the modeller can begin to feel confident that the majority of technical errors have been identified and eliminated. The next stage is to attempt to replicate historic known results.

Replicate actual results

The modeller should populate the model's input assumptions with recent historic data and the outputs of the model should be compared with the actual results. This stage of the testing process begins to examine the model's predictive power. Any significant differences between the model's outputs and the actual results are likely to be caused by conceptual flaws in the model design, although some technical errors may remain and the modeller should be on guard for them.

The process of solving the conceptual issues is an iterative one, and it can be a valuable part of the modelling experience. Attempting to reproduce actual results both tests and challenges the understanding of the economics of the business and may provide new insights. Modellers should re-examine initial assumptions regarding the critical factors and logic flows that they believed characterised the business. Alternative structures should be considered and tested in the model. Eventually, a revised set of critical factors and relationships will evolve which, once incorporated into the model, reproduce the historic results. Any significant changes to the model may have introduced new errors, so the modeller should repeat step 1 of the checking strategy for any amended code. The purpose of the modelling exercise is to examine possible future environments, and the next step explores model performance over a range of different future operating conditions.

STEP 2: RANGE TEST THE MODEL

Step 2 is as much about learning as it is about testing the model's ability to produce intuitive results. It consists of two stages.

- Stage one examines the performance of the model under a number of possible or likely scenarios.
- Stage two examines the model's performance at the extreme edges of the expected possible future environments in which the business may operate.

Test likely scenarios

Once the model has been populated with data representing a scenario, modellers should compare the results from the model with their expectations. Any significant differences should be examined and either the model's design altered or the expectations and understanding of the possible future environments amended.

Test the model's performance under extreme inputs

A crucial requirement for the model is the ability to produce meaningful results over a full range of possible future scenarios. The modeller should identify a number of key model inputs and produce a test dataset that covers the extremes for these variables. Price levels will often be such a variable, and the modeller may use major price reductions, or even giving the product away for free, as one of the extreme inputs. These extreme values should be examined individually by placing each input, in turn, in the model and recording the results. Although the results from the model may be unlikely, they should at least be plausible and intuitive. The causes of implausible results should be identified and the model amended as required.

Combine a number of extreme inputs

The extreme inputs were originally entered separately. In order to examine the model at the limit, a number of extreme inputs should be entered simultaneously. Once again, the results will be unlikely, but they should remain intuitive. It is worth examining the results of these tests closely as they may shed light on an entirely new business design structure. The concept of free Internet access, as first developed by Freeserve in the UK, could easily have evolved from a similar testing exercise as the one described here.

Having eliminated most technical errors and examined the predictive power of the model, the third stage of the testing process begins.

STEP 3: STRESS TEST THE MODEL

The objective of this testing stage is to examine the model's ability to cope with inappropriate or unexpected inputs that might be made by an inexperienced user. Of course, error checking should already be in place to prevent erroneous entries by the user. Inevitably user errors will occur, however, and the typical input errors detailed below should be tested:

- Negative values when positive values were expected and vice versa.
- Text when numbers were expected and vice versa.
- Wide ranges of inputs.
- Very large or very small values.
- Decimals when an integer was required.
- Decimal places in the wrong place.
- Date ranges in reverse order; for example, from 31/12/2000 to 12/31/2000.
- Zero inputs.
- All inputs deleted so that the cell is blank.

Clear documentation, and the use of checks on inputs (see Chapter 8), can reduce the incidence of user error. As the model is tested using the common entry mistakes described above, whenever an error arises the modeller can incorporate error-trapping techniques, such as the ISERROR function, to prevent the model from failing completely. The modeller can also test the feedback the model gives to the user, such as warning messages.

Having completed steps 1–3, the modeller is ready to beta test the model. Beta testing involves a typical user testing the model for ease of use.

STEP 4: USER TESTING

A number of potential users, with differing levels of ability and from different disciplines, should be given one of the historic or scenario-based datasets used earlier in the testing phase and asked to populate the model with the data and produce a set of results. Using the same datasets that were employed in earlier testing will allow the quick identification of any errors.

The modeller should observe how the user interacts with the model. In particular, the modeller should observe and make notes on the following important areas for modification:

- Whether the model's layout and design are intuitive.
- How easily the user navigates around the model.
- Whether the user finds the flow of data entry logical.
- Whether the user is certain of the type of input and format required.
- Whether the model provides useful feedback during use.
- Whether the model produces the results the user was expecting.
- Whether the model's documentation is appropriate and sufficient.

The modeller can debrief the users after the testing period for their feedback on the design. They will be able to make suggestions on how to improve the structure and layout, and the modeller can then make the required changes. The same users can then review the amended interfaces. Once this group of users is comfortable with the design, a new user should be invited to test the model. At this stage little further development work should be required.

At the end of this four-stage testing process nearly all the technical errors within the model will have been identified and eliminated. Some errors will inevitably persist, but the ability to reproduce a historic set of results in step 1 and the intuitive results produced in step 2 will provide reasonable assurance for the modeller that the model is a useful representation of reality. The modeller can now add the finishing touches described in Chapter 18 to ensure that the integrity of the model is maintained when it is finally used in practice.

SUMMARY OF FOUR-STEP TESTING PROCESS

Step 1: eliminate technical and conceptual flaws
- Use simple test data
- Perform manual checks
- Deconstruct complex formulae
- Use the auditing toolbar
- Examine mathematical operations
- Check column and row consistency
- Use FIND to locate hidden errors
- Set all inputs to zero
- Manage circular references
- Replicate actual results

Step 2: range test the model
- Test likely scenarios
- Test the model's performance under extreme inputs
- Combine a number of extreme inputs

Step 3: stress test the model
- Use inappropriate or unexpected inputs

Step 4: user testing
- Observe users interacting with the model
- Obtain users' feedback

18 Turning a spreadsheet into an application

CHARACTERISTICS OF A GOOD SPREADSHEET APPLICATION

Until now this book has focused on the individual elements within a model that have been developed to address a specific business problem. During the development of the model it is easy to forget that the ultimate user may not have been involved in the development process. Users have a task, project or business problem that they need to address, and they require a tool to make the process easier and more efficient and to help them produce better final results. Unfortunately, many spreadsheets are almost impossible for anyone other than the developer to use. A well-structured, bug-free spreadsheet requires a number of additional characteristics if it is to become a useful and valuable spreadsheet application that can be used by someone other than the developer.

A good spreadsheet application should be:

- easy to navigate;
- easy to enter data accurately;
- difficult to corrupt;
- easy to view on the screen;
- able to produce good-quality printed outputs.

NAVIGATION

Basic navigation

The nature of spreadsheet models is such that only a small number of spreadsheet windows can easily be viewed at any one time, which can often make navigation difficult. With only a list of sheet names at the bottom of a spreadsheet window for guidance it is easy to become disoriented in large, complex models. The problems of navigation are eased by the separation of inputs, outputs and workings and by adopting a logical sequence to the sheets within the model. The use of informative sheet names can also aid navigation. However, the first step in turning a spreadsheet into a spreadsheet application is to provide the user with specific navigation tools.

Hyperlinks

One of the quickest and easiest methods is to place a series of hyperlinks on a separate navigation page within the model. Hyperlinks, like the links on an Internet web page, allow the user to "jump" to a specific sheet.

The steps involved in creating a hyperlink are described below. The example produces a "Menu" page that contains a hyperlink to the sheet called "Results".

- Name two separate sheets "Menu" and "Results".

▰ Move to the Menu sheet and select a cell in which to place the hyperlink (cell B2 in the example).

▰ From the INSERT menu select HYPERLINK.

▰ Select BOOKMARK.

▰ Select the Results sheet and a cell reference A1 should automatically appear (this can be overwritten if desired); click OK.

▰ In "Text to Display" at the top of the dialog box enter "Results Page".

▰ Click OK.

An example of the Menu sheet is presented in Chart 18.1. Clicking on the link moves the user to cell A1 on the results sheet. The hyperlinks appear with a line underneath the text and are initially blue in colour. Once a link has been activated for the first time it changes from blue to maroon. The change in colour can act as a useful auditing device when the model is being populated with data. The user will easily be able to identify those sheets that have not been completed, as the links will still be blue. In a complex model there will be a large number of hyperlinks and they can be placed on the Menu sheet in the order that the model must be completed. Text boxes can also be added to make navigation clearer. A text box has been added in Chart 18.1. Alternatively, the text within the hyperlink itself could simply have been changed to read "Click here to review the results".

Chart 18.1 **Navigation using hyperlinks**

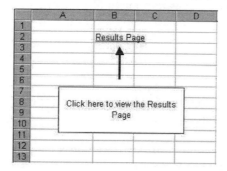

Creating a menu using Visual Basic or another macro language

Spreadsheet packages incorporate programming languages, such as Excel's Visual Basic, which allow the modeller to write a set of commands that collectively are called a program or macro. These macros allow the modeller additional control over the behaviour of the spreadsheet package. Macros can become highly complex, but some simple macro programming can create impressive navigation menus. The example in Chart 18.2 can be produced in Excel with only a limited knowledge of Visual Basic for Applications.

Chart 18.2 **Navigation menu using Visual Basic for applications**

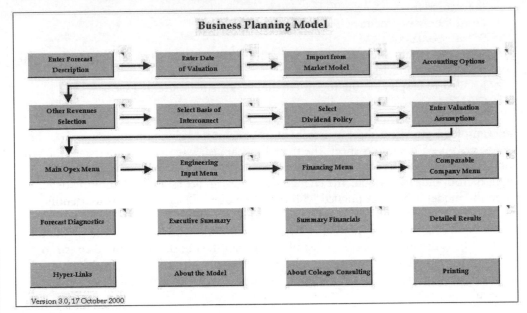

Before examining the macro code required to produce a navigation menu like the one in Chart 18.2, the next section describes how to record simple macros using Excel's macro recording feature.

Recording simple macros

The procedure for recording simple macros was introduced in Chapter 7. Here it is briefly summarised before more complex examples are considered.

The following macro is designed to place the author's name in the active cell on a spreadsheet. The first series of instructions records the macro:

- From the TOOLS menu select MACRO→RECORD NEW MACRO→OK (you can enter a different macro name if you wish).
- Type your name and press ENTER.
- From the TOOLS menu select MACRO→STOP RECORDING.

This simple set of actions will have recorded the macro. The macro does not appear like conventional code in a spreadsheet. It appears in its own language and format and must be viewed in a different type of window from the conventional spreadsheet window. The window for viewing macros is called a Visual Basic Editor.

Viewing macro code

To view the code associated with the macro, follow the steps below:

- From the TOOLS menu select MACRO→VISUAL BASIC EDITOR.

- Two windows will appear; the one on the left is called the Project Window.
- Identify the name of the workbook and double click on it.
- "Microsoft Excel Objects" appears and within that folder are all the sheets in the workbook. There is also a "Modules" folder. Double click on the modules folder to reveal all the modules. Double click on module one. The code will appear in the window on the right.

The code will be similar to the code shown in Chart 18.3.

Chart 18.3 **Recording a simple macro**

```
Sub Macro1()
'
' Macro1 Macro
' Macro recorded 20/02/2001 by A N Author
'

'
    ActiveCell.FormulaR1C1 = "A N Author"
    Range("F25").Select
End Sub
```

The start of each new macro begins with the word Sub followed by the name of the macro. The spreadsheet package automatically allocates a name to the macro unless in the steps described above the user enters a specific name for the macro being recorded. The lines commencing with an apostrophe are for information only. The line that actually performs the task is:

$$ActiveCell.FormulaR1C1="A N Author"$$

The following line

$$Range("F25").Select$$

moves the cursor to cell F25, the cell below the one in which the name was originally entered. Highlight "Range ("F25"). Select" and press DELETE, as you do not want to move cells when you run the macro.

To inform the package that the macro has ended the command "End Sub" must be present. Sub is an abbreviation for subroutine.

To return to the familiar spreadsheet window simply click on the EXCEL tab.

Running a macro

Once the macro has been recorded and the code reviewed the macro can be used to perform the task of entering the author's name into the active cell. To run a macro, follow the steps below:

▨ In the spreadsheet select a cell where you want the name to appear.
▨ From TOOLS menu select MACRO→MACROS.
▨ Select MACRO 1 (or the name of the macro you used).
▨ Press RUN.

The macro will place the author's name into the active cell. Selecting another cell and repeating the steps above will, once again, place the author's name in that cell.

Amending macro code

Once a macro has been recorded the original code can be modified to perform different tasks from the one originally recorded. Modellers can return to the Visual Basic Editor and type their own name in the code in place of the author's. When the macro is run again the newly entered name will appear. It is often easier to record and then amend a macro rather than type in the specific code.

Using Visual Basic to provide navigation

The code in Chart 18.4 can be typed directly into the Visual Basic Editor window. This code activates a sheet called "Executive Summary" and then moves to the range name *ExecStart* within that sheet. Before creating and running the macro, the modeller must set up a sheet with the name Executive Summary and type a range name, *ExecStart*, in cell A1. In the Visual Basic Editor select the workbook in the Project Window and from the INSERT menu select MODULE. The code in Chart 18.4 can be typed directly into the module.

Chart 18.4 **Navigation macro**

```
Sub ExecMove()

Sheets("Executive Summary").Activate
Application.Goto Reference:=Range("ExecStart"), scroll:=True

End Sub
```

The macro has been given the name "ExecMove". The first line of code

Sheets("Executive Summary").Activate

activates the Executive Summary sheet. The line of code beneath moves the user to the cell with the range name *ExecStart*.

Running this macro in the normal way will navigate the user to cell A1 on the Executive Summary sheet. The same code can be copied and amended, within the Visual Basic Editor, to produce a separate macro for each sheet name. For example, the following changes in the code would be required in a macro to navigate to cell A1 in a sheet called "Summary Results":

▨ Change the macro title "ExecMove" to "Summary Results".
▨ Change *ExecStart* to *SummaryResultsStart*.

A sheet name and a range name must also be created consistent with the new sheet and range names introduced above.

Attaching a macro to a button

Using the toolbar to initiate the use of a macro can be a little cumbersome. An alternative is to create a button on the spreadsheet to which the macro can be attached. Whenever the macro button is pressed the macro code will be activated.

The following steps create a button and then attach the "ExecMove" macro to the button:

- Right click in the toolbar area and from the menu select FORMS.
- Click on the BUTTON icon.
- Move to the spreadsheet and draw a rectangle.
- Select the macro "ExecMove" and press OK.
- Click on the text of the button and change it to "Executive Summary".
- Click outside the button on the spreadsheet.

The text, font and colour of the text on the button can be altered by right clicking on the macro and then clicking inside the button to access the text. If the user clicks on the button, the cursor moves to cell A1 on the Executive Summary sheet. An example of a macro button, is shown in Chart 18.5.

Chart 18.5 **A macro button**

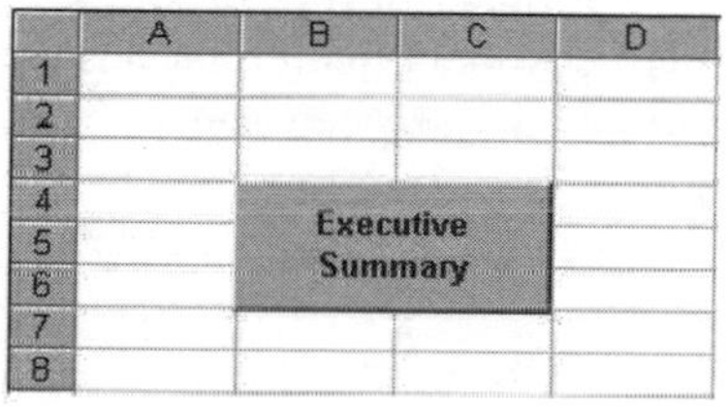

A number of buttons can be placed on a sheet to create a navigation menu. Within the body of the model itself buttons entitled "Next" and "Previous" can be used to direct the user through the model in the correct order. On each sheet a "Return to Main Menu" option should be provided. Once a button has been created with a macro attached, that button can be copied and pasted to other sheets (right click on the button and select, then paste). The same button can be reused many times and will continue to perform the same macro.

USER INPUTS

Input cell design

A good spreadsheet application should make entering the appropriate data in the right format and units in the right cell as easy as possible. The first step in achieving this goal is to make the identification of the input cells straightforward.

All input cells should look the same and should be easily distinguishable from workings or output cells. This can be achieved by giving input cells a different background colour, a different text colour and even by placing an outline around the box. The format of a cell can be altered by right clicking on the cell and selecting FORMAT CELLS. The dialog box provides a wide range of formatting options.

The user should also be given guidance on how to complete the model, possibly through cell comments and text boxes. Model documentation is discussed in detail in Chapter 20.

Built-in checks on inputs

Despite the modeller's best efforts, users will inevitably make errors in their data entry. A spreadsheet application should provide extensive entry checking. This concept was introduced in Chapter 7, where the model checked whether inputs were within a specified range.

Additional checks should be put in place. For example, the LEN function can be employed to ensure that the description used to identify a currency does not exceed three characters. Excessively long descriptions can interfere with the layout of the model.

The LEN function counts the number of characters in an input.

$$=IF(LEN(\textit{Input\_cell})>3,\text{"Error"},\text{"OK"})$$

Often a model may require the user to allocate a total across a number of subcategories. For example, the total number of gross additions to a mobile network (a figure that has already been calculated elsewhere in the model) may have to be analysed between different segments. It is important that the total of all the percentages sum to 100%. The example below checks that a range of percentage inputs, *Sum_percentages*, sums to 100%.

$$=IF(SUM(\textit{Sum\_percentages})<>1,\text{"Error"},\text{"OK"})$$

An alternative to this error-checking device is to replace the final input percentage of a range of inputs with a calculation of 100% less the sum of all the other inputs. This technique guarantees that the total will sum to 100%.

When users are required to enter selling prices to the customer as well as costs to the business, the model's documentation should make it clear what sign convention is expected from the user. The modeller may design the model so that all revenue-related inputs have a positive sign and all cost-related items have a negative sign. If this approach is adopted, the model should check that erroneous sign entries are not made. The following example examines whether an input cell is negative and reports an error if this is the case.

$$=IF(\textit{Input\_cell}<0,\text{"Error"},\text{"OK"})$$

An alternative to the error-checking techniques described above is provided by Excel's DATA VALIDATION function. To activate the Data Validation dialog box:

◪ From the DATA menu select VALIDATION.

This will bring up a three-tab dialog box. Most types of input validation can be performed simply by using the defaults for whole numbers, decimals, lists, dates, time and text length. The modeller can select the relevant criteria and also the permitted ranges. An error message is given if an input falls outside the permitted range. The message itself can be customised to provide additional feedback to the user by selecting the ERROR MESSAGE tab. The dialog box also gives the modeller the opportunity to provide guidance to the user about the nature of the inputs by selecting the INPUT MESSAGE tab. Using the in-built validation function can provide more immediate feedback to the user.

PROTECTING THE MODEL

The flexibility and openness of spreadsheets unfortunately makes them easy to corrupt. However, once the model has been completed a number of actions can be taken to make it more robust and prevent users from intentionally or unintentionally altering the fragile code.

Protecting non-input cells

Through the use of cell protection users can be prevented from making entries in cells that are not input cells. Cells are locked for data entry by default, so that when a sheet is protected the contents of the cells cannot be altered. For input cells the default needs to be altered to allow data entry. To allow data entry into a particular cell the following two steps must be completed:

◪ From the FORMAT menu select CELLS→PROTECTION.
◪ Uncheck the "Locked" box.

When the sheet is protected all but the input cells will be locked. To protect the sheet, follow the three steps below:

◪ From the TOOLS menu select PROTECTION→PROTECT SHEET.
◪ Enter a password and then click OK.
◪ Enter the same password and click OK.

The cells are now locked and only the contents of input cells can be altered. Any attempt to enter information in other cells will result in an error message.

To unprotect the sheet and release all cells these two steps are required:

◪ From the TOOLS menu select PROTECTION→UNPROTECT SHEET.
◪ Enter the password and click OK.

Even when sheets have been protected, the user can still change other elements within the model, such as sheet names, or reveal sheets, formulae, rows and columns that have been hidden. Changing sheet names can prevent the navigation macros from functioning correctly as the text in the macro does not update automatically when the sheet names are changed (this must be done manually in the Visual Basic Editor). To prevent the underlying structure of the model being altered the entire workbook can be protected.

The procedure for protecting a workbook is as follows:

- ◪ From the TOOLS menu select PROTECTION→PROTECT WORKBOOK.
- ◪ Enter a password and then click OK.
- ◪ Enter the same password and click OK.

To unprotect the workbook only two steps are required:

- ◪ From the TOOLS menu select PROTECTION→UNPROTECT WORKBOOK.
- ◪ Enter the password and click OK.

One of the disadvantages of protecting a workbook is that the ability of compression software, such as WinZip, to reduce the size of a file is diminished when the entire workbook has been protected. Protecting only the sheets does not have the same effect, however.

IMPROVING THE APPEARANCE OF THE MODEL

Consistency

Chapter 8 discussed a number of important presentational issues. One of the most important is preserving a consistent appearance across all sheets, as this makes the model easier to use and gives a more professional appearance when printed.

Simple layout

The modeller should ensure that each sheet has a simple layout and that only the minimum required information is presented on each sheet. Ideally, all the information on input and output sheets should be visible without having to scroll down the screen. Providing too much information can be confusing and makes the model difficult and frustrating to use. In designing the layout of the sheet the user should consider whether the application is likely to be used on a desktop or laptop. Laptop screens are usually smaller, so less information should be presented on a sheet.

Freezing the screens

The title and subtitle should be placed in the top left-hand corner of each sheet. The column headings should also be near the top of the sheet. Unfortunately, in sheets with a large amount of information the model title and column headings can disappear from view as the user scrolls down the sheet. To avoid this happening the user can use the FREEZE PANES command to lock the titles and column headings in view when scrolling.

FREEZE PANES effectively divides the screen into four quadrants. To use the FREEZE PANES option, imagine that the sheet has already been divided into the desired four quadrants and select the cell in the upper-left corner of the bottom-right quadrant. In the example in Chart 18.6 this is cell E6.

To freeze the panes around cell E6:

- ◨ Select cell E6.
- ◨ From the WINDOW menu select FREEZE PANES.

The block of cells A1 to D5 will now remain permanently in view. The user can continue to scroll within the remaining quadrants, but rows 1 to 5 and columns A to D will always be visible.

To unfreeze the panes:

- ◨ From the WINDOW menu select UNFREEZE PANES.

Chart 18.6 **Freezing panes**

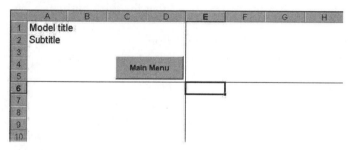

Placement of macro buttons

When macro buttons have been created these should be placed in the top-left quadrant of a screen with frozen panes so they will always be visible and accessible to the user irrespective of where, within the sheet, the user is.

Removing the gridlines

The presence of gridlines is one of personal preference. To remove gridlines use the following commands:

- ◨ From the TOOLS menu select OPTIONS→VIEW.
- ◨ Uncheck the "Gridlines" box.

It is also possible to remove the row and column headings and even the scroll bar. These changes can make the spreadsheet look much more like a dedicated application. However, this is useful only if all the information is presented on the screen at once because the user will have lost the ability to scroll within the screen.

GIVING THE USER OPTIONS

The modeller may want to give the user choices in some of the outputs from the model. For example, the user could be given the option of whether the results are presented in US dollars or UK pounds. Radio or Option buttons can be incorporated into a model to allow the user to select different options – for example, to choose one result or another, such as outputs in real or nominal terms.

To create the buttons the FORMS toolbar must be available. To reveal the FORMS toolbar, right click in the main toolbar area and select the FORMS option. The following steps create the option buttons:

1 Click on GROUP BOX.
2 Draw a large rectangle.
3 Click on the rectangle title and type in "Currency selection".
4 Click on an option button.
5 Draw a rectangle inside the group box.
6 Click on the title and change to GB£.
7 Repeat for the second option button using US$.
8 Right click on an option button within the group box so that the thick outline appears.
9 Select FORMAT CONTROL→CONTROL then select the sheet icon.
10 Select a cell for the selection results to be entered and click on the sheet icon.
11 Click OK.
12 Range name the cell from step 10 *Macro_result*

Once these steps have been completed, clicking on the buttons in turn should switch the number in the macro result cell between 1 and 2. The macro result cell can now be used in the spreadsheet formulae to present the required results. The spreadsheet is presented in Chart 18.7. The panes have been frozen in cell D7 and the gridlines removed. All the figures in rows 6 and 8 are inputs, as is the exchange rate in cell F4.

Chart 18.7 **Option buttons**

	A	B	C	D	E	F	G	H
1	┌ Currency selection ─							
2								
3	○ GB£				Macro_result	2		
4					Exchange_rate	1.6		
5	● US$							
6						2000	2001	2002	2003
7								
8	Base revenues (GB£)					1,000	1,500	2,000	3,000
9								
10	Revenue – selected currency					625	938	1,250	1,875
11								

The model's original results are in UK pounds, so if the GB£ button had been selected no change to the results would be required. The US$ button has actually been selected and so the results are divided by the US$/GB£ exchange rate. The detailed code is presented in Chart 18.8 and relates to column F.

Chart 18.8 **User options**

Row	Calculation	Actual Calculation	Answer
Row 3, cell F3	Selection based on the radio buttons	2	2
Row 4, cell F4	Input	1.6	1.6
Row 6	Input	2001	2001
Base revenue (GB £)	Input	Input	1,500
Revenue – selected currency	=IF(Macro_result=1,F8, F8/Exchange_rate)	=IF(2=1,1500,1500/1.6)	938

PRODUCING THE OUTPUTS

Setting print ranges

Eventually, the user will want to print the output sheets from the model. If the print ranges have already been set appropriately, the user can simply use the print command from the toolbar to print a sheet or a collection of sheets.

To set a print range the user should highlight all the cells that are to be printed and then follow the commands below:

◪ From the FILE menu select PRINT AREA→SET PRINT AREA.

If a sheet is likely to require more than one page, the user can view the print areas by following the commands below:

◪ From the VIEW menu select PAGE BREAK PREVIEW.

The thick blue lines indicate the boundaries of the print ranges. The print ranges can be adjusted by simply clicking and dragging the blue lines to the required position. Additional print options can be found in the FILE menu in PAGE SET-UP. The orientation of the paper can be chosen (landscape or portrait), the size of the print can be adjusted, and headers and footers can be created.

Creating a print macro

It is possible to write a macro that automatically prints out the required sheets at the click of a button. The macro code in Chart 18.9 on the next page prints the print area on the Executive Summary sheet. The modeller will still have to set the appropriate print ranges.

Chart 18.9 **Print macro**

```
Sub PrintMacro()

'Activate the sheet to be printed
Sheets("Executive Summary").Activate

'Print the sheet
ActiveWindow.SelectedSheets.PrintOut Copies:=1, Collate:=True

End Sub
```

The print macro can be attached to a button so that whenever the button is pressed the Executive Summary sheet is printed. The print macro button can be placed on the sheet itself in the top-left quadrant. Alternatively, a number of print macro buttons that relate to different sheets can be placed on one sheet that then acts as the print menu.

19 Using the model

At the outset a model is built to provide decision support to enable the consequences of implementing a project to be evaluated. The exploration of scenarios and alternatives ensures that conclusions can be drawn in the knowledge of the likely results that can be expected. This chapter details ways to structure the exploration of a project's potential so that a decision can be made on whether to accept or reject the project.

SENSITIVITY ANALYSIS

However accurately generated are the assumptions in a model, it is unlikely that reality will yield the same result as the model. Indeed, the further into the future the result is projected the less accurate the result is likely to be. Therefore it is perhaps more relevant to identify the "arena of likely outcomes" than to rely on a specific numerical result for a project. Each combination of realistic alternative assumptions will yield a different result. Being comfortable with the perimeter of this arena will give confidence that it is acceptable to implement this project. If the arena is large and has negative potential, the sanctioner of a project needs to focus on the risks and likelihood of failure.

With the model structured in the way described in Chapter 8, the establishment of scenario columns, as shown in Figure 19.1, easily enables the development of alternative sets of data to explore a wide range of alternative outcomes and the sensitivity of the projected result.

Chart 19.1 **Setting up an input page to handle scenarios**

	A	B	C	D	E	F	G	H
1	Model title							
2						Scenarios		
3	Dataset	1	Dataset		1	2	3	4
4					Expected	Best case	Worst case	
5	Revenue							
6	Price	5.0	Input_price		5.0	5.5	5.0	7.0
7	Price growth	3%	Input_price_growth		3%	3%	5%	5%

The simplest and most common way to explore the project potential is to have three sets of data:

- ◪ An expected outcome comprising the modeller's most realistic set of assumptions.
- ◪ A best case that illustrates the potential should the project exceed expectations.
- ◪ A worst case should conditions be adverse and the project matures less fast.

These can be set up as scenarios 1, 2 and 3, with row 4 being used to provide a narrative heading for each column. This method is sometimes seen as simplistic and a more comprehensive process is required.

Some companies like to see the separate impact of effects such as 10% increase on capital, 10% increase on operating costs, 10% decrease in revenue and 1-year deferral of revenue commencement. This is perhaps more formal, but better still is to understand and develop dependency rankings.

DEPENDENCY RANKING

This is the process of ranking the input assumptions in order of their importance to the final outcome. It can help focus attention on the assumptions that must be validated to ensure that a project should proceed.

To identify this ranking, follow the steps below:

- ◪ Identify an output number that defines success for the project, perhaps a net present value (NPV) or return on capital employed (ROCE) level.
- ◪ Quantify a value for this number that would prevent the project proceeding, such as an NPV of zero or a ROCE of less than 10%.
- ◪ Calculate as a percentage the amount each variable needs to change for the projected result to reach the failure point.
- ◪ Rank the input assumptions in order of the amount of percentage change that can be tolerated (the smallest being the most critical to the project).

For example, revenue could be created from the inputs shown in Chart 19.2.

Chart 19.2 **Setting up an input page to evaluate dependency ranking**

	A	B	C	D	E	F	G
1	**Model title**						
2						Scenarios	
3	Dataset	1	Dataset		1	2	3
4							
5	Revenue						
6	Price	5.0	Input_price		5.0		
7	Price growth	3%	Input_price_growth		3%		
8	Units	1,000	Input_unit		1,000		
9	Units growth	4%	Input_unit_growth		4%		

GOAL SEEK

Using NPV as the success factor and zero as the failure value, the GOAL SEEK function can be used to test the amount each variable needs to change for the projected result to reach the failure point.

GOAL SEEK is used to find a specific result for an output cell by adjusting the value of an input cell. For the function to work the numbers must be linked through formulae.

GOAL SEEK can be found in the TOOLS menu. The function has three inputs:

- Set cell – the result value (or in the example the cell on the output sheet that displays the NPV amount).
- To value – the amount that the result value should reach (or 0 in the example). This cell must be an entered value and not a cell reference.
- By changing cell – the input value that will be changed (one of the revenue assumptions). This cell must contain a value and not a formula. Hence in the example it would be linked to column E, where the number is entered, and not column B, where there is an offset formula to pick up the number to drive the model.

Once set, press OK and the function will try to find a solution.

Chart 19.3 **GOAL SEEK input box**

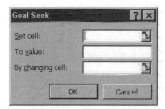

If GOAL SEEK is successful, it will state that it has "Found a solution". The input will now have the value required for the "Set cell" to equal the "To value". If OK is pressed at this stage, the new input value will be retained. This would be a mistake, as the aim of this dependency ranking is to explore the project's sensitivity to each input individually and not collectively. By pressing CANCEL the original input value will be restored. It would be helpful to enter the GOAL SEEK value manually into column F in order to rank the impact of each input.

If GOAL SEEK is unsuccessful, it will state that it "May not have found a solution", showing the target value and how near it has managed to get. This may imply that the project is not sensitive to the input and that the input is not critical to its success. Alternatively, the sensitivity of the search criteria may need to be adjusted.

To adjust the sensitivity of the search, select OPTIONS→CALCULATION tab from the TOOLS menu. In the middle section of this box are the criteria for iteration calculation, the basis on which GOAL SEEK works. Checking the iteration box allows you to adjust the number of iterations and the maximum change in the result that is acceptable before iteration stops. Maximum iterations is best left at 100, but Maximum change should be changed to reflect the properties of "Set cell". For an NPV the value could be 1, as +/−1 will not be material to the answer. However, for a ROCE of 10% (held in Excel as 0.1) the value should be 0.001 or even 0.0001.

Repeating the operation

GOAL SEEK has a frustrating property in that it has to be called up each time it is used and the three inputs have to be re-entered. For a small model this is not onerous, but for 50 or more inputs it may be worth writing a small macro to automate much of the process. Chapter 18 describes how to record a simple macro. For more advanced macros the "follow me principle" can be used. For this set up a new macro, and perform the key strokes described below to record the repetitious stages. To the code can be added a small loop to enable it to run a set number of times.

The following macro can be used:

- ◪ In column E have the base assumptions.
- ◪ Copy the same data into column F so it is replicated (these should be values not formulae linking to column E).
- ◪ Clear column G to store the sensitivity data.

The macro is shown in Chart 19.4.

Chart 19.4 **Macro for automating GOAL SEEK selection**

```
Dim count as integer
For count = XX To YY (the row numbers of the first and last lines of inputs)
    Range("E" + Trim(count)).Select
    If ActiveCell.Value <> "" Then
        Range("Cell co-ordinates of NPV value").GOALSEEK_
        Goal:=0, ChangingCell:=Range("E" + Trim(count))
        Range("E" + Trim(count)).Select
        Selection.Copy
        Range("G" + Trim(count)).Select
        ActiveSheet.Paste
        Range("F" + Trim(count)).Select
        Selection.Copy
        Range("E" + Trim(count)).Select
        ActiveSheet.Paste
    End If
Next
```

Here the code will run from lines XX to YY performing a GOAL SEEK calculation on the data in column E. After each GOAL SEEK the answer is copied from column E to column G, and the base assumption in column F is copied back to column E to continue with the data in the next row.

Run the macro and column G will have all the sensitivity factors. Calculate the percentage change from the base data and rank in order. (Having saved the spreadsheet, DATA→SORT can be used to rank the findings.) Be aware of the need to take the absolute value of the percentage changes. The negatives are as important as the positives. The =ABS(value) function can be used around the percentage calculation to remove the sign.

In analysing the results of this process it will be important to focus on the principal drivers of the value in the project. Any assumption that can cause failure with a swing of less than 10% will bring a high degree of risk to the project and require careful validation.

MONTE CARLO ANALYSIS

Monte Carlo analysis provides a way of exploring a huge number of scenarios through the model and being able to evaluate statistically the "arena of likely outcomes". Instead of setting one assumption for each input, the principle is based on setting a range within which the input value should lie. For example, the revenue growth rate may not be 4%, but it probably lies between 3% and 5%. Using the random number generator, the model can randomly select an input value from each input range and then use this to derive a model result. By operating several hundred or more iterations, an expected value and standard deviation can be calculated. The standard deviation enables the model result to be quoted with a confidence level. One standard deviation away from the expected value is 66% confidence, two standard deviations away is 95% confidence and three standard deviations away is 99% confidence.

This enhanced statistical presentation of a model's results may seem helpful to the sanctioning and approval process, but the wider the ranges of input ranges, the larger is the standard deviation number and the bigger is the arena of likely outcomes. Hence a narrow range of well-researched assumptions is still the way to derive a realistic result from the model.

Setting up a Monte Carlo analysis requires a macro to operate and calculate the scenarios.

Monte Carlo macro

On the input page set up two columns that will contain the maximum (for example, column E) and minimum (for example, column F) values of the range for each assumption. In a third column (for example, column G) calculate the random number within the input range. This can be achieved by the following formula (as applied to row 8):

$$=RAND()*(E8-F8)+F8$$

Excel has a function RANDBETWEEN that can make this simpler, but it only works in integers and hence would be inappropriate for models where percentages are involved.

Set the model to be driven from the dataset in this Monte Carlo column (column G). Every time the spreadsheet is recalculated a new set of input values will be generated. To force a recalculation press F9.

A Monte Carlo results page

This can be done with a simple macro or developed further by using a Visual Basic form that can automate much of the data gathering and statistical evaluation.

Open a new sheet and set up a row that captures all the key attributes of the project that are required, such as NPV, IRR, payback, ROCE, gearing, and so on. The references to the output page need to be absolute, as this row of data needs to be copied down the sheet for 200 lines with every row reading the same value.

Set up a macro that is linked to a button, as shown in Figure 19.5.

Chart 19.5 **Macro for Monte Carlo analysis**

```
Dim count as integer
For count = 1 To 200
    Calculate
    Range("A" + Trim(count) + ":C" + Trim(count)).Select
    Selection.Copy
    Selection.PasteSpecial Paste:=xlValues, Operation:=xlNone, SkipBlanks:= _
    False, Transpose:=False
Next
```

The C in the line "Range …" code is the column of the last piece of data that is required to be captured.

Set the macro to RUN. It will recalculate the model with new data, store the information and move down a row. The loop will continue 200 times capturing a set of data on which statistics can be applied.

To calculate a mean value use the =AVERAGE function over the range of data, and for the standard deviation use the =STDEV function over the range of data.

EXCEL SCENARIO MANAGER

In Excel there is a built-in Scenario Manager that can be used to achieve much of the functionality described here. The disadvantage is that only 32 variables can be held in any scenario, which limits the capacity of this function to support large models.

In practice, few modellers use the function as the visibility created by the offset method enables a high degree of clarity and user friendliness.

DISPLAYING THE ASSUMPTION DATASET ON THE OUTPUT SHEET

As the input page builds with datasets and scenarios, users can become confused about which output they are viewing or have printed out. At the top of the output sheet it can be helpful to put a detailed narrative explanation of what the scenario illustrates. Using the OFFSET function triggered from the dataset value, the title can be placed on the output page.

The contents of the cell under the title of the output page could be set up as follows:

=CONCATENATE("Output generated from the dataset: ",OFFSET
(Inputs!D4,0,*Dataset*))

RISK AND ITS MANAGEMENT

The benefit of many models in providing decision support is to reduce the risk of embarking on projects that will fail. To manage this risk it is helpful to divide it into three categories and have appropriate strategies to manage each category:

- Assumption risk – that the estimates and assumptions used in the model are significantly flawed and that the project benefits will never materialise.
- Operational risk – that in implementing the project there are unforeseen events, complexities and skills that will require resource and cost to resolve.
- Environmental risk – that the environment will change in terms of government policy and economic conditions.

These risks have to be managed through appropriate responses that might be as follows:

- Assumption risk – exploration of sensitivity analysis and validation of key dependent variables as described above.
- Operational risk – find appropriate mitigating factors to reduce potential exposure such as insurance, supplier quality guarantees and performance bonds.
- Environmental risk – identify potential exit options during the life of the project that can limit losses and continuing commitments, such as flexible property leases that can be terminated rather than signed for 25 years.

20 Documenting the model

INTRODUCTION

The need for documentation

The changing needs of a business may require an existing model to be altered long after the original development work was completed. Gaining the required understanding of a model to allow further development work is a challenging task for the modeller, even when that modeller did the original work. The most unenviable task for any modeller, however, is to attempt to understand and then further develop somebody else's poorly structured and documented model. In nearly all cases, the modeller abandons the original and develops an entirely new model from scratch, representing a significant waste of resources.

The existence of relevant, accurate documentation, at the appropriate level of detail, makes these tasks considerably easier. It will also be invaluable to whoever else may have to develop or maintain the model in the future. The preparation of documentation material throughout the development process also provides reassurance to the sponsor of the project. If the original modeller is unable to continue to develop the model, for whatever reason, the sponsor will be able to pass the uncompleted model and the accompanying documentation to a new modeller, who will quickly be able to continue the work. Lastly, documentation makes the reviewing and testing process more effective and efficient.

As well as development documentation, a user guide and training material are essential if the model is to be successfully used by someone other than the modeller.

When to document

Documentation should ideally take place throughout the development process. As well as allowing a simple handover of development from one modeller to another, documenting the model alongside the development process helps to instil discipline, rigour and structure. Preparing documentation material throughout the build stage also makes writing the final document, after the model is completed, less onerous.

Unfortunately, producing detailed documentation often proves too cumbersome during the initial stages of development, especially if the early workings of the model are evolving through a number of iterations. However, particularly complex areas of the model should be documented as soon as they have reached a reasonable degree of stability. Inevitably, most of the work on preparing the documentation will be done once the model has been completed. The modeller should therefore ensure that sufficient time has been included in the project plan to allow for this important task.

Where to document

The modeller must decide whether to produce the documentation within the model itself or whether to use a separate file. Maintaining the documentation within the model makes the spreadsheet solution more self-contained. The material is always accessible and there is no risk of the documentation file becoming separated from the model it supports. Retaining all the material within the model also makes version control between the model and the documentation easier to manage. Unfortunately, spreadsheet packages are not specifically designed for document production, so the presentation of the material is not always as clear as it would be if it had been produced in a separate, dedicated piece of software such as a word-processing package. Furthermore, the user or reviewer of the model may prefer to have a printed version of the documentation available while they work through the model, which may be more effectively accomplished through the use of a separate file. The ultimate decision will depend on the preference of the user and the complexity and usability of the model. Ideally, extensive documentation within the model should be combined with a well-presented model development document and a high-level user guide produced in a word-processing package.

DOCUMENTATION WITHIN THE MODEL

A number of options for online documentation and user help are available to the model developer. At the simplest level, "cell comments" (text boxes attached to a particular cell that appear when the user hovers over the cell) can be used. At the other end of the scale, dedicated software can be purchased to help create Windows-based help systems. For most modelling exercises, however, the use of cell comments and text boxes (discussed below), supplemented by a well-written manual, is more than adequate.

Cell comments

During the build stage of the model development process, cell comments are probably the most effective method of documenting the model. They are quick and easy to create and can be tagged to a particular cell. If the model has to be restructured, and cells moved to new locations, the cell comments will move with the cells. The use of cell comments is made even easier if informative variable range names have been used. The cells can refer to the names rather than cell references, which makes understanding the formulae easier. The content of the cell comments can also be used as the basis for preparing the detailed documentation at the end of the development process. The content of the cell comments can simply be copied and pasted directly into a word-processing document, saving considerable time and effort.

To create a cell comment using Excel, follow the steps below:

- Select the cell in which the comment is to be placed.
- From the INSERT menu select INSERT COMMENT.
- Type the comment directly into the comment box.
- Click on any other cell to close the cell comment box.
- To read a comment, hover over the cell and the comment will appear.
- To edit a comment, select the cell and right click the mouse to reveal EDIT COMMENT.

Within the comment box there is considerable flexibility to alter the font, style and presentation. This flexibility also makes cell notes useful for providing user guidance and help, as they are unobtrusive and immediately available within the model. Cell comments can help the user understand the input requirements, such as appropriate units and currency.

Text boxes

Text boxes are more useful for providing user help than for providing model documentation, as they are not tagged to a specific cell. They are permanently visible on the face of the spreadsheet, which makes them ideal for alerting the user to important tasks associated with using the model. They also offer increased formatting and presentation options compared with cell comments. As they are not attached to particular cells, their creation should wait until the model's structure is fairly stable.

To create a text box using Excel, follow the steps below:

- Ensure that the DRAWINGS toolbar is visible by right clicking in the main toolbar area and selecting DRAWING.
- Click on the TEXT BOX icon.
- Create an appropriately sized rectangle on the spreadsheet in the preferred location by left clicking and dragging the mouse to draw the required shape.
- Click on the text box to enter text and use the standard formatting functions.

Dialog boxes

Dialog boxes are a more time-consuming method of providing user help, although they do make a model seem much more sophisticated. They can give the model the appearance of being a dedicated application rather than a spreadsheet. The modeller can place instructions and information in the dialog box, although compared with text boxes the formatting and text capabilities are limited. Dialog boxes also require macro code to reveal them to the user. The easiest approach is to place a button on a particular sheet that reveals the dialog box when it is clicked. Another alternative is to create a dedicated toolbar with a number of help options, each associated with a particular dialog box. Unfortunately, creating dialog boxes is beyond the scope of this book, but most books on Visual Basic for applications provide a detailed explanation of this process.

Specific help software

A more elegant alternative to the creation of a series of dialog boxes is to purchase software specifically designed to create user help systems. The software provides simple wizards that enable the modeller to develop help screens that resemble those of any Windows application.

Macro comments

If the modeller has incorporated macros as part of the modelling solution, it is vital to ensure that these macros are well documented. Attempting to understand the actions of an undocumented macro is even more challenging than reviewing poorly structured and undocumented spreadsheets. Comments should be placed liberally throughout any macro code. The comments should identify and describe any variables used and their characteristics, as well as the tasks performed by each section of code. The example in Chart 20.1 uses the macro code from Chapter 18, but it has been embellished with comments. The comments begin with an apostrophe to indicate that the text is for information only and is not part of the operational code.

Chart 20.1 **Macro code comments**

```
Sub ExecMove()

'Macro to move the user to the Executive Summary Sheet
'Recorded by A N Author

'Select the Executive Summary sheet and make this the active sheet

Sheets("Executive Summary").Activate

'Move to the cell with the range name ExecStart

Application.Goto Reference:=Range("ExecStart"), scroll:=True


End Sub
```

DOCUMENTATION OUTSIDE THE MODEL

Fit for the purpose

Irrespective of the format used for providing development documentation or user guides, the material must be written with the ultimate objectives of the audience in mind. Development documentation is aimed at those who will have to review, develop or maintain the model. Documentation for these audiences will be more detailed than a user guide and will explain how the model is structured, the key input variables, the logical flow of the workings and especially any critical relationships between variables that must be maintained. User guides and any training material, however, will be at a much higher level and will focus more on the nature of the data inputs, the order in which the model must be completed and how to run sensitivities and scenarios, before explaining how to interpret and analyse the results.

Good document form design

The format and style of any documentation should be carefully considered. The following information should be clearly visible and in the same position on every sheet of the document, ideally in the top right-hand corner:

- Title
- Reference or version number
- Author
- Page number
- The date of preparation and issue
- File name including the directory file path

The document should also provide a sufficient margin on the left-hand side to allow it to be read, even once it has been filed. A standard paper size is important to allow for easy reproduction, and plenty of space should be provided for additional information that might be recorded by hand. An example of the layout of a typical model documentation page is shown in Chart 20.2.

Chart 20.2 **Typical documentation layout**

		Title:	Mobile Business Planning Model	Page Number:	14
		Developer:	A N Author	Issue Date:	17/07/2000
		File Name:	C:\My Documents\Models\BP M_V3.2.xls	Version Number:	3.2

Structure

The structure of the document should flow naturally from the model, provided that the model itself has been carefully designed. The documentation should also be structured to reflect the modular design of the model. If the documentation is modular, any changes to a particular module within the model can easily be reflected in the corresponding section of the documentation. For example, if a module within the model becomes redundant and is removed, it should be possible to remove the appropriate section from the report without damaging the flow and readability of the overall document.

Modeller's documentation

Documentation for a modeller should contain, as a minimum, the following information:

- A contents page.
- An overview of the model, including its objectives, approach, structure and limitations.
- A review of the data input requirements, including definitions, variable names and their appropriate units.
- A commentary on the logical flow of the model, which would include: identification of critical variables and relationships; a discussion of key workings.
- Details of macros used to perform specific tasks, with a line-by-line review of the code where appropriate.
- A review of the main outputs and guidance on interpreting the results.
- Additional features in the model such as printing and navigation macros.
- Areas identified for future development.

User's documentation

The level of detail contained in the documentation produced for users will depend on the skill level of the users, the complexity of the model, and the sophistication and extent of the user interface and online help within the model. Documentation for the users will usually involve the production of a user guide or manual and, occasionally, training material.

Contents of a typical user's guide

The contents of a typical user's guide should include the following:

- A contents page.
- An overview of the model's objectives, key features and limitations.
- An overview of the structure of the model and the tools in place to help the user navigate around the model to ensure that it is completed in the correct order.
- A list of key milestones for completing the model.
- The data input requirements, including definitions, units and currencies.
- A section-by-section guide to completing the model. The level of information contained in the user guide will depend on the level of detailed support provided online within the model.
- Guidance on reviewing the model's outputs to ensure that the model has been populated correctly.
- How to run scenarios and sensitivities through the model.
- How to print the final outputs.
- An appendix or glossary of technical terms.

Training material

To avoid an unnecessary duplication of effort, any training material that the modeller is required to produce should draw heavily on the contents of the user guide. The presentation should be at a reasonably high level of detail, as the combination of the online help within the model and the user guide will provide all the required information. The training material should focus on the structure of the model, the design of the user interfaces and the steps involved in completing the model. If possible, the training should include extensive, practical worked examples where the user practices completing each section in turn.

Continuing user support

Inevitably, users will raise questions about the model that cannot be answered by reference to the online help within the model, the documentation or user guide. The modeller should decide how the continuing support will be provided and inform the users of the process for gaining access to user support.

21 Writing and presenting the business plan

The financial model generated through this book will be able to evaluate a wide range of scenarios for the potential of a business or project. These will form the backbone of a business plan to seek approval for a venture from investors (either internal to an organisation or external).

Although the outputs from the model will be the basis of the financial strength of the project, the numbers will have to be supported by a business plan – a written document that describes and summarises the opportunity. This chapter gives guidance on the questions a business plan should seek to address, the potential contents and the presentation of financial information.

KEY ISSUES TO ADDRESS IN A BUSINESS PLAN

The typical issues that investors want to see explored and explained in a business plan document are as follows:

- What is the determinant of the value in this proposal – which factor(s) will deliver and sustain the success/competitive advantage that is offered?
- What is the evidence that the determinants of value will deliver the projected results – the surveys, past history or success of similar ventures in other places?
- What other options have been considered to achieve the same aim (and why is do nothing not the best option)?
- What are the risks that the investors will take on by backing the project, and what is the worst possible scenario?
- What returns and rewards are available if the venture should prove successful?
- What is the experience of the people involved, and do they have the skills to realise the potential in the project?
- Do the managers understand the business, its markets, its customers and its competition?

Many investors would cite the most important ingredient in the success of any venture as the managers, the people responsible for delivering success. Therefore most investors need to "believe" and "trust" the managers. Belief can be conveyed through the rigour and quality of the business plan. Trust will often take more: interaction at meetings, the ability to answer questions and harmony of thinking – a set of interpersonal factors that no model or paperwork can cover.

The business plan will open the door to a project being heard; the meeting has to bring it alive and convince the investors that management can deliver.

TYPICAL CONTENT OF A BUSINESS PLAN DOCUMENT

To answer these questions and provide the details of a proposal, the typical contents page for a business plan might include the following:

Executive summary
An overview of the opportunity available, summarising the management team, the products or services proposed, key financial information and the investment required.

Strategic importance
- Importance to the individual, organisation or group
- The competitive advantage offered in the market
- Links to other products and markets
- Links to other processes
- Why "do nothing" is not a better option
- Other options considered to achieve some aims

Market
- Actions of competitors that could have a detrimental impact
- Competing alternatives
- Likely future demand in the light of competitor actions
- A detailed SWOT (strengths, weaknesses, opportunities and threats) analysis will form a useful summary of the marketing proposition

Commercial risk
- Key business risks in the project
- Impact of a shortfall in revenue and an overrun in costs
- Mitigation of risks including exit options should all go wrong
- Competition – strengths and weaknesses
- Political and legal issues
- Regulation
- Monopoly

Financial
- Projected cashflows
- Valuation measures of payback, NPV (net present value) and IRR (internal rate of return)
- ROCE (return on capital employed), ROS (return on sales), RONA (return on net assets), EBITDA (earnings before interest, tax, depreciation and amortisation)
- Accounts presenting projected profit and loss and balance sheets

Assumptions
- Key assumptions and how they have been checked to be robust

- ☑ Research completed
- ☑ Reference for data
- ☑ Benchmark validity

Economic
- ☑ Exchange rates
- ☑ Inflation
- ☑ Growth of economy
- ☑ Funding sources

Taxes
- ☑ Impact of tax – corporate, withholding, capital gains and others

Sensitivity
- ☑ Alternative scenarios
- ☑ Results of sensitivity analysis to changes in key variables
- ☑ Timescale changes

Technical
- ☑ Type of plant and/or computer
- ☑ Capability and compatibility
- ☑ Yields and unit times
- ☑ Processes
- ☑ Maintenance and reliability

Milestones
- ☑ Approval as start date
- ☑ Commencement of investment
- ☑ Production and delivery
- ☑ End date or terminal value

Manning
- ☑ Human resources implications
- ☑ Scheduling
- ☑ Dependencies
- ☑ Utilisation of plant
- ☑ Utilisation of property

Safety, health and environment
- ☑ Key issues
- ☑ Approvals

Report style

In preparing a business case for approval, the content should be written in a selling style that influences and persuades the reader as to the merits of the opportunity. If the authors are not excited by the opportunity, then why should the investors want to back it?

The length of the business plan should be proportional to the size of the investment. It is a fine balance between demonstrating that the authors have done a thorough investigation and a conciseness that is efficient for the reader. Often when the proposals are submitted internally the sanctioners will offer:

- limited time
- short attention span
- low boredom threshold
- potential expertise in non-critical areas

Therefore the layout should allow readers to grasp quickly the principal issues as well as having clear references to supporting papers in a supplementary appendix.

PRESENTING THE MODEL OUTPUTS

Financial results can be effectively presented with a lively analysis that uses pictorial or graphical charts to convey information.

In his book on data reduction, A.S.C. Ehrenberg[1] describes several methods for communicating data through manageable tables and charts to enable it to be visibly easier to read, assimilate and act upon. Some of his techniques include the following:

Rounding

Most people cannot manipulate long numbers in their heads. To enable readers to analyse the data presented, it is helpful to round each number to two effective digits. Although this may seem a reduction in detail, it will probably be within the accuracy of model projections that can be realistically made.

For example, if the IRR for two projects were 18.86% and 38.12%, they would be difficult to compare. However, with two effective digits the IRR becomes 19% and 38%, making it quicker to see that one number is half the other.

Tables of data

Tables of data are much easier to read if they are sorted into ascending or descending order of the most critical item, such that the top few items of data convey the critical information.

---

1   *A Primer in Data Reduction*, John Wiley & Sons, 1982.

It is also helpful to leave a gap every few rows to enable the eye to travel easily across the table without jumping a row.

An example is reworking the data in Chart 21.1 into Chart 21.2.

Chart 21.1 **Sales by country**

	2001	2002	2003	2004
Canada	578.1	553.2	654.2	765.4
France	177.9	241.4	472.9	632.8
Germany	384.1	429.4	556.1	642.9
India	185.4	278.3	335.6	432.8
Japan	165.4	145.2	185.4	176.4
Spain	0.0	0.0	25.2	64.1
UK	153.2	171.6	183.6	234.6
USA	1,473.2	1,321.5	1,659.0	1,854.3

This table would be better presented rounded to two effective digits, sorted by size of sales in 2004 (not alphabetically by country), with a gap inserted between the two blocks of four rows, as shown in Chart 21.2.

Chart 21.2 **Sales by country**

	2001	2002	2003	2004
USA	1,500	1,300	1,700	1,900
Canada	580	550	650	770
Germany	380	430	560	640
France	180	240	470	630
India	190	280	340	430
UK	150	170	180	230
Japan	170	150	190	180
Spain	0	0	25	60

This can be achieved as follows.

To *round to two significant figures*
Providing numbers are mainly greater than zero, copy them from a source area through the following formula:

$$=ROUND(number,MIN(2-LEN(ROUND(number,0)),0))$$

To *order*
Highlight the whole block of data (from top left country name to bottom right value for 2004). From the menu select DATA→SORT and sort by the right-hand column in descending order.

To insert the blank line
This must be done manually by inserting rows as appropriate.

Rows versus columns

It is usually easier to read down a column of numbers than across a row. This is because the leading digits in each number are then close to each other for direct comparison.

An example is Chart 21.3.

Chart 21.3 **Age profile of customers**

	Under 15	15–30	30–50	Over 50
Buyers	8%	23%	48%	21%

If this table is swapped round, it is much easier to see where the key segment of the market resides, as shown in Chart 21.4. Furthermore, the superfluous percentage sign has been removed and added to the heading, making the numbers clearer.

Chart 21.4 **Age profile of customers**

	Buyers (%)
Under 15	8
15–30	23
30–50	48
Over 50	21

Graphs

Graphs are useful to tell a story, not necessarily to convey detail (for which a table would be better). For clarity, keep a graph to a maximum of three lines or stacks on a bar chart and then summarise the key trend that emerges to help the reader interpret what is being shown. Try to avoid a detailed description of each rise and fall along the line.

An example is Chart 21.5 on the next page.

Chart 21.5 **Forecast sales**

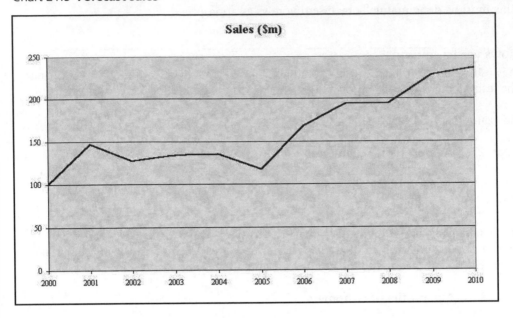

An appropriate narrative might be as follows:

"The sales rise by an average of 9% per year over the ten years, although much of the growth is achieved in the second half of the decade."

Appendix 1 **Spreadsheet functions**

ABS

Definition	Returns the absolute value of a number, that is, the number without the sign
Examples of use	Used in the calculation of the mean square error to assess the goodness of fit of a model
Syntax	=ABS(*number*) where *number* is the real number of which you want to have returned the absolute number
Example	=ABS(10)=10
	=ABS(−10)=10
Reference	Chapter 10, page 93

AVERAGE

Definition	Returns the arithmetic mean of a series of arguments
Examples of use	1. Calculating the average customer base from the opening and closing customer-base positions from which a revenue figure can be derived
	2. Calculating the average cash balance from an opening and closing position from which an interest charge can be calculated
Syntax	=AVERAGE(*number1,number2,...numbern*) where *number1,number2...* are arguments for which you want to calculate the arithmetic average
Example	=AVERAGE(1,2,3)=2
	If cells A1 to A3 are 1,2,3
	=AVERAGE(A1:A3)=2
	Range names can also be used in this function
Reference	Chapters 7, 10 and 14, pages 47, 109 and 153

CONCATENATE

Definition	Joins a number of string (text) variables into a single text variable
Examples of use	When labelling results the description of the results can be combined with the currency name, which can be a user input
Syntax	=CONCATENATE(*text1,text2,...*) where *text1,text2...* are strings
Example	If *Currency* is a range name for the currency description (for example, UK£), then
	=CONCATENATE("Total profit − ",*Currency*) would return
	Total profit − UK£
	Cells, range names and text can be used in this function
Reference	Chapter 7, pages 44 and 46

COUNTIF

Definition	Counts the number of cells within a specified range that meet given criteria
Examples of use	Examining whether user input data is valid

Syntax	=COUNTIF(*range,criteria*) where *range* is the range in which you want to count the cells and *criteria* is the form of a number, expression or text that defines which cells will be counted
Example	If cells A1 to A4 contain "red", "blue", "red" and "green" respectively, then =COUNTIF(A1:A4,"red") would return 2
Reference	Chapter 8, page 54

EXP

Definition	Returns E raised to the power of the number where E is the constant base of the natural logarithm
Examples of use	Fitting product life cycle curves
Syntax	=EXP(*number*) where *number* is the exponent applied to base E
Example	=EXP(1)=2.7181282
Reference	Chapter 10, page 103

IF

Definition	Returns one value if a specified condition is true and another value if the condition is false
Examples of use	1. Determining whether the balance on a cash account should be reflected as an overdraft or a positive cash balance in the balance sheet 2. Determining whether a formula should be altered to reflect the first year of a forecast
Syntax	=IF(*logical test,value if true,value if false*) where *logical test* is any expression that can be evaluated on the basis of true or false. *Value if true* is the value returned if the test is true and *value if false* is the value returned if the result of the test is false
Example	If the range name *Cash* is 125, then =IF(Cash<0,"Overdraft","Positive cash balance") would return "Positive cash balance"
References	Chapter 7, page 44

INDEX

Definition	Returns a value or a reference to a value from within a table or range. Can be used either in an array or in a reference form. In the array form the function always returns a value or an array of values; in the reference form a reference is always returned
Examples of use	Extracting linear regression coefficients and statistics from the LINEST worksheet function
Syntax	Array Syntax – INDEX(*array,row number,column number*) where *array* is an array of cells and *row number* and *column number* specify a cell or an array of cells
Example	=LINEST({1,9,5,7},{0,4,2,3}) produces the array {2,1} =INDEX(LINEST({1,9,5,7},{0,4,2,3}),2) returns the second result from the array, 1
Reference	Chapter 7, page 45, and the uses of the LINEST function

IRR

Definition	Returns the internal rate of return for a series of cashflows
Examples of use	Investment evaluation
Syntax	IRR(values,gross). Values is an array or reference to cells that hold numbers for which you want to calculate the IRR. Gross is a number close to the expected IRR
Example	If B1 to B6 contains $−70,000, $12,000, $15,000, $18,000, $21,000 and $26,000 respectively, then IRR(B1:B6) equals −2.12%
Reference	Chapter 15, page 184

ISERROR and ISSER

Definition	Tests whether a value or reference contains an error, but ISERR does not detect the error of #N/A!
Examples of use	To avoid errors elsewhere in the model rendering the balance sheet incapable of balancing itself as a result of circular references in cash and taxation workings
Syntax	=ISERROR(value) where value is a value or reference
Example	If the result of a calculation in cell A5 results in a division by zero, then =IF(ISERROR(A5),"Division by zero error","Result OK") returns "Division by zero error"
Reference	Chapter 7, page 45

LEN

Definition	Returns the number of characters in a text string
Examples of use	To test whether a user input exceeds a specified number of characters
Syntax	=LEN(text) where text is the string for which you want to count the number of characters
Example	If cell A5 contains the user input "GBP£", then =IF(LEN(A5)>3,"Entry must be three characters or less","Entry correct") would return "Entry must be three characters or less"
Reference	Chapter 18, page 216

LINEST

Definition	Calculates the statistics for a line of best fit for a set of data through the application of ordinary least squares regression. As the function returns an array of variables that describe the line it must be entered as an array function
Examples of use	Determining the coefficients of a regression line fitted to a set of observations that can be used to predict future sales. Useful for multiple regression exercises
Syntax	If the equation of a straight line is given by the formula $y=m_1x_1+m_2x_2+...+b$ then =LINEST(known-y's,known-x's,constant,statistics) will produce the statistics describing the line. A block of cells (at least 5 by 5) should be highlighted and the formula entered. Hold down the CTRL and SHIFT keys and press ENTER – this will enter the formula as an array.

Known-y's represent the existing, known dependent variables. *Known-x's* represent one or more explanatory variables. *Constant* is a logical value (either true or false). If true or omitted, b is calculated normally. If false, b is set to zero. *Statistics* is a logical value that if true returns the additional regression statistics

Example	=LINEST({1,9,5,7},{0,4,2,3}) produces the array {2,1} where 2 represents the slope of the line and 1 gives the intercept
Reference	Chapter 10, page 94

LN

Definition	Returns the natural logarithm of a number
Examples of use	Fitting a product life cycle curve
Syntax	=LN(*number*) where *number* is a positive real number for which a natural logarithm is required
Example	=LN(86) returns the value 4.454347
Reference	Chapter 10, page 103

MAX

Definition	Provides the largest value among a set of values
Examples of use	Calculating the number of credit controllers required to manage a maximum number of accounts
Syntax	=MAX(*number1,number1,...*) where *number1* and *number2* and so on are a collection of numbers from which the largest is sought
Example	If A1 to A5 contain the values 1, 4, 15, 6 and 12, then =MAX(A1:A5) would return the value 15
Reference	Chapter 7, page 44

MIN

Definition	Returns the smallest number among a set of numbers
Examples of use	Calculating the replacement level of fixed assets
Syntax	=MIN(*number1,number2...*) where *number1, number2 ...* are a collection of numbers
Example	If cells A1 to A5 contain 2, 4, 5, 3 and 9, then =MIN(A1:A5) will return 2
Reference	Chapter 7, page 44

MOD

Definition	Returns the remainder of a division calculation
Examples of use	Calculating when to replace a fixed asset based on its economic life
Syntax	=MOD(*number,divisor*) where *number* is the numerator and *divisor* is the denominator of a division calculation
Example	=MOD(3,2) returns the answer 1
Reference	Chapter 7, page 47

NPV

Definition	Calculates the net present value of a series of cashflows
Examples of use	Evaluating investment projects
Syntax	=NPV(rate,value1,value2,...valuen) where rate is the discount rate and value 1, value 2 to value n are cashflows
Example	=NPV(10%,−10000,3000,4200,6800) equals $1,188.44, and you must format the cell for currency
Reference	Chapter 10, page 170

OFFSET

Definition	Returns the reference to a range that is a specified number of rows and columns away from a cell or a range of cells
Examples of use	1. Selecting datasets for different scenarios 2. Fixed asset disposal calculations
Syntax	=OFFSET(*reference,rows,columns,height,width*) where reference is the start point from which the offsets are made. Rows is the number of rows (up or down) from the reference cell that you want the upper-left cell to refer to. *Columns* is the number of columns (left or right) that you want the upper-left cell to refer to. *Height* and *width* specify the size of the returned reference – these can be excluded and only the single cell will be returned
Example	=OFFSET(C3:E5,−1,0,3,3) gives cells C2 to F4
Reference	Chapter 7, page 46

RANK

Definition	Returns the rank of a number from a list of numbers where rank examines the size of the number relative to the others in the list
Examples of use	Comparing current performance against the results of previous years
Syntax	=RANK(*number,reference,order*) where *number* is the number to be ranked, *reference* is a list of numbers that may be in an array or a reference and *order* indicates how to rank the number. If order is zero or omitted, then the ranking assumes the numbers are in descending order
Example	If A1 to A5 contains the numbers 6, 3.2, 3.2, 2, 1, then =RANK(A2,A1:A5,1) gives 3
Reference	Chapter 16, page 191

ROUND

Definition	Rounds a number to the specified number of digits
Examples of use	Improving the presentation of results
Syntax	=ROUND(*number, number of digits*) where *number* is the number to be rounded and *number of digits* is the number of digits you want to round the number to
Example	=ROUND(5.1234,2) returns 5.12
Reference	Chapter 8, page 58

ROUNDDOWN

Definition	Rounds a number to the specified number of digits towards zero
Examples of use	Improving the presentation of results
Syntax	=ROUNDDOWN(*number, number of digits*) where *number* is the number to be rounded and *number of digits* is the number of digits you want to round the number to
Example	=ROUNDDOWN(5.1234,2) returns 5.12
Reference	Chapter 8, page 59

ROUNDUP

Definition	Rounds a number to the specified number of digits away from zero
Examples of use	Improving the presentation of results
Syntax	=ROUNDUP(*number, number of digits*) where *number* is the number to be rounded and *number of digits* is the number of digits you want to round the number to
Example	=ROUNDUP(5.1234,2) returns 5.13
Reference	Chapter 9, page 66

SIN

Definition	Calculates the SINE of a given angle
Examples of use	Forecasting business cycles in the calculation of GDP growth rates
Syntax	=SIN(*number*) where *number* is the angle in radians. To convert from degrees to radians multiply it by PI()/180
Example	=SIN(30*PI()/180) gives 0.5 the SIN of the 30 degrees
Reference	Chapter 9, page 66

SUM

Definition	Adds all the numbers in a range
Examples of use	Calculating totals
Syntax	=SUM(*number1, number2, ...*) where *number1, number2* and so on are numbers to be added
Example	If cells A1 to A5 contain the numbers 1, 2, 3, 4 and 5, then =SUM(A1:A5) gives the result 15
Reference	Chapter 10, page 107

TREND

Definition	Returns values along a linear trend using ordinary least squares regression (see also FORECAST and LINEST)
Examples of use	Forecasting future revenue
Syntax	=TREND(*known-y's,known-x's,new-x's,constant*) where *known-y's* are the known dependent variables, *known-x's* the known, existing explanatory variables and the *new-x's* the explanatory variables for which new y values will be forecast. *Constant* is a logical value: if true or omitted, then the constant is calculated normally; if false, then it is forced to zero

Example	=TREND({1,2,3,4},{1,2,3,4},{5;6;7}) would generate the result 5;6;7
Reference	Chapter 10, page 92

VLOOKUP

Definition	Searches for a value in the left-most column of a table and then returns a value from the same row in a column from within the table specified by the user
Examples of use	Look-up tables can be used to generate price tables
Syntax	=VLOOKUP(*lookup value,table array,column index number,range lookup*) where *lookup value* is the value to be located in the first column of the array. *Table array* is the data table from which the value will be looked up. *Column index number* is the column number in the table from where the value will be retrieved; the first column of the table is column one. *Range lookup* (optional) is a logical value: if true, you are requesting an exact match, if false, then you require the closest match. If you specify true, then the values in the first column of the table must be sorted in ascending order
Example	For a detailed example see Chapter 11, page 000, Charts 11.7 and 11.8
References	Chapter 11, page 114

Appendix 2 Other platforms

Other platforms on which business models can be constructed are described in Chart A1.

Chart A1 **Other platforms for constructing business models**

Platform	Description	Typical use
Database	Contains vast sets of data that can be analysed by a variety of attributes and criteria to evaluate results.	Common applications are for summarising the results of historic records such as customer orders or product trends. Takes time to analyse and works at a level of detail that is often irrelevant to many strategic models.
SPSS Inc.	Leads the data mining market. Data mining is a process, or methodology, for discovering patterns and trends in large datasets to find useful, decision-making information. The analytical methods used in data mining include traditional statistical analysis and statistical graphics, as well as software designed to perform new types of analysis such as data visualisation, decision trees and neural networks.	Provides a more sophisticated database evaluation such that trends and behaviour patterns can be used to understand and plan the use of marketing techniques such as promotions. Common applications include customer segmentation analysis and behavioural analysis.
Manufacturing models	Monitor the flow of materials through a manufacturing process. These models start at the order stage, through goods in, inspection, drawn from stores, use in work in progress and outflow of finished goods. They can scan and track consumption and automate reordering of stock.	Help to reduce stock levels in the supply chain and explore optimum levels of orders and frequencies. Additional evaluations can be used to understand patterns of wastage and operational performance of key activities.

Platform	Description	Typical use
Neural network	A distributed processor that has a natural propensity for storing experiential knowledge and making it available for use. It resembles the brain in two respects: knowledge is acquired by the network through a learning process; inter-neurone connection strengths known as synaptic weights are used to store the knowledge.	An emerging technology to simulate the brain and explore the correlation and interrelation of data.
Online analytical processing	Data warehousing is the process of integrating and transforming disparate operational data into strategic business information. Organisations are deploying data warehouses as the backbone for delivering analytical applications to optimise business performance.	With businesses collecting vast amounts of point-of-sales and e-commerce data, trends in customer behaviour can be evaluated to enhance marketing effort and minimise waste.

Index